Front Pages, Front Lines

THE HISTORY OF
COMMUNICATION

Robert W. McChesney and
John C. Nerone, editors

*A list of books in the series appears
at the end of this book.*

Front Pages, Front Lines

Media and the Fight
for Women's Suffrage

Edited by
LINDA STEINER, CAROLYN KITCH,
AND BROOKE KROEGER

**UNIVERSITY OF
ILLINOIS PRESS**
Urbana, Chicago, and Springfield

Library of Congress Control Number: 2019956849

ISBN 978-0-252-04310-9 (hardcover)
ISBN 978-0-252-08497-3 (paperback)
ISBN 978-0-252-05198-2 (e-book)

Contents

Acknowledgments

This project began when a team of nine women, inspired by Brooke Kroeger, planned a special issue for *American Journalism*, the journal of the American Journalism Historians Association, on media of the US women's suffrage movement and about media coverage of that movement. Having recruited, reviewed, and shaped the articles for that special issue, the team members and others were invited to contribute essays for this book, also timed to mark the ratification of the Nineteenth Amendment enfranchising women a century ago. The contributors were spectacular: they produced thoughtful critiques of the media strategies, the politics and strategizing, and, more generally, the successes and blind spots of editors, publishers, suffrage supporters, and antisuffrage activists. Meanwhile, they met every deadline along the way.

Among the people deserving thanks are Ford Risley and Vanessa Murphree, then the editor and associate editor of *American Journalism*, who granted permission for this book's inclusion of chapters based on three articles from its Winter 2019 issue (volume 36, issue 1):

Linda J. Lumsden, "Historiography: Woman Suffrage and the Media"
Linda M. Grasso, "Differently Radical: Suffrage Issues and Feminist
    Ideas in *The Crisis* and *The Masses*"
Teri Finneman, "Covering a Countermovement on the Verge of Defeat:
    The Press and the 1917 Social Movement against Woman Suffrage"

We also thank the Humanities New York project for funding a Women's Suffrage and the Media website (http://suffrageandthemedia.org/) that includes a database of primary and secondary sources that can be used at every learning level, news of relevant suffrage events and exhibits, and even Dolly Parton singing "Nineteenth Amendment." The site contains video and podcast interviews with suffrage historians, including contributors to the *AJ* special issue and to this book. New links to suffrage-related events, exhibits, and research will be added throughout the centennial year.

We also thank our own team at the University of Illinois Press: Danny Nasset, for his calm support and useful suggestions; Marika Christofides, the associate acquisitions editor who helped us with the illustrations; and Marilyn Campbell, our copyeditor.

We want to acknowledge the support of New York University's Faculty of Arts and Science and the NYU Arthur L. Carter Journalism Institute, the University of Maryland's Philip Merrill College of Journalism, and Temple University's Klein College of Media and Communication.

LS, CK, and BK

Introduction

LINDA STEINER

The centennial commemoration of the ratification of the constitutional amendment enfranchising women calls for serious consideration—or reconsideration—of the role of media in the contentious debates not merely over women's suffrage, but also women's rights and even womanhood more generally. The time is ripe for thinking about new ways to tell and retell suffrage history, including its communication history. Historians have long treated both mainstream and specialized media merely as information sources, to be mined for relevant facts and quotes. Suffragists and antisuffragists, however, realized from the start that media were crucial to their success. For this reason, suffragists issued dramatic posters, clever postcards, broadsides with enormous headlines, and yellow sashes proclaiming "Votes for Women." To garner publicity they staged events—parades and pageants, hikes and strikes. They cast ballots and picketed the White House, knowing this would send them to jail. Positive coverage cannot ensure success nor does notoriety automatically spell a movement's defeat. Nonetheless, media operate with some degree of agency, so women activists have long made journalism part of their strategies.

This book's contributors approach the relevant media issues from multiple angles, thereby bringing into view many intertwined issues, theories, and problems. In addition to a historiographic assessment of scholarly work on media coverage of the suffrage movement, the book touches on the entire life span of the "woman's rights question," from the antebellum suffrage periodicals even before suffragists coalesced around an organized movement, to the political journals for women in the 1920s, after ratification of the Nineteenth Amendment establishing women's right to vote. Furthermore, in contrast to the undertheorized suffrage histories of old, contributors incorporate contemporary theories and concepts: social-movement and countermovement strategies; status conflict and status politics; competing notions of identity, including white masculinity; the intersections of race, class, and gender; and public sphere questions about citizenship, among others.

Women's rights advocates first focused on launching their own periodicals as mechanisms through which they could develop and elaborate arguments on behalf of both the cause and their evolving identity, and then recruit and mobilize converts. After the turn of the century, suffragists primarily concentrated on attracting positive publicity from regional and national mass-market newspapers, so chapters included here examine how they cultivated attention from a variety of news outlets. Other chapters highlight the distinctive approaches and dilemmas of the black press, radical newspapers, religious periodicals, and women's magazines. Antisuffragists likewise used niche and mass-circulation media to attract supporters and undermine adversaries. Analyses of these media issues explain critical challenges that both suffragists and antisuffragists faced and provide theoretical and historical lessons for and about all sorts of social and political causes, including for twenty-first-century feminism and feminist media.

News media's importance to suffragists was already evident in the first volume of the three-volume *History of Woman Suffrage*, published in 1881. The prominence of "Woman in Newspapers"—it was chapter 2—was perhaps predictable given that the *History*'s authors were Elizabeth Cady Stanton, Susan B. Anthony, and Matilda Joslyn Gage, that is, suffrage leaders who themselves edited or published suffrage periodicals.[1] That chapter featured many women involved in journalism, including Frances Wright, who edited the reform-minded *Free Enquirer*, 1828–35; Clarina Howard Nichols, the triune activist (temperance, antislavery, and women's rights) who edited the *Windham County (VT) Democrat*; and Frances Dana Barker Gage, who edited the "Ladies Department" of the *Ohio Cultivator* and later wrote for a variety of general interest and women's periodicals, as well as reform periodicals such as the *National Anti-Slavery Standard*. Stanton, Anthony, and Gage mentioned women editors and journalists going back to the colonial era, foreign-language papers for women in the United States, and women's rights papers in other countries. They featured reform papers in the 1850s and 1860s, such as *The Commonwealth*, the abolitionist and free thought newspaper that Julia Ward Howe and her husband coedited; and Anna W. Spencer's *Pioneer and Woman's Advocate*, dedicated to "Liberty, Truth, Temperance, Equality." Stanton and Anthony, who had never promised to be modest, bragged that their own suffrage paper, *The Revolution*, attracted national press attention.

FIGURE 0.1. Photograph taken during three-week inaugural meeting of the International Council of Women, Washington, DC, March 1888. Seated, front row: Laura Ormiston Chant (UK); Susan B. Anthony (US); Isabelle Bogelot (France); Elizabeth Cady Stanton (US); Matilda Joslyn Gage (US). Item 12941, The Huntington Library, San Marino, California.

Nevertheless, they also commended a host of other suffrage papers, including the *Woman's Journal*, which represented a rival faction. They even mentioned the *True Woman*, a Baltimore antisuffrage monthly that "soon died of inanition and inherent weakness of constitution."

A chapter on women journalists included in an 1891 book, *Woman's Work in America*, mentioned many of the same women journalists and women's papers as had the *History*.[2] This chapter emphasized that "Anglo-African sisters are awakening to a comprehension of the use of the press as an instrument of value to themselves and their race," and were writing for leading East Coast dailies as well as race papers.[3] Furthermore, the 1891 chapter's author, who was associated with the suffrage movement's moderate wing, was even-handed regarding *The Revolution* and the *Woman's Journal*, crediting both papers "as potent factors in woman's education, industrial and social advancement, in helping to secure the repeal of unjust laws" and especially in "awakening women to a sense of their solidarity as a sex—to the truth that 'where one of the members suffers all the members suffer with it.'"[4]

Below I make two points about the suffrage press specifically. First, I use the example of a suffrage paper outside the East Coast, the *Missouri Woman*, to suggest the highly typical swath of suffragist experiences; this news organ illustrates both suffrage editors' strategic creativity in the face of money problems, an issue that scholars rarely address, and the decision-making of the editors to largely (but not entirely) abandon periodicals for, by, and about a movement's insiders. Second, *The Lily*, a twenty-first-century case of using and misusing suffragists' media experiments, shows the postfeminist depoliticization of suffrage politics. Then, after summarizing the individual chapters, I will sketch out a few of the broad themes of the book.

The *Missouri Woman*: A Case Study

Already in 1920, the year the Nineteenth Amendment was finally ratified, a history journal published an issue on the "History of the Woman Suffrage Movement in Missouri." In it, Mary Semple Scott described the *Missouri Woman*, which she edited from 1916 to 1919.[5] Scott's account of the *Missouri Woman* essentially addresses every dilemma that suffragists faced organizationally, interpersonally, tactically, technically, politically, and financially. Scott underscores the agonizing trade-off between investing in suffragist-run periodicals and attracting positive coverage in mass-circulation papers, when the goal was supporting both kinds of media. Scott began by explaining the "great difficulty" in convincing local papers to run suffrage news: "The suffragists were continually obliged to do something spectacular in order to be mentioned. This was felt to be a great drawback to the cause; moreover, the leaders were women who abhorred the sensational."[6] Only the *St. Louis Post-Dispatch*'s progressive editor published, "when occasion warranted, strong pro-suffrage editorials." By 1913, other leading Missouri dailies as well as several weeklies were publicly supporting suffrage. Publicity went so well that editors grew much more sympathetic: women were able to produce special suffrage editions for three newspapers, which they personally sold on street corners. Nevertheless, "constructive propaganda . . . was almost entirely barred, and we were sadly in need of better and more frequent publicity."[7]

In 1915, a journalist offered to publish a magazine devoted to women's issues, the *Missouri Woman*. This suffrage monthly "was greeted with great enthusiasm by all who were active in suffrage work because they understood the great value of such a publication. All went well for a few months. . . . Then the publisher failed."[8] Luckily, Flint Garrison, the president of a printing company (an "ardent suffragist," he was editor-in-chief of the *Drygoodsman*), stepped in. Because the founding editor could not travel to the new printer's St. Louis premises, Scott took over as editor. The newly constituted twenty-page magazine had many contributing editors, including prominent club women who induced the Missouri Federation of Women's Clubs to adopt the magazine as its official organ.

Because the Democrats held their 1916 national convention in St. Louis, Scott went all out to produce an issue that would "impress the public." Volunteer "newsies" sold 10,000 copies. Local department stores advertised generously, so for the first time, the *Missouri Woman* could pay its printing bill. Indeed, it managed to incorporate: Garrison and other officers bought half the stock; suffragists bought the rest. By 1916 subscriptions reached the "coveted" 5,000 mark—and attracted retail advertisers. During World War I, the magazine devoted several pages each issue to Council of Defense propaganda, news, and advertising. In 1919 when the national suffrage convention came to St. Louis, and the Missouri Senate passed the suffrage bill, the paper "received full credit for the sentiment it had created for suffrage throughout the state."[9] The state suffrage association decided, however:

> The great need for an official suffrage organ had passed. . . . The need of the future lay in wider publicity through the daily and weekly press. . . . Whereas in the old days it had been impossible to get our news into the papers, at this time it was impossible to keep it out. Reporters listened eagerly to every word of our opinions; our leaders were accurately photographed; everything we did was featured and not on the Woman's Page, but in the general news.[10]

The Lily: Then and Now

In the 1960s and 1970s, during what is often called the women's movement's second wave, feminists involved in establishing newspapers, magazines, and broadcast public affairs shows often looked back to nineteenth-century (i.e., first-wave) suffrage outlets for inspirations and models. In the twenty-first century, however, not only are the specific platforms very different, the third- and fourth-wave versions usually cater to audiences with far blander politics albeit sharper consumer angles. In 2017, the *Washington Post* launched *The Lily*, "an experimental, visually driven product designed for millennial women that will boldly reimagine The Post's award-winning journalism for distributed platforms."[11] Its title commemorates a journal launched in 1848 as one of the earliest periodicals to advocate women's suffrage.

The original *Lily* editor Amelia Bloomer earnestly explained in 1853 that the publication aimed to challenge women to reinvent themselves as citizens who deserved political rights; it was "a needed instrument to spread abroad the truth of a new gospel to woman."[12] In contrast, Amy King, the (new) *Lily*'s editor-in-chief and creative director, says: "We wanted to go all-in on distributed platforms because it's where millennial women are getting most of their news. We decided it made sense to find people where they already are and make it really easy for people to find the content that we think that they would enjoy."[13] King says the site "surfaces" both freelance and *Post* stories and its "brand aesthetic" makes art and creative direction just as important as the stories; after one year, *The Lily* apparently had over 276,000 followers on Facebook and 26,000 followers on Instagram.[14] Notably, Team Lily's eight members' online bios mention their various food preferences (vegetarian), style (six tattoos), and previous jobs (King had helped launch the *Post*'s national apps and Snapchat Discover channel; a multiplatform editor had covered real estate). Among the other obvious differences between the two *Lily*s, not one staffer mentioned feminism or political commitment.

Chapter Overview

These kinds of uses, misuses, and myth-making regarding women's political communications underscore the value of continuing research. The historical accounts in this volume point to the importance of incorporating media theory, new approaches to social movements, and historiography, and of tackling the complex, vexed relationship between the media and women's suffrage debates. Chapters accordingly analyze the suffrage press and other women's periodicals that were dedicated to women's rights; mainstream press coverage of the suffrage and antisuffrage campaigns at national and local levels; and treatment of the issue in other kinds of "alternative" or niche periodicals.

In Chapter 1, Linda J. Lumsden offers a comprehensive historiography that highlights the near one-dimensionality of much of the early suffrage scholarship. Lumsden analyzes what historians, journalism studies researchers, and sociologists have found—and what they have ignored—beginning in the 1970s, when feminist scholars began to look back at both suffrage editors and mainstream news media coverage of the suffrage campaign. More recent scholarship pays valuable attention to visual rhetoric and spectacle. In general, Lumsden shows, contemporary researchers no longer conflate the entire women's suffrage movement with the leadership efforts of a few white middle-class northeasterners. Instead, they now appreciate how diverse activists across the country engaged with the issues in significantly different ways.

In Chapter 2, Linda Steiner argues that—in the face of challenges to women's lives wrought by industrialization, urbanization, a lowered birth rate, and a shift to a monetary economy—the suffrage and women's rights papers of the nineteenth century created and experimented with very different versions of a new woman, and then dramatized and celebrated these identities. Referencing theory that treats political conflicts as proxies for debates over status and deference paid to a group's particular way of being, she argues that suffrage was primarily important to the new women because a constitutional amendment enfranchising women would symbolize the increased legitimacy of the new women, regardless of how they might vote, if they voted at all.

In Chapter 3, one of several chapters that correct the erasure of regional differences that has marked much suffrage literature, Sherilyn Cox Bennion shows how the prosuffrage arguments of the *Women's Exponent*, published for Mormon women, were reformulated in response to regional political shifts. From its start in 1872, two years after the Utah legislature enfranchised Utah's women, the *Exponent* used various rationales to counter attempts to disenfranchise polygamous women. In the 1880s, however, women in polygamous marriages and then all Utah women were disenfranchised. In 1896, when Utah was admitted as a state, its constitution re-enfranchised women. Bennion contrasts the *Exponent* with the *Anti-Polygamy Standard*, which opposed suffrage for Utah's (mostly Mormon) women but supported women's suffrage in general.

Certainly, one of the major criticisms of the mainstream suffrage movement was that white middle-class suffrage leaders failed to embrace women of color and to partner with them, and likewise failed to recognize how their own articulations of suffrage arguments ignored the concerns of African Americans. Similarly, a major criticism of much suffrage/media scholarship is that it has ignored those failures; it rarely noticed its own whiteness. Several chapters here correct those omissions. Among those most prominently addressing this, Robin Mazyck Sundaramoorthy and Jinx Coleman Broussard address black women journalists and coverage of black women's positions on suffrage; Linda M. Grasso and Jane Rhodes focus on early twentieth-century black publications.

In chapter 4, Sundaramoorthy and Broussard look at both the suffrage activities of black journalists such as Ida B. Wells-Barnett, Mary Church Terrell, and Frances Ellen Watkins Harper and the black press coverage of black women's participation in the movement, which was controversial among black communities across the country. Sundaramoorthy and Broussard find that the black press celebrated women suffragists such as the poet Bettiola Fortson for their persistence, passion, determination to push back against discrimination by white women, and their oratorical and writing skills. Yet, black newspaper and magazine editors' personal support for the cause was lackluster at best; they avidly published essays and articles both pro and con.

Rhodes, in chapter 5, examines the positions of black periodicals attached to socialism or the Communist Party, as well as black nationalist papers, regarding suffrage and black women's suffrage activism. She focuses on the post–World War I era, when black periodicals conveyed the anxiety and grievances about a widespread backlash against black American soldiers, urban antiblack violence, and lynching. The editors of *The Messenger*, for example, viewed black women's suffrage as part of a larger political and social transformation that would give the masses a voice and equal opportunity. A. Philip Randolph and Chandler Owen boasted, soon after they founded *The Messenger*: "The Editors have supported woman suffrage by voice and pen for the last eight years. . . . We shall fight hereafter to help them make the most profitable and desirable use of that same ballot."

Grasso, in chapter 6, compares the approaches to women's suffrage adopted by the NAACP's *Crisis*, under the leadership of W. E. B. Du Bois, and *The Masses*, edited by Max Eastman and primarily serving white readers. Both magazines vigorously supported women's suffrage, but Grasso analyzes their respective 1915 special suffrage issues in terms of their "differently radical" perspectives on gender discrimination and disenfranchisement. This exposes the fraught conflicts between the nineteenth-century abolitionist and black freedom movements and the women's rights movement. It illustrates "race in gendered radicalism and gender in race radicalism."

In chapter 7, Teri Finneman draws on US news coverage to examine anti-suffragists' rhetorical strategies for representing themselves and their adversaries in 1917, when antis began to lose significant ground while suffragists' progressive arguments gained more traction with journalists. She finds that, consistent with many countermovements, the antis used negative, emotional rhetoric, focusing more on what they opposed than what they advocated. Moreover, by lobbying during the First World War, the antis were caught in a Catch-22, undercutting the very myths about women's role that they tried to promote; women's valuable wartime contributions manifestly contradicted the antisuffragists' published argument that women did not belong in the public sphere.

In chapter 8, Jane Marcellus also complicates the reading of race, gender, and geography by highlighting opposing understandings of white masculinity as these were articulated in competing newspapers in Tennessee. Marcellus offers a close reading of a crucial state in 1920, when the entire country was watching to see whether Tennessee would become the thirty-sixth and final state to ratify the Nineteenth Amendment. The relatively liberal *Nashville Tennessean*, roughly aligned with progressive "New South" views, supported ratification; the "Old South" *Nashville Banner* remained opposed. Offering a counterpoint to the usual emphasis on competing versions of womanhood, Marcellus contends that instead, for both newspapers, competing views of southern white masculinity were at stake.

Brooke Kroeger, in chapter 9, shows the importance and influence, especially during the suffrage movement's final decade, of high society women and men who enjoyed elite status as socialites, businessmen, and professionals, especially as editors and publishers of important newspapers and magazines. Suffrage leaders cultivated elite recruits who brought useful resources: the ability to present the movement in the popular press in a flattering light; political and financial assets for statewide and national campaigns; and access to powerful social, professional, and political contacts. Kroeger shows that social elites directly influenced the mainstream press; their participation drew useful publicity for the suffrage movement.

Finally, a couple of chapters usefully extend the account beyond the 1920 ratification of the Nineteenth Amendment. Maurine Beasley examines how suffrage organizations and their news outlets shifted their policies, positions, and philosophies during the 1920s. Carolyn Kitch considers the editorial legacies and deployment of suffrage memories in the later twentieth century and even into the contemporary era. In chapter 10, Beasley analyzes efforts of suffrage activists, once women were enfranchised in 1920, to decide whether they should attempt to enter the existing male power structure or should concentrate on advancing women's causes outside it. Beasley looks at *Equal Rights*, the magazine of the National Woman's Party; the *Woman Citizen*, produced by the League of Women Voters; and *Independent Woman*, representing the National Federation of Business and Professional Women. In the 1920s and 1930s, she finds, these publications fractured the suffragists' idealism yet also kept alive the idea that women would use the vote to build a better society.

In chapter 11, Carolyn Kitch analyzes how *Time*, *Life*, and *Newsweek* cover stories, in the context of reporting on the so-called second wave of the women's movement, both remembered and forgot the women's suffrage movement. She identifies three stages of coverage: puzzled and cautious concern over women's unhappiness; a period of acknowledging gender inequities; and finally, coverage of women as political candidates, politicians, and voters. Reporting on the women's movement of the 1970s, these three weekly newsmagazines alternated (and sometimes combined) celebration and dismissal of feminism, using suffrage memory toward both ends.

Kathy Roberts Forde's Afterword returns to white southern suffragists' "unholy alliance" with white supremacy, including through the support of the leading suffragist periodical in the South. Indeed, she points out that in the early twentieth century, the National American Woman Suffrage Association (NAWSA) capitulated to southern prejudice, for example, by acknowledging the right of southern chapters to exclude black women from membership. The black suffragist Ida B. Wells-Barnett's pamphlet *Southern Horrors*, Forde notes, decried the fantasy of a New South put forth in the "malicious and untruthful white press" that, among other problems, tolerated lynching.

Geography, Politics, and Social Movements

Taken collectively the chapters in this book clarify intersections of suffrage ideas with other social and political movements as well as differences by geography and culture. Especially with the expansion of transportation systems across the country, several suffrage movement founders based on the East Coast frequently traveled across the United States, thus drawing considerable publicity and nationalizing the movement to a degree; meanwhile, as Kroeger points out in chapter 9, a Colorado judge repeatedly came east to rally support for enfranchisement. More to the point, with the development of telegraphy as well as the railroads, suffrage ideas moved independently of suffrage leaders, sometimes through niche or mainstream newspapers and magazines (that themselves were transported across vast spaces), taking on different inflections given the political and social contexts.

Indeed, suffragists and suffrage ideas enjoyed transatlantic interaction. Men's Leagues started forming in the United States soon after they formed in Holland and England. To take another example, in 1907, Alice Paul moved to England, where she soon joined a militant suffrage group, the Women's Social and Political Union (WSPU). Paul was arrested repeatedly during suffrage demonstrations in England and Scotland; during three jail terms, she learned about civil disobedience, demanding to be treated as a political prisoner and engaging in hunger strikes. In 1910, she returned to the United States, bringing with her the WSPU's militancy. Notably, as several chapters suggest, the "social utility" argument, with its "tamer" conception of new women, had gradually become more salient in the United States than "natural rights" arguments for enfranchisement. But the latter did not disappear. Given disagreements over strategy and tactics with the National American Woman Suffrage Association, for whom she initially worked, Paul formed the Congressional Union for

FIGURE 0.2. "At Last," cover illustration for *The Suffragist*, official organ of the National Woman's Party.

Woman Suffrage and later the National Woman's Party; she deployed some of the same dramatic tactics and suffered the same forced feeding in prison she had in England. The house organ for both of Paul's organizations was *The Suffragist*; after ratification, to promote the Equal Rights Amendment (ERA), the weekly became *Equal Rights*. *The Suffragist's* "official cartoonist," Nina Allender, famously produced 287 suffrage cartoons, depicting suffragists as stylish, attractive, bold, passionate young women. Moreover, despite Paul's adamant rejection of moderation and reform approach, *The Suffragist* enjoyed mainstream attention and even healthy advertising revenue.

More specifically, several chapters highlight how suffrage logic—and, for that matter, antisuffrage argumentation—developed quite differently in the Northeast, South, Midwest, West, and Pacific Northwest. It's worth bringing to the fore how, for all suffragists' attempts (in their own periodicals and for other news outlets) at strategic self-presentation, suffrage often served as a political football for another cause. Brewers and distillers opposed women's enfranchisement because they assumed that women would vote to prohibit alcoholic beverages, and businesses that employed children opposed it because they assumed women would vote to eliminate child labor. Already in the nineteenth century, as Bennion points out, both support for and opposition to women's suffrage in the Territory of the Deseret were based on the shared assumption that women would vote according to their Mormon beliefs and support polygamy. Likewise, although with far more tragic consequences, as Forde emphasizes, women's suffrage drew support in the South only in the 1890s, when southerners supposed that white women would vote to maintain white political control. That said, the tension between black and white suffragists in the North should not be exaggerated into a totalizing binary. Some black suffragists and black editors maintained cordial supportive relationships with white suffragists. Similarly, notwithstanding suffragists' critique of men who would deny women political agency, as Kroeger emphasizes, some men were actively supportive of women's suffrage.

A second subpoint deserving mention in this context is that among suffragists, rhetoric about suffrage rarely turned solely on *whether* women should vote, although, as already noted, *why* they should vote was a matter of debate. What caused more friction and mutual criticism were the various other causes that could be and were associated with suffrage. Some prominent suffrage editors, at least at some point, advocated temperance; others, especially on the West Coast, were disinclined to endorse prohibition or even temperance. Many prominent suffragist founders from the North were associated with the abolition movement, but they varied in their support of political-economic reforms regarding land, currency, and labor rights; later they fractured over pacifism. Debates over dress reform, nutrition, free love, and coeducation were also woven into the discussion of the cause, sometimes to endorse, sometimes to push for greater dedication, and sometimes as a way to attack and undermine individual "new women" or groups of women. Having in 1869 transformed a San Francisco paper into the West's first suffrage periodical, Emily Pitts Stevens abandoned *The Pioneer* within ten years. At least part of the reason was that rival suffragists managed to associate her with the free-love movement, despite her vehement denial of the heretical accusations that her critics essentially leaked to the *San Francisco Chronicle*.[15]

Finally, the conduct of the suffrage movement from the mid-nineteenth century to 1920, and then beyond, shows how, after a long, rocky and uneven journey requiring the participation of many people with different ideas and different ways of working, radical ideas can be made acceptable, not merely officially ratified.[16] The media are crucial in making converts, in normalizing ideas formerly ridiculed, and in sustaining dedication that otherwise flag in the face of internal setbacks as well as defeats and challenges at the hand of opponents. Individual suffragists, including suffrage editors, were stubborn. Dissension and outright division among suffrage leaders and organizations was undoubtedly unproductive. Yet, the multiplicity, flexibility, and adaptability of the movement, suffragists' energetic willingness to experiment with a wide range of media, and their openness to working with an array of reform-minded partners were probably all, taken together, crucial to the eventual success. This explains the continuing relevance and significance of this history not only to other social and political movements, but to understanding cultural conflict and cultural politics broadly.

This book offers new perspectives on the past and suggests potential paths for future research. Several media-related topics relevant to the suffrage debate deserve additional study, from the importance of visual elements (cartoons, engravings, news photographs, among others) and the materiality of suffrage and antisuffrage media (physical appearance, advertising, technological affordances and new mechanisms for production and support) to popular culture representations of suffragists and women's rights activists more generally. Although the platforms of choice for contemporary activists now include blogs, podcasts, and instantaneous vehicles such as Twitter and Instagram, media still matter.

Notes

1. Elizabeth Cady Stanton, Susan B. Anthony, and Matilda Joslyn Gage, eds., *The History of Woman Suffrage*, Vol. 1, *1881*. All references here to the Project Gutenberg eBook #28020, released 2009.

2. Susan E. Dickinson, "Woman in Journalism," in *Woman's Work in America*, ed. Annie Nathan Meyer (1891; reprint, New York: Arno Press, 1972), 128–38.

3. Dickinson, "Woman in Journalism," 137.

4. Dickinson, "Woman in Journalism," 133.

5. Mary Semple Scott, "The *Missouri Woman*," *Missouri Historical Review* 14, no. 3–4 (1920): 372–77.

6. Scott, "*Missouri Woman*," 372.

7. Scott, "*Missouri Woman*," 372.

8. Scott, "*Missouri Woman*," 372.

9. Scott, "*Missouri Woman*," 376.

10. Scott, "*Missouri Woman*," 376–77.

11. "The *Washington Post* announces *The Lily*," *WashPostPR* blog, January 18, 2017, https://www.washingtonpost.com/.

12. Amelia Bloomer, "Why We Publish," *The Lily*, January 1853, 12.

13. Laura Hazard Owen, "With *The Lily*, the *Washington Post* Wants to Draw Young Women In (but Won't Do a Subscription Hard Sell)," *NiemanLab*, June 19, 2017, http://www.niemanlab.org/2017/06/with-the-lily-the-washington-post-wants-to-draw-young-women-in-but-wont-do-a-subscription-hard-sell/?relatedstory.

14. Sarah Penix, "Building *The Lily*, the Washington Post Project Designed for Millennial Women," September 1, 2018, https://studybreaks.com/culture/reads/building-lily-washington-post-project-designed-millennial-women/.

15. Sherilyn Cox Bennion, *Equal to the Occasion: Women Editors of the Nineteenth-Century West* (Reno: University of Nevada Press, 1990). Bennion suggests that the true reason for the attacks on Stevens, otherwise known to be a devoted homemaker, was her published support of a controversial financier, George Francis Train, and of the "liberal" wing of the suffrage movement.

16. For this point, as well as for other helpful suggestions, we thank two anonymous reviewers of this manuscript.

1

Historiography

Women's Suffrage and the Media

LINDA J. LUMSDEN

Culture. Multiculturalism. Spectacle. Public sphere. Interdisciplinary studies. Those terms sum up the major directions of the media historiography of the suffrage movement since the 1990s.

This chapter traces the evolution of diverse scholarship on a wide range of media in relation to the American suffrage movement. Scholars began investigating the role of suffrage periodicals in the early 1970s, when women's history emerged from the second wave of feminism as an exciting new field within the historical profession. The first decades concentrated on retrieving to public memory the many periodicals and personalities that shaped the suffrage press. Cultural historical approaches began to appear in the 1980s. Black feminist scholars in the 1990s challenged the racist assumptions that tinged earlier Whiggish accounts of persevering white suffrage editors. Visual rhetoric studies emerged as scholars rediscovered the spectacle of suffrage. Journalism scholars, however, have lagged in recognizing the central role of the suffrage press in reshaping the public sphere.

Since the dawn of the twenty-first century, the historiography of suffrage media has grown exponentially, but it has been driven largely by disciplines outside of journalism history. Interdisciplinary studies have offered the most comprehensive accounts. Literary scholars, art historians, anthropologists, black studies scholars, and even cartographers have put new spins on the history of suffrage media, which besides newspapers and magazines encompass theater, film, and fiction; cartoons and postcards, cookbooks and costumes, banners and songs. Three strands weaving through interdisciplinary suffrage media scholarship are: an embrace of cultural approaches; the retrieval of excluded voices and a scourging of racism; and a celebration of suffrage as spectacle in myriad forms. My essay begins by tracing early suffrage media scholarship, then surveys major directions of the past twenty years (especially innovative British cultural approaches to suffrage media), followed by suggestions on how US journalism historians can reinvigorate the field.

Journalism historians Catherine Mitchell in 1993 and Elizabeth V. Burt in 2000 critiqued the historiography of suffrage journalism, providing precursors to this essay on American suffrage media in the broadest sense. Mitchell urged scholars to interrogate the white, middle-class suffrage press's performance on issues of race and class.[1] Burt similarly invoked multiculturalism but also suggested more interdisciplinary studies and new theoretical frameworks.[2] Both called for more cultural approaches, echoing James Carey's oft-quoted appeal in the inaugural issue of *Journalism History* in 1974.[3] Thirty years later, women's historian Kathi Kern likewise called for more cultural analysis in women's history.[4] Cultural history currently dominates studies of diverse suffrage media.

Pioneers of Suffrage Media History

The history of American suffrage media began with what pioneering scholar Gerda Lerner terms compensatory studies of forgotten individual journals and their editors.[5] Lynn Masel-Walters launched the field with her groundbreaking analyses in 1976 of two key suffrage newspapers, Susan B. Anthony and Elizabeth Cady Stanton's *The Revolution* (1868–70), and the *Woman's Journal* (1870–1917), official organ of what became the National American Woman Suffrage Association (NAWSA).[6] (Marion Marzolf summarized the suffrage press in four paragraphs in *Up from the Footnote: A History of Women Journalists*, the first detailed work of women's journalism history.)[7] Sherilyn Cox Bennion followed, identifying more than a dozen western suffrage newspapers and editors.[8] Suffrage editors beginning with Oregonian Abigail S. Duniway attracted scholarly attention as early as 1971. Duniway continues to attract interest for both her writing and her speeches.[9]

Masel-Walters also led the move beyond compensatory history in her 1980 investigation of suffrage newspapers' internal workings, for which she delved into nineteenth-century suffrage newspaper records.[10] Burt also utilized suffrage organization records and correspondence, analyzing them through the prism of social movement theory to detail how power struggles within the Wisconsin Woman Suffrage Association were mirrored in its organ, the *Woman Citizen*.[11] The encyclopedic *Women's Periodicals in the United States: Social and Political Issues*, edited by Kathleen L. Endres and Therese L. Lueck, includes sixteen suffrage journals as well as three antisuffrage periodicals.[12]

Studies on mainstream press coverage of the suffrage movement began in 1980 with Lauren Kessler's content analysis of the *Portland Oregonian*, which, she concluded, reported on suffrage only after it perceived the movement as legitimate.[13] Anne Messerly Cooper found that ten daily newspapers put passage of the Nineteenth Amendment on page one, regardless of whether their state ratified the amendment. The suffrage movement did not exist in isolation: Janet Cramer discovered that turn-of-the-century women's periodicals connected four themes to suffrage: motherhood, women's moral superiority, female altruism, and women's equality with men.[14] Similarly, Nancy Burkhalter's analysis of coverage from 1918 to 1920 in the *Ladies' Home Journal*, *Good Housekeeping*, the *New Republic*, and *Literary Digest* concluded that editors appeared most concerned with minimizing any impact the vote might have on the traditional role of women valorized in their magazines.[15] Burt's studies of the Wisconsin press found newspapers conveyed diverse views variously influenced by their publishers and editors, political affiliations, competing interests, regional demographics, circulation, place of publication, and suffrage story sources.[16] Rodger Streitmatter, who has outlined the importance of several suffrage periodicals, dissected the hostility of nineteenth-century media toward woman's suffrage.[17] In a study of *The Delineator*, a hugely successful women's magazine in the 1910s, Sidney Bland demonstrated that the popular magazine fostered community among suffragists seeking to redefine themselves for the modern age.[18]

I examined ten dailies' coverage of the 1913 national suffrage parade and pageant in Washington, DC, and found that newspapers offered a forum for a broader debate on women's place after a drunken mob broke up the parade. Editorial indignation over the women's ill treatment conferred legitimacy upon women's right of assembly, moving mainstream media closer toward the conclusion that women should have a right to vote.[19] The 2017 Women's March in Washington drew parallels to the 1913 parade, although Teri Finneman's analysis of 1913 press previews concluded that their episodic approach resulted in shallow diagnostic framing of the suffrage issue.[20] Tiffany Lewis similarly observed that reporters covering a small band of suffragists who hiked from New York City to Albany in 1912 to urge passage of a suffrage amendment depoliticized the transgressive protest by framing it as entertainment.[21]

A shortcoming of all these works is their piecemeal approach to mass media coverage of one of the nation's largest social movements. Many suffrage histories rely heavily on mainstream media as sources but never address their relationship to the movement. Just one example is Elna C. Green's fine *Southern Strategies: Southern Women and the Woman Suffrage Question*, whose bibliography lists nineteen commercial periodicals.[22] Several books deal briefly with suffrage and the media in the course of discussing other aspects of the movement, since media are so enmeshed with history, culture, and politics. Sally G. McMillen's *Seneca Falls and the Origin of the Women's Rights Movement* devoted three pages to mainstream reactions to the convention.[23] In *Rampant Women: Suffragists and the Right of Assembly*, I sporadically discussed the importance of newspaper coverage of suffrage conventions, soapboxers, parades, and the White House pickets.[24]

Susan E. Marshall discussed the antis' *Remonstrance* newspaper and the press tactics of antisuffragists in her *Splintered Sisterhood*.[25] Brooke Kroeger's *The Suffragents: How Women Used Men to Get the Vote*, mines myriad newspaper accounts.[26] Two other books reflect on wealthy white suffragists' golden media effect, including Johanna Neuman's *Gilded Suffragists: The New York Socialites Who Fought for Women's Right to Vote*.[27] Joan Marie Johnson describes the energizing effect of Mrs. Frank Leslie's $1 million bequest to NAWSA; Johnson maintains, "The publicity and NAWSA's winning plan were essential to the passage of the Nineteenth Amendment."[28]

The most comprehensive look at US mainstream media so far is Genevieve G. McBride's examination of how Wisconsin women marshaled the press in their fight for suffrage and other reforms; her book is a model for taking a deep dive into journalism's role in a state, regional, or national suffrage campaign.[29]

Cultural History Emerges

Cultural history began to emerge in suffrage press studies in 1983 with Linda Steiner's seminal analysis of how nineteenth-century newspapers forged an independent identity and created community among far-flung women. Steiner built on William Goode's theorization of professions as communities to argue that periodicals played a central role in sustaining and solidifying suffragist identity. The suffrage press, she concluded, played a key role in the move from the Victorian selfless "true woman" to the twentieth century's independent "new woman."[30] Steiner offered a more structural analysis a decade later that found suffrage journals were nonhierarchal, unconcerned with objectivity, and disinclined to separate editorial and business departments.[31]

In *A Voice of Their Own: The Woman Suffrage Press, 1840–1910*, editor Martha Solomon advanced scholarship in 1991 with a collection of essays by assorted authors that analyzed the rhetorical functions of eight suffrage periodicals. Solomon identified their two main functions as raising women's consciousness about their subjugation and providing information to support the suffrage movement.[32] Ann Russo and Cheris Kramarae's collection of early women's rights newspaper articles that same year contextualized them in relation to the intellectual and social currents of the 1850s. They argued that the anthology showed that a significant segment of women challenged the nineteenth-century's self-denying "cult of true womanhood."[33] Kramarae edited a similar collection of *Revolution* articles with Lana K. Rakow; the useful introductory materials position the short-lived newspaper at the nexus of a transnational "web of interconnections" among women's communications.[34] Maurine H. Beasley contrasted the radical, short-lived *Revolution* with the more conservative, long-lived *Woman's Journal* in a 1993 anthology of women's journalism.[35] Lee Joliffe focused on how the *Woman's Journal* popularized suffrage, and traced how the growth of nineteenth-century women's magazines facilitated the movement's important shift from relying on oratory to engaging mass media.[36]

Moving into the twentieth century, I studied the wartime strategies of the *Woman's Journal*, which in 1917–18 emphasized women's war work to prove their worthiness of the vote, contrasted to the National Woman's Party's (NWP) recalcitrant *Suffragist*, which ignored the war while publicizing its scandalous picketing of the White House.[37] Scrutinizing antisuffragist periodicals, Manuela Thurner refuted the notion that men controlled them and their publishers rejected women in the public sphere.[38] Burt incorporated social movement theory in her study of *The Remonstrance*, voice of the Massachusetts Association Opposed to the Further Extension of Suffrage to Women, whose exclusively reactive rhetoric doomed the antis.[39]

The cultural emphasis generated new perspectives on old periodicals. Mary M. Carver's study of *Woman's Journal* letters to the editor in the 1880s and 1890s argued they were precursors of second-wave feminist consciousness-raising. Carver's suggestion that "the press was an interactive communication partner" that provided community for geographically dispersed women, however, basically reiterates Steiner's findings in 1983.[40] In another study of the *Woman's Journal*, Todd H. Richardson cited twenty-three references to Walt Whitman, whom contributors extolled as a progressive feminist whose poetry had helped conceptualize new possibilities for women in civic affairs.[41]

Amber Roessner demonstrated how scholars can discover new insights about familiar individuals in her reexamination of Jane Cunningham Croly, better known in the Reconstruction era as popular women's columnist "Jenny June." Taking a cue from feminist theorist Diana Fuss, Roessner reconsidered why some successful career women who championed women's rights opposed enfranchisement. The article also demonstrated how searchable, digitized collections can advance research in suffrage and the media. Using two of ProQuest's online databases, Roessner located more than sixty of Croly's newspaper and magazine articles published over four decades.[42]

Other scholars made inroads into transitional history. Maurine H. Beasley examined the positive impact the suffrage movement exerted on women journalists' careers in Washington, DC, in the 1920s. She calls the suffrage campaign "a godsend" to women because it gave them entry into writing political news.[43] Sheila Webb's inquiry into the *Woman Citizen*'s struggle to remain relevant after women won the vote makes a provocative connection between the political climate of the 1920s and the 2008 presidential election, when mainstream media fumbled to reframe women's role in the public sphere. According to Webb, press coverage of Hillary Clinton and Sarah Palin resorted "to the same archetypes found of women in public life in the 1920s."[44] Donna Harrington-Lueker connects *The Revolution* to *Ms.* magazine in her examination of the former's evolving editorial, advertising, and circulation practices in search of new audiences and financial solvency.[45] A. Cheree Carlson finds advice for modern feminists in her analysis of Lucretia Mott's use of the Quaker concept of "inner light" as a bridging device between her conservative audience and her radical goals in "Discourse on Woman." Carlson suggests Mott's technique could help modern feminists unite women with widely disparate cultural roots.[46]

Scholars continue to identify contributions of important individual suffragists like Alice Duer Miller, chair of NAWSA's resolutions committee and author of a popular weekly column for the *New York Tribune* intriguingly titled, "Are Women People?"[47] Feminist scholar Jennifer Thompson went back to *Queen Bee* editor Caroline Nichols Churchill's early experiences as a travel writer to understand the origins of her forceful arguments for the inherent equality between the sexes.[48] Candi Carter Olson recently revisited another nineteenth-century journal in her framing analysis of how the Utah Woman's Press Club capitalized on its connections to the *Woman's Exponent* (the club's founder edited it) to advance its views.[49]

The oldest work of suffrage history remains fodder for historians. Julie Des Jardins used the prism of public memory to dissect the ideological clashes and personal antagonisms that biased *The History of Woman Suffrage* (1881–1922), a six-volume work comprising more than 5,700 pages.[50] Ellen Gruber Garvey includes a fascinating analysis of the role of the humble scrapbook in suffrage history in a chapter of *Writing with Scissors: Scrapbooks from the Civil War to the Harlem Renaissance*, observing that the thirty-three scrapbooks Anthony filled during her long career provided the foundation for the monumental *History* (Eleanor Flexner called Anthony, Stanton, and

Gage "inveterate hoarders").[51] Garvey reframes the private, parlor-room pursuit as an extraordinary claim to act in the public sphere.[52] Lisa Tetrault's bold reassessment of the *History* described it as a "stunning act of historical imagination."[53] She argued, however, that the tome also enshrined in public memory the editors' dominance of the suffrage movement, even as they battled among themselves, contributors, and American Woman Suffrage Association leaders whose role in suffrage history they erased.[54]

Tetrault's more significant critique is that the editors' "whitening" of the suffrage movement "insisted that educated, white, middle-class women could, and should, speak for all women."[55] Racism within the white-dominated suffrage movement has been much scrutinized in the twenty-first century. Jen McDaneld analyzed Stanton's "racist rhetoric." She claims black women appear in *The Revolution* only as the "supreme victims of the atrocities of slavery," a device to associate privileged white suffragists with slavery's subjugation.[56] Louise Michele Newman parsed the equally racist writings of antisuffrage leader Mary Abigail Dodge.[57] Teresa Zackodnik elaborated on racism in her thoughtful interrogation of the *History*'s representation of Sojourner Truth in *Press, Platform, Pulpit: Black Feminist Publics in the Era of Reform.*[58]

In the 1990s, black feminist scholars demanded more inclusivity and intersectionality in studies of the suffrage movement.[59] The most important figure retrieved may be Frances Ellen Watkins Harper. For over sixty years her work appeared in diverse white and black publications. Harper directly addressed suffrage in print in only a few articles, however, writing more about abolition before the Civil War and temperance and race after. Best known as a novelist, she inserted her prosuffrage views in her fiction, whose republication in 1994 sparked a resurgence of interest in her.[60]

Nell Irvin Painter contrasted Stanton's erasure of the literate Harper, born a free black, with her co-optation of Truth, the former slave, in *The History of Woman Suffrage*.[61] Painter detailed the impossible choice forced upon the pioneering black feminist by the double burden of race and sex discrimination. During the divisive debate on the Fifteenth Amendment (which enfranchised black men), Harper concluded that she had to choose between her identity as a woman and "as a Negro."[62] Alison Parker, tracing how Harper's popular novels presented political debates on women's voting rights and temperance, quotes one of Harper's characters in *Minnie's Sacrifice*: "When they are reconstructing the government why not lay the whole foundation anew, and base the right of suffrage not on the claims of service or sex, but on the broader basis of our common humanity. . . . Is it not the negro woman's hour also?"[63]

Race and Suffrage Media

Full-fledged biographies of black suffragists/journalists remain rare. The best remains Jane Rhodes's biography of Mary Ann Shadd Cary (1823–93), the first black woman in North America to edit and publish a newspaper, the *Provincial Freeman*. Rhodes makes clear the gender and racial barriers Cary overcame to launch the weekly publication for African Americans, especially escaped slaves. Passage of the Fugitive Slave Law spurred Cary to flee to Canada in 1850, even though she was born free in Delaware. A suffrage advocate after the Civil War, Cary addressed the 1878 convention of the National Woman Suffrage Association and worked with Anthony and Stanton.[64]

Ida B. Wells-Barnett is probably the most famous African American journalist and suffragist, but those two passions seem never to have converged. By the time the antilynching muckraker founded the Alpha Suffrage Club of Chicago in 1913, she had left journalism behind.[65] Jinx C. Broussard has highlighted the journalism of black activist Mary Church Terrell, who supported suffrage but concentrated on racial issues.[66] Streitmatter has profiled clubwoman and publisher Josephine St. Pierre Ruffin, whose *New Era* newspaper supported votes for women.[67]

Zackodnick analyzed writing by Anna Julia Cooper, the radical black journalist, feminist, educator, and leader of the black women's club movement. Cooper pioneered intersectionality a century before the term existed by examining the interlocking systems of race, gender, and class oppression in a collection of essays, *A Voice from the South by a Black Woman of the South* (1892). The book includes an 1891 essay that Cooper penned after attending the National Council of Women's meeting in Washington, DC, where she was dismayed by the racist rhetoric of the white women who dominated the meeting. Cooper condemned suffrage leader Anna Howard Shaw's ugly screed against South Dakota's recent enfranchisement of male Indians, calling for the natural inherent rights of all people.[68]

Suffragists both romanticized and denigrated Native Americans in their campaign for the vote. An ambitious project might be a study of how the suffrage press framed native culture. Kristin Mapel Bloomberg addresses suffragists' paradoxical views of Native Americans in her profile of *Woman's Tribune* editor and publisher Clara Bewick Colby, a Kansan who advocated full equality for both women and Indians. Colby used her adopted Sioux daughter in the *Tribune*'s pages to link whites and people of color and engage them in "a conscious understanding of the gendered intersections of race and class."[69] Anthropologist Gail Landsman's nuanced look at the evolution of suffragists' use of native people as a political symbol found that Indian women served both as a symbol of women's past power and natural rights, on the one hand, and a validation of women's special "civilizing" influence on the other. Landsman recounts how suffragists appropriated Sacajawea as a symbol, culminating in their unveiling of the scout's statue during a NAWSA convention in Portland in 1905, the same year as the Lewis and Clark Centennial Exposition: Sacajawea, with a baby on her back, points to the land that she was helping to open up to white civilization.[70] Suffrage periodicals' accounts of this activity could shed additional light on movement views.

Perhaps not surprisingly, prosuffrage commentaries by black men (editors) received attention a generation earlier than did the suffrage writings of black women. As early as 1940, Benjamin Quarles wrote about Frederick Douglass's role in the women's rights movement, pointing out that the inaugural issue of his *North Star* abolition newspaper in 1847 declared, "Right is of no sex." Quarles's recounting of the Fifteenth Amendment split is more benign than recent scholarship. He states Douglass's relationship with Anthony and Stanton "became very cordial again" after the furor died. A footnote attributes the split not to racism but to "bitter personal animosities" among suffrage leaders.[71]

Several scholars have discussed W. E. B. Du Bois's vocal support for woman suffrage in *The Crisis*, the newspaper he edited for the National Association for the Advancement of Colored People (NAACP), including Kroeger's *The Suffragents*. Jean Fagan Yellin and then Garth E. Pauley each described the remarkable number of materials in *The Crisis* that championed women's rights.[72] Gary L. Lemons positions Douglass and Du Bois as "womanist forefathers" to later generations of feminist black men.[73] Valethia Watkins emphasizes his stinging critiques of movement racism and argues that Du Bois sought to rebuild linkages between suffragists and the black civil rights struggle by emphasizing their common ground. Her claim that Du Bois's advocacy challenges the myth that black men did not support enfranchising women, however, seems a bit outdated.[74]

Visual Rhetoric and Consumer Culture

The colorful spectacle of suffrage has made the biggest splash in suffrage media history, beginning with British art historian Lisa Tickner's lavish *The Spectacle of Women: Imagery of the Suffrage Campaign 1907–14*. Tickner convincingly demonstrated the preeminent role of visual spectacle in the British campaign for the vote.[75] By producing their own posters, banners, leaflets, and plays, she observes, suffragists created positive images of female activism in rallies, pageants, and demonstrations that also provided visual proof of wide-scale support for the movement. Visual rhetoric was the organizing theme of rhetoricians Katharine H. Adams and Michael L. Keene's book about Alice Paul's theatrical techniques. They assert that images of the White House pickets she organized in 1917 and other spectacular but nonviolent protests pressured President Woodrow Wilson to eventually support a federal suffrage amendment.[76]

Alice Sheppard's lush illustrated study of suffrage cartoons testifies to the centrality of imagery in American suffrage print media. She contextualizes dozens of suffrage cartoonists' images by explaining the history of political cartoons and the suffrage movement.[77] The edifying introduction by Elizabeth Israels Perry highlights how the cartoonists adroitly used humor and horror to galvanize suffrage newspaper readers. The political cartoons—Sheppard's book includes 200 of them—subvert stereotypes of suffrage activists as unfeminine, dour, or dangerous. Cartoonists' emphasis on suffragists' youth, beauty, and femininity, however, reinforced stereotypes of women as decorative rather than as powerful political players. Thus, the cartoons "helped win the battle for the vote but never shook loose long-entrenched views of how men and women should interact once the vote was won."[78]

Other scholars since have put suffrage cartoons under the microscope to good effect. Katharina Hundhammer compared cartoons in the *Woman's Journal*, *The Suffragist*, and the *Woman Voter* with those in the general interest magazines *Life*, *Harper's Weekly*, and the *Literary Digest* to trace sociocultural changes in the concept of femininity in the early twentieth century.[79] Catherine H. Palczewski determined that a twelve-card set of antisuffrage cartoon postcards in 1909 visually made the argument that voting women would feminize men (and the nation).[80] Jaqueline McLeod Rogers compared the antisuffrage cartoons of John Tinney McCutcheon, an American whose cartoons valorize the peaceful tactics of American suffragists, and Newton McConnell, a Canadian whose cartoons depict the militant British suffragettes as a mob that could tear apart Canadian society.[81]

Carolyn Kitch dug deeper into the ramifications of gender stereotypes in early twentieth-century American magazine illustrations (especially covers) of the New Woman, who invariably was a suffragist. Instead of portraying them as citizens, however, Kitch found mass magazines stereotyped new women as consumers.[82] E. Michele Ramsey built on Kitch's analysis of the *Woman Citizen*'s (successor to the *Woman's Journal*) construction of women as strong, competent, and essential to winning World War I in a series of cover illustrations depicting women performing a variety of war work. Ramsey argues the illustrations' merger of traditional conceptions of women—sewing bandages, for example—with the masculine act of waging war stands as the "most rhetorically inventive representation of woman by the suffrage movement."[83] Rachel Schreiber studied what she terms the "graphic satire" of the *Woman's Journal* wartime cartoons.[84] She traces how suffrage cartoonists subverted gendered ideals of citizenship. Schreiber overgeneralizes, however, in her claim that toward the end of the war the suffrage press reverted to conventional images of women. At the time, *Suffragist* cartoons championed the NWP's unladylike pickets even as police hauled them off to Occoquan workhouse.

Opening the doors to a fertile new line of research, Margaret Finnegan's *Selling Suffrage: Consumer Culture and Votes for Women* (1999) illuminated how suffragists looked to mass media, advertising, and entertainment for ideas on new ways to promote their ideas and began securing more public space than ever before.[85] Suffrage products such as newspapers, Kewpie dolls, and "Womanalls" (overalls for the new woman) helped make suffrage a household word, according to Finnegan, as well as suffrage pageants, fashionable window displays, "newsies," and other devices. Finnegan convincingly argues such entertaining activities and commodities helped suffragists claim legitimacy in a consumer capitalist society. Pursuing a tangent of this theme but challenging studies that cite the auto's positive influence on women, Laura L. Behling argues the male-dominated automobile and advertising industries reinforced the same traditional sex and gender roles that much of society feared votes for women would destroy.[86]

Kenneth Florey cataloged some 700 imaginative and ideological postcards that suffragists exchanged, wrote about, and sold; they even organized "postcard day" campaigns. While postcards produced by suffragists argued for enfranchisement and countered antisuffrage broadsides, Florey found that cards produced by commercial publishers frequently conveyed negative stereotypes. Florey also published an illustrated history of suffrage memorabilia that relies on period accounts to understand their role in the United States and England.[87]

Some visual rhetoric studies have inventively ventured farther afield. Christina Elizabeth Dando describes the maps that American suffragists used to illustrate the spread of women's suffrage on posters, pamphlets, and broadsides as an example of "critical cartography," in which a minority adopts "the master's tools" to advance their own interests.[88] If dress can be considered media, Katherine Feo Kelly artfully incorporated issues of class and race into her fascinating analysis of how the NWP exploited the shocking sight of white, elite suffragists who were jailed for picketing the White House wearing coarse prison uniforms. Women repurposed these prison smocks as costumes on the NWP's "Prison Special" campaign tour in 1919.[89]

Enlivening Literary, Film, and Theater Scholarship

Literary approaches also have breathed fresh air into suffrage media studies. Political scientist Barbara A. Bardes and drama scholar Suzanne Gossett
coauthored the survey *Declarations of Independence: Women and Political
Power in Nineteenth-Century American Fiction*.[90] Ann L. Ardis connected
suffrage texts and literary modernism in her study of novels with prosuffrage
new women characters.[91] Victoria Olwell's creative analysis of "typewriter fiction" quotes a 1914 advertisement in New York's *Woman Voter* that declares
the typewriter has done "much toward gaining 'Women's Rights'" by giving
women economic independence.[92] Amy Easton-Flake concluded that fiction
and poetry played "an integral, polemical role" in both the *Woman's Journal*'s
and *The Revolution*'s visions of new womanhood.[93] American suffragists were
keenly aware of literature's power to persuade. Mary Chapman and Angela
Mills find "startling affinities between popular literature and propaganda"
in their analysis of literary texts that experimented with genre, aesthetics,
humor, and sex appeal to win suffrage support.[94]

Retrieval work on suffrage film and theater beginning in 1987 with Bettina Friedl's collection of twenty forgotten suffrage plays in *On to Victory:
Propaganda Plays of the Woman Suffrage Movement*, enabled scholars to paint
a richer picture of the theater's considerable role in shaping feminism. Attention went to Hazel MacKaye, author of the 1913 suffrage pageant on the US
Treasury Building that followed the national parade,[95] and Elizabeth Robins,
an American novelist, playwright, actress and suffragist, who in 1888 moved
to London, where she wrote the popular play *Votes for Women!*[96] Susanne
Aitsch included suffrage plays in her analysis of the gender tensions enacted
onstage in plays by women between 1910 and 1930.[97] Connecting these works
to the present, Susan A. Glenn demonstrated how the stage proved pivotal
in the emergence of modern feminism.[98] Christine Woodworth argues that
a 1910 New York City performance of suffrage plays, poetry, and speeches
united US and British artists and activists.[99]

Film scholars also traced the importance of silent films in suffrage campaigns, first in the inaugural issue of *Women and Film*.[100] Few of dozens of
suffrage films survived, so Kay Sloan's ground-breaking analysis of them
relied largely on film magazines. She concluded that theater screens became a
battleground for an ideological war on gender roles that extended far beyond
the vote.[101] Shelley Stamp Lindsey analyzed the 1913 feature *Eighty Million
Women Want—?*, coproduced by the Women's Political Union (and featuring a rousing suffrage speech by founder Harriot Stanton Blatch). Lindsey
observed that the urban melodrama's potentially radical rewriting of gender

roles is compromised by reliance on traditional separate spheres, a perpetual dilemma for suffrage advocates. Amy Shore positioned suffragists among the earliest US activists to harness the power of cinema for social change. Suffrage films, she argues, including four full-length, nationally distributed feature productions, represent the birth of a feminist political filmmaking tradition.[102]

Although none cast a critical eye on the movement they honor, documentary films have become another medium for suffrage history, beginning with the BBC six-part "Shoulder to Shoulder" series on the British suffrage movement in 1974. Twenty years later Ruth Pollak's *One Woman, One Vote* for PBS offered a sweeping look at the US suffrage movement, a topic revisited by Ken Burns in his trademark style in *Not for Ourselves Alone: The Story of Elizabeth Cady Stanton and Susan B. Anthony*.[103] California filmmaker Martha Wheelock similarly combined archival photographs, stock footage, and reenactments set to narration and suffrage music in several short celebratory films, including a 2016 profile of suffrage martyr Inez Milholland.[104] Yoshie Lewis told the story of Tennessee's crucial role in the ratification of the Nineteenth Amendment in his 2017 film, *The Perfect 36: When Women Won the Vote*.[105]

An embryonic branch of inquiry considers the treatment of suffrage history in current popular culture. Krista Cowman chronicled factual and fictional film portrayals of the British Women's Social and Political Union's militant protests from newsreels in the 1910s through *Suffragette* (2015), the first feature film about the campaign.[106] HBO's 2004 feature film, *Iron Jawed Angels*, a Hollywoodized re-creation of Alice Paul's campaign, won popular and industry acclaim for making the suffrage movement relevant to young women. Kristy Maddux praised director Katja von Garnier's rock music score but feared the film deflated possibilities for radical feminist activism directed at structural change.[107] Despite the film's shortcomings and inaccuracies, cinema scholar Suzanne Bouclin deemed it a feminist legal text that remains relevant.[108] Jill Lepore made fascinating connections between the female superhero and the suffrage movement in *The Secret History of Wonder Woman*.[109] Digital media also holds promise for original suffrage studies, as evident in an article connecting political memes today to suffrage and antisuffrage imagery.[110]

British Suffrage Media Studies Offer New Directions

The field's greatest need, however, is research on suffrage in the big picture—how movement media influenced and interacted with the larger political and cultural climates. Scholars here can find worthy models in studies of the British suffrage press as a major force in shaping society. An exemplar is Maria DiCenzo, Lucy Delap, and Leila Ryan's exploration of how the British suffrage press advanced women's role in the public sphere. Challenging Jürgen Habermas's claim that the public sphere declined with the rise of mass media, they argue that suffrage periodicals were integral in forging a British feminist public sphere.[111] DiCenzo has been especially innovative; her insights about suffragette newsies, for example, demonstrated they did much more than sell newspapers. On the symbolic and political levels, she writes, the newsie "embodied the 'respectable' woman's foray into the public sphere, and, as a result, contributed in significant ways to the construction and visibility of the politically active, modern woman."[112] Finnegan made similar observations about newsies in *Selling Suffrage*, but opportunity exists for a much broader and deeper look at suffrage media and the American public sphere.

The 2016 special issue of the *Women: A Cultural Review* suggests other new avenues for the study of American suffrage journals, beginning with Victoria Bazin and Melanie Waters's linkage between suffrage and second-wave journals in their introduction.[113] American contributor Barbara Green, who wrote pioneering work on British suffrage as performance in the 1990s, demonstrates how new theoretical frameworks can revitalize familiar topics. For example, she deploys affect theory to the infamous split over militant tactics in 1912 that severed the WSPU organ *Votes for Women* from its publisher, showing how emotions affected feminist periodical networks.[114] (Green's *Feminist Periodicals and Daily Life: Women and Modernity in British Culture* is kind of the flip side of her work on suffrage as spectacle.[115]) As the premier medium of the UK suffragette movement, *Votes for Women* has been the subject of several studies, notably John Mercer's analysis of how its ability to challenge and compete with mainstream media prior to the split demonstrated the WSPU's broader press strategy.[116] Katherine E. Kelly's study of how the symbiotic relationship between London's changing commercial press and the publicity-hungry suffragists gave readers a thrilling new sense of urban life offers a template for a similar investigation in New York.[117]

A new collection on the relationships among artists, political activists, and commerce in Edwardian England may inspire interdisciplinary scholars in the United States. One enticing entry is coeditor Miranda Garrett's chapter, "Window Smashing and Window Draping: Suffrage and Interior Design."[118] Other work also suggests how suffrage media studies can extend beyond journalism.[119]

The most significant British studies exposed unexpected connections between suffrage media and literary modernism. Carol Barash first made the case in her artful tracing of the gender politics at play in the transformation of the *Freewoman: A Weekly Feminist Review* (1911–12) into the literary modernist little magazine *The Egoist* (1914–19), edited by Ezra Pound.[120] Her work influenced the most engaging, innovative, and ambitious work on American suffrage media, Canadian scholar Mary Chapman's *Making Noise, Making News: Suffrage Print Culture and U.S. Modernism.* Both cultural history and literary criticism, Chapman's interdisciplinary foray links a broad range of suffrage media to the modernist literature movement in the early twentieth century.[121] She asks large questions that put suffrage print culture front and center; several of her themes have been plumbed by British cultural scholars.[122] Chapman, who coedited *Treacherous Texts*, argues suffragists finally won the vote largely because they moved from a nineteenth-century reliance on oratory and polemic to a twentieth-century focus on engaging mass media. "Whether modern suffragists fashioned their own counterpublic through advocacy journals or caught the attention of mainstream newspapers and journals," Chapman observes, "print offered them a way of reaching large numbers of people across the country quickly."[123]

In a chapter that applies modernist literary scholar Juan Suarez's notion of "sonic modernity," Chapman found the *American Suffragette* newspaper deployed noise—"'loud' fonts, hectoring editorial personae, noisy hurdy gurdy organs, and barking suffrage newsies"—in a way that marked them politically modern and aesthetically modernist. Conversely, the second chapter shows how three genres of suffrage silence—tableaux, "voiceless speeches," and banners—transformed women's lack of political voice from a symbol of weakness into active participation in the public sphere. The mainstream press found these publicity stunts irresistible, garnering positive news coverage for the suffrage campaign. Other chapters compare the work of Alice Duer Miller, author of "Are Women People?," the popular *New York Tribune* suffrage poetry column, with that of modernist poet Marianne Moore. A chapter on the work of Chinese North American writer Edith Eaton/Sui Sin Far helps diversify suffrage history by highlighting Far's challenge to US suffragists' often xenophobic outlook.

The lack of a work as ambitious as *Making Noise, Making News* in the United States is a glaring omission from nearly a half-century of American suffrage media history. No book-length treatment yet explores US suffrage print culture. A model framework for a national study might be found in a 2014 study of how thousands of pamphlets, leaflets, and flyers shaped suffrage campaigns in the Midwest, where vast spaces and difficult travel conditions stymied face-to-face conversations. Author Sara Egge concludes print culture was vital to midwestern suffragists, who "planned their political campaigns around small papers with big messages."[124] Alice Fahs's lively *Out on Assign-*

ment: Newspaper Women and the Making of Modern Public Space, in which the suffrage press occasionally pops up, offers another model for exploring the key question of how suffrage media drew women into the public sphere—and changed both.

Notes

1. Catherine Mitchell, "Historiography: A New Direction for Research on the Woman's Rights Press," *Journalism History* 19 (Summer 1993): 59–63. See also Mitchell, "Historiography on the Woman's Rights Press," in *Outsiders in 19th-Century Press History: Multicultural Perspectives*, ed. Frankie Hutton and Barbara Straus (Bowling Green, OH: Bowling Green State University Popular Press, 1995), 159–68.

2. Elizabeth V. Burt, "Journalism of the Suffrage Movement: 25 Years of Recent Scholarship," *American Journalism* (Winter 2000): 73–85.

3. James W. Carey, "The Problem of Journalism History," *Journalism History* 1 (1974): 3–5, 27.

4. Kathi Kern, "Productive Collaborations: The Benefits of Cultural Analysis to the Past, Present, and Future of Women's History," *Journal of Women's History* 16, no. 4 (2004): 34–40.

5. See Gerda Lerner, "Placing Women in History: Definitions and Challenges," *Feminist Studies* 3 (Autumn 1975): 5–14.

6. Lynne Masel-Walters, "Their Rights and Nothing More: A History of the Revolution, 1868–1870," *Journalism Quarterly* 53 (Summer 1976): 242–51; and Masel-Walters, "A Burning Cloud by Day: The History and Content of the *Woman's Journal*," *Journalism History* 3 (Winter 1976–77): 103–10. See also Part 2 in Lee Jolliffe, "Women's Magazines in the 19th Century," *Journal of Popular Culture* 27, no. 4 (1994), 125–40; Katharine Rodier, "Lucy Stone and *The Woman's Journal*," in *Blue Pencils and Hidden Hands: Women Editing Periodicals, 1830–1910*, ed. Sharon M. Harris and Ellen Gruber Garvey (Boston: Northeastern University Press, 2004), 99–120; and Rodger Streitmatter, "Setting a Revolutionary Agenda for Women's Rights," in *Voices of Revolution: The Dissident Press in America* (New York: Columbia University Press, 2001), 36–53.

7. See Marion Marzolf, "The Feminist Press Then and Now," in *Up from the Footnote: A History of Women Journalists* (New York: Hastings House, 1977), 219–47.

8. Sherilyn Cox Bennion, "Woman Suffrage Papers of the West, 1869–1914," *American Journalism* 3 (1986): 125–39; Bennion, "The *New Northwest* and *Woman's Exponent*: Early Voices for Suffrage," *Journalism Quarterly* 54 (1977): 286–92; Bennion, "*The Pioneer*: The First Voice of Women's Suffrage in the West," *Pacific Historian* 25 (1981); 15–21; and Bennion, "The *Woman Exponent*: Forty-two Years of Speaking for Woman Suffrage," *Utah Historical Quarterly* 44 (1976): 222–30. See also Bennion, "The Woman Suffrage Press of the West," in *Outsiders in 19th-Century Press History: Multicultural Perspectives*, ed. Frankie Hutton and Barbara Straus (Bowling Green, OH: Bowling Green State University Popular Press, 1995). Bennion discusses several suffrage editors in her *Equal to the Occasion: Women Editors of the Nineteenth-Century West*

(Reno: University of Nevada Press, 1990). See also Marilyn Dell Brady, "Populism and Feminism in a Newspaper by and for Women of the Kansas Farmers' Alliance, 1891–1894," *Kansas History* 7 (Winter 1984–85): 280–90.

9. D. M. Mansfield, "Abigail S. Duniway: Suffragette with Not-So-Common Sense," *Western Journal of Speech Communication* 35 (1971): 24–29. See also Lauren Kessler, "A Siege of the Citadels," *Oregon Historical Quarterly* 84 (Summer 1983): 117–49; Tiffany Lewis, "Winning Woman Suffrage in the Masculine West: Abigail Scott Duniway's Frontier Myth," *Western Journal of Communication* 75, no. 2 (2000): 127–47; Ruth Barnes Moynihan, *Rebel for Rights: Abigail Scott Duniway* (New Haven: Yale University Press, 1983); and Jean M. Ward and Elaine A. Maveety, "Introduction," in *Yours for Liberty: Selections from Abigail Scott Duniway's Suffrage Newspaper*, ed. Ward and Maveety (Eugene: Oregon State University Press, 2000), 1–38.

10. Lynne Masel-Walters, "To Hustle with the Rowdies: The Organization and Functions of the American Woman Suffrage Press," *Journal of American Culture* 3 (Spring 1980): 167–83.

11. Elizabeth V. Burt, "Dissent and Control in a Woman Suffrage Periodical: Thirty Years of the *Wisconsin Citizen*," *American Journalism* 16, no. 2 (Spring 1999): 39–62.

12. Kathleen L. Endres and Therese L. Lueck, eds., *Women's Periodicals in the United States: Social and Political Issues* (Westport, CT: Greenwood Press, 1996).

13. Lauren Kessler, "The Ideas of Woman Suffragists and the *Portland Oregonian*," *Journalism Quarterly* 57, no. 4 (December 1980): 597–605. Ronald Schaffer alludes to California suffragists' cognizance of appealing to the mainstream press in "The Problem of Consciousness in the Woman Suffrage Movement: A California Perspective," *Pacific Historical Review* 45 (1976): 469–93. See also Lauren Kessler, "The Ideas of Woman Suffrage and the Mainstream Press," *Oregon Historical Quarterly* 84 (Fall 1983): 257–75.

14. Janet M. Cramer, "Woman as Citizen: Race, Class, and the Discourse of Women's Citizenship, 1894–1909," *Journalism and Mass Communication Monographs* 165 (March 1998): 1–39.

15. Nancy Burkhalter, "Women's Magazines and the Suffrage Movement: Did They Help or Hinder the Cause?" *Journal of American Culture* 19, no. 2 (Summer 1996): 13–24.

16. Elizabeth V. Burt, "The Wisconsin Press and Woman Suffrage, 1911–1919: An Analysis of Factors Affecting Coverage by Ten Diverse Papers," *Journalism & Mass Communication Quarterly* 73, no. 3 (Autumn 1996): 620–34; and Burt, "Conflicts of Interest: Covering Reform in the Wisconsin Press, 1910–1920," *Journalism History* 26 (Autumn 2000): 94–107.

17. Rodger Streitmatter, "Slowing the Momentum for Women's Rights," in *Mightier Than the Sword: How the News Media Have Shaped American History* (Boulder, CO: Westview Press, 1997), 30–44.

18. Sidney Bland, "Shaping the Life of the New Woman: The Crusading Years of *The Delineator*," *American Periodicals* 19, no. 2 (2009): 165–88.

19. Linda J. Lumsden, "Beauty and the Beasts: the Significance of Newspaper

Coverage of the 1913 National Suffrage Parade," *Journalism and Mass Communication Quarterly* 77 (Autumn 2000): 593–611. See also Katharine H. Adams and Michael L. Keene, "Parades and Other Events: Escalating the Nonviolent Pressure," in *Alice Paul and the American Suffrage Campaign* (Champaign: University of Illinois Press, 2008), 76–117; Lucy G. Barber, *Marching on Washington: The Forging of an American Political Tradition* (Los Angeles: University of California Press, 2004), 1–353; Jennifer L. Borda, "The Woman Suffrage Parades of 1910–1913: Possibilities and Limitations of an Early Feminist Rhetorical Strategy," *Western Journal of Communication* 66, no. 1 (2002): 25–52; Sarah J. Moore, "Making a Spectacle of Suffrage: The National Woman Suffrage Pageant, 1913," *Journal of American Culture* 20 (Spring 1997): 89–103; Belinda A. Stillion Southard, *Militant Citizenship: Rhetorical Strategies of the National Woman's Party, 1913–1920* (College Station: Texas A&M Press, 2011); and Jim Stovall, *Seeing Suffrage: The Washington Suffrage Parade of 1913, Its Pictures and Its Effects on the American Landscape* (Knoxville: University of Tennessee Press, 2013).

20. Teri Finneman, "'The Greatest of Its Kind Ever Witnessed in America': The Press and the 1913 Women's March on Washington," *Journalism History* 44, no. 2 (Summer 2018): 109–16. See also Rebecca Boggs Roberts, *Suffragists in Washington, DC: The 1913 Parade and the Fight for the Vote* (Charleston, SC: History Press, 2017).

21. Tiffany Lewis, "Mediating Political Mobility as Stunt-Girl Entertainment: Newspaper Coverage of New York's Suffrage Hike to Albany," *American Journalism* 36, no. 1 (April 2019): 99–123.

22. See Elna C. Green, *Southern Strategies: Southern Women and the Woman Suffrage Question* (Chapel Hill: University of North Carolina Press, 1997).

23. Sally G. McMillen, *Seneca Falls and the Origin of the Women's Rights Movement* (London: Oxford University Press, 2008). See also Elaine Weiss, *The Woman's Hour: The Great Fight to Win the Vote* (New York: Viking, 2018).

24. Linda J. Lumsden, *Rampant Women: Suffragists and the Right of Assembly* (Knoxville: University of Tennessee Press, 1997). See also Lumsden, *INEZ: The Life and Times of Inez Milholland* (Bloomington: Indiana University Press, 2004).

25. Susan E. Marshall, *Splintered Sisterhood: Gender and Class in the Campaign against Woman Suffrage* (Madison: University of Wisconsin Press, 1997); Marshall, "Ladies against Women: Mobilization Dilemmas of the Antifeminist Movement," *Social Problems* 32 (April 1985): 348–62; and Louise Stevenson, "Women Anti-Suffragists in the 1915 Massachusetts Campaign," *New England Quarterly* 52 (March 1979): 80–93.

26. Brooke Kroeger, *The Suffragents: How Women Used Men to Get the Vote* (Albany: SUNY Press, Excelsior Editions, 2017).

27. Johanna Neuman, *Gilded Suffragists: The New York Socialites Who Fought for Women's Right to Vote* (New York: NYU Press, 2017).

28. Joan Marie Johnson, *Funding Feminism: Monied Women, Philanthropy, and the Women's Movement, 1870–1967* (Chapel Hill: University of North Carolina Press, 2017), 76. When magazine publisher Frank Leslie died, his widow changed her name to Frank Leslie and inherited his business. Joan Marie Johnson, "New Yorker Mrs.

Frank Leslie's Million-Dollar Gift to Women's Suffrage," *Gotham: A Blog for Scholars of New York City*, November 14, 2017, https://www.gothamcenter.org/blog/new-yorker -mrs-frank-leslies-million-dollar-gift-to-womens-suffrage.

29. Genevieve McBride, *On Wisconsin Women: Working for Their Rights from Settlement to Suffrage* (Madison: University of Wisconsin Press, 1993).

30. Linda Steiner, "Finding Community in 19th-Century Suffrage Periodicals," *American Journalism* 1 (Summer 1983): 1–15. Steiner expanded on this theme in "Evolving Rhetorical Strategies/Evolving Identities," in *A Voice of Their Own: The Woman Suffrage Press: 1840–1910*, ed. Martha Solomon (Tuscaloosa: University of Alabama Press, 1991), 183–97.

31. Linda Steiner, "19th Century Suffrage Periodicals: Conceptions of Womanhood and the Press," in *Ruthless Criticism: New Perspectives in U.S. Communication History*, ed. William Solomon and Robert McChesney (Minneapolis: University of Minnesota Press, 1993), 66–97. She looks at *The Lily* (1849–56); *The Una* (1853–55); *The Revolution* (1868–70); the *Woman's Journal* (1870–1931); the *New Northwest* (1871–87); the *National Citizen and Ballot Box* (1876–81); and the *Woman's Tribune* (1883–1909).

32. See also Martha Solomon, "Autobiographies as Rhetorical Narratives: Elizabeth Cady Stanton and Anna Howard Shaw as 'New Woman,'" *Communication Studies* 42 (1991): 83–92.

33. Ann Russo and Cheris Kramarae, eds., *The Radical Women's Press of the 1850s* (New York: Routledge, 1991). See also Barbara Welter, "The Cult of True Womanhood: 1820–1860," *American Quarterly* 18 (Summer 1966): 151–74.

34. Lana F. Rakow and Cheris Kramarae, eds., *The Revolution in Words: Righting Women 1868–1871* (New York: Routledge, 1990).

35. Maurine H. Beasley, "Suffrage Newspapers," in *Taking Their Place: A Documentary History of Women and Journalism*, ed. Maurine H. Beasley and Sheila J. Gibbons, 1st ed. (Washington, DC: American University Press, 1993).

36. Lee Joliffe, "Women's Magazines in the 19th Century," *Journal of Popular Culture* 27 (Spring 1994): 125–40.

37. Linda J. Lumsden, "'Excellent Ammunition': Suffrage Newspaper Strategies during World War I," *Journalism History* 25 (Summer 1999): 53–63.

38. Manuela Thurner, "'Better Citizens without the Ballot': American Anti-Suffrage Women and Their Rationale during the Progressive Era," *Journal of Women's History* 5, no. 1 (Spring 1993): 33–60. Reprinted in *One Woman, One Vote: Rediscovering the Woman Suffrage Movement*, ed. Marjorie Spruill Wheeler (Troutdale, OR: NewSage Press, 1995), 203–20.

39. Elizabeth V. Burt, "The Ideology, Rhetoric, and Organizational Structure of a Countermovement Publication: *The Remonstrance*, 1890–1920," *Journalism Quarterly* 75 (Spring 1998): 69–83.

40. Mary M. Carver, "Everyday Women Find Their Voice in the Public Sphere: Consciousness Raising in Letters to the Editor of the *Woman's Journal*," *Journalism History* 34, no. 1 (Spring 2008): 15–22.

41. Todd H. Richardson, "From Syphilitic to Suffragist: The *Woman's Journal* and

the Negotiation of Walt Whitman's Celebrity," *Walt Whitman Quarterly Review* 28 (2010): 36–53.

42. Amber Roessner, "'The Great Wrong': 'Jennie June's' Stance on Women's Rights," *Journalism History* 38 (Fall 2012): 178–88.

43. Maurine H. Beasley, *Women of the Washington Press: Politics, Prejudice, and Persistence* (Evanston, IL: Northwestern University Press, 2012), esp. 25–56.

44. Sheila M. Webb, "The *Woman Citizen*: A Study of How News Narratives Adapt to a Changing Social Environment," *American Journalism* 29, no. 2 (Spring 2012): 9–36.

45. Donna Harrington-Lueker, "Finding a Market for Suffrage," *Journalism History* 33, no. 3 (2007): 130–39.

46. A. Cheree Carlson, "Defining Womanhood: Lucretia Coffin Mott and the Transformation of Femininity," *Western Journal of Communication* 58, no. 2 (1994): 85–97.

47. Mary Chapman, "'Are Women People?': Alice Duer Miller's Politics and Poetry," *American Literary History* 18, no. 1 (Spring 2006): 59–85.

48. Jennifer A. Thompson, "From Travel Writer to Newspaper Editor: Caroline Churchill and the Development of Her Political Ideology within the Public Sphere," *Frontiers: A Journal of Women Studies* 20, no. 3 (1999): 42–63. See also Patricia Grimshaw and Katherine Ellinghaus, "'A Higher Step for the Race': Caroline Nichols Churchill, The *Queen Bee* and Women's Suffrage in Colorado, 1879–1893," *Australasian Journal of American Studies* 20, no. 2 (December 2001): 29–46.

49. Candi Carter Olson, "'We Are the Women of Utah': The Utah Woman's Press Club's Framing Strategies in the *Woman's Exponent*," *Journalism & Mass Communication Quarterly* 95 (Spring 2018): 213–34.

50. See Julie Des Jardins, "Remembering Organized Feminism," in *Women and the Historical Enterprise in America: Gender, Race, and the Politics of Memory, 1880–1970* (Chapel Hill: University of North Carolina Press, 2003), 177–213.

51. Eleanor Flexner, *Century of Struggle: The Woman's Rights Movement in the United States,* enlarged ed. (Cambridge, MA: Belknap Press of Harvard University Press, 1996), 338.

52. Ellen Gruber Garvey, *Writing with Scissors: Scrapbooks from the Civil War to the Harlem Renaissance* (New York: Oxford University Press, 2012), 173. Garvey also has detailed how her scrapbook illuminates the suffrage work of African American poet, journalist, and activist Alice Moore Dunbar-Nelson. See Ellen Gruber Garvey, "Alice Moore Dunbar-Nelson's Suffrage Work: The View from Her Scrapbook," *Legacy: A Journal of American Women Writers* 33, no. 2 (2016): 310–35, https://muse.jhu.edu/.

53. Lisa Tetrault, *The Myth of Seneca Falls: Memory and the Women's Suffrage Movement, 1848–1898* (Chapel Hill: University of North Carolina Press, 2014), 115. Editors of *The History of Woman Suffrage* changed as the originals died: Ida Usted Harper replaced Gage as coeditor for Volume 4 of the *History*; Stanton and Harper edited Volume 5, and Harper was sole editor of Volume 6. See also Lisa Tetrault, "We Shall Be Remembered: Susan B. Anthony and the Politics of Writing History,"

in *Susan B. Anthony and the Struggle for Equal Rights*, ed. Christine L. Ridarsky and Mary M. Huth (Rochester: University of Rochester Press, 2012), 15–58.

54. See also Grace Farrell, "Beneath the Suffrage Narrative," *Canadian Review of American Studies* 36, no. 1 (2006): 45–65; and Leila R. Brammer, *Excluded from Suffrage History: Matilda Joslyn Gage, Nineteenth-Century American Feminist* (Westport, CT: Greenwood Press, 2000).

55. Tetrault, *Myth of Seneca Falls*, 135.

56. Jen McDaneld, "White Suffragist Dis/Entitlement: *The Revolution* and the Rhetoric of Racism," *Legacy: A Journal of American Women Writers* 30, no. 2 (2013): 243–64.

57. Louise Michele Newman, *White Women's Rights: The Racial Origins of Feminism in the United States* (New York: Oxford University Press, 1999).

58. Teresa Zackodnik, "'I Don't Know How You Will Feel When I Get Through': Racial Difference, Symbolic Value, and Sojourner Truth," in *Press, Platform, Pulpit: Black Feminist Publics in the Era of Reform* (Knoxville: University of Tennessee Press, 2011), 93–126. See also Zackodnik, ed., *"We Must Be Up and Doing": A Reader in Early African American Feminisms* (Peterborough, ON: Broadview Press, 2010).

59. See Patricia Hill Collins, *Black Feminist Thought: Knowledge, Consciousness, and the Politics of Empowerment* (New York: HarperCollins, 1990); and Kimberlé Crenshaw, "Demarginalizing the Intersection of Race and Sex: A Black Feminist Critique of Antidiscrimination Doctrine, Feminist Theory and Antiracist Politics," *University of Chicago Legal Forum*, no. 1 (1989): 139–67, https://philpapers.org/archive /CREDTI.pdf?ncid=txtlnkusaolp00000603. For foundational accounts of black women suffragists, see Rosalyn Terborg-Penn, *African American Women in the Struggle for the Vote, 1850–1920* (Bloomington: Indiana University Press, 1998); and Ann Dexter Gordon with Bettye Collier-Thomas, eds., *African American Women and the Vote, 1837–1965* (Amherst: University of Massachusetts Press, 1997).

60. Frances Harper, *Minnie's Sacrifice, Sowing and Reaping, Trial and Triumph: Three Rediscovered Novels*, ed. Frances Smith Foster (Boston: Beacon Press, 1994). See also Foster, "Gender, Genre, and Vulgar Secularism: The Case of Frances Ellen Watkins Harper and the AME Press," in *Recovered Writers/Recovered Texts: Race, Class, and Gender in Black Women's Literature*, ed. Dolan Hubbard (Knoxville: University of Tennessee Press), 46–59; and Bettye Collier-Thomas, "F.E.W. Harper: Abolitionist and Feminist Reformer 1825–1911," in *African American Women and the Vote*, ed. Gordon and Collier-Thomas, 41–65.

61. Nell Irvin Painter, "Difference, Slavery, and Memory: Sojourner Truth in Feminist Abolitionism," in *The Abolitionist Sisterhood: Women's Political Culture in Antebellum America*, ed. Jean Fagan Yellin and John C. Van Horne (Ithaca, NY: Cornell University Press, 1994), 139–58.

62. Nell Irvin Painter, "Voices of Suffrage: Sojourner Truth, Frances Watkins Harper, and the Struggle for Woman Suffrage," in *Votes for Women*, ed. Jean H. Baker (New York: Oxford University Press, 2002), 51.

63. Alison Parker, "Frances Watkins Harper and the Search for Women's Inter-

racial Alliances," *Susan B. Anthony and the Struggle for Equal Rights*, ed. Christine L. Ridarsky and Mary M. Huth (Rochester: University of Rochester, 2012), 145–71.

64. Jane Rhodes, *Mary Ann Shadd Cary: The Black Press and Protest in the Nineteenth Century* (Bloomington: Indiana University Press, 1999). See also Jim Bearden and Linda Jean Butler, *The Life and Times of Mary Ann Shadd Cary* (Toronto: NC Press, 1977); Jane Rhodes, "Race, Money, Politics, and the Antebellum Black Press," *Journalism History* 20, no. 3–4 (1994): 21–43; and Rodger Streitmatter, "Mary Ann Shadd Cary: Advocate for Canadian Emigration," in *Raising Her Voice: African-American Women Journalists Who Changed History* (Lexington: University Press of Kentucky, 1994), 25–36.

65. Rodger Streitmatter, "Josephine St. Pierre Ruffin: Pioneering African American Newspaper Publisher," in *A Living of Words: American Women in Print Culture*, ed. Susan Albertine (Knoxville: University of Tennessee Press, 1995), 49–64; and Streitmatter, "Josephine St. Pierre Ruffin: Driving Force in the Women's Club Movement," in *Raising Her Voice: African-American Women Journalists Who Changed History*, 61–72.

66. Jinx C. Broussard, "Mary Church Terrell: A Black Woman Journalist and Activist Seeks to Elevate Her Race," *American Journalism* 19 (Autumn 2002): 13–35.

67. Rodger Streitmatter, "Josephine St. Pierre Ruffin: Pioneering African American Newspaper Publisher," in *A Living of Words: American Women in Print Culture*, ed. Susan Albertine (Knoxville: University of Tennessee Press, 1995), 49–64; and Streitmatter, "Josephine St. Pierre Ruffin: Driving Force in the Women's Club Movement," in *Raising Her Voice: African-American Women Journalists Who Changed History*, 61–72.

68. Teresa Zackodnik, "Conclusion: Feminist Affiliations in a Divisive Climate: Anna Julia Cooper's 'Woman versus the Indian,'" in *Press, Platform, Pulpit*, 225–48.

69. Kristin M. Bloomberg, "Cultural Critique and Consciousness Raising: Clara Bewick Colby's *Woman's Tribune* and Late-Nineteenth-Century Radical Feminism," in *Women in Print: Essays on the Print Culture of American Women from the Nineteenth and Twentieth Centuries*, ed. James P. Danky and Wayne Wiegand (Madison: University of Wisconsin Press, 2006), 27–63. See also C. S. Lomicky, "Frontier Feminism and the *Woman's Tribune*: The Journalism of Clara Bewick Colby," *Journalism History* 28, no. 3 (2002): 102–11.

70. Gail H. Landsman, "The 'Other' as Political Symbol: Images of Indians in the Woman Suffrage Movement," *Ethnohistory* 39, no. 3 (Summer 1992): 247–84.

71. Benjamin Quarles, "Frederick Douglass and the Woman's Rights Movement," *Journal of Negro History* 25, no. 1 (January 1940): 43, 41n28. S. Jay Walker addresses but does not dwell on the suffragists' racist reaction to the Fifteenth Amendment. See S. Jay Walker, "Frederick Douglass and Woman Suffrage," *Black Scholar* 4, no. 6–7 (March–April 1973): 24–31. Reprinted in *Black Scholar* 14, no. 5 (September–October 1983): 18–25. Philip Foner also edited a collection of Douglass's speeches and writings on women's rights. Philip Foner, ed., *Frederick Douglass on Women's Rights* (Westport, CT: Greenwood Press, 1976).

72. Jean Fagan Yellin, "Dubois' 'Crisis' and Woman's Suffrage," *Massachusetts Review* 14, no. 2 (1973): 365–75; Garth E. Pauley, "W. E. B. Du Bois on Woman Suffrage: A Critical Analysis of His *Crisis* Writings," *Journal of Black Studies* 30, no. 3 (January 2000): 383–410.

73. Gary L. Lemons, *Womanist Forefathers Frederick Douglass and W. E. B. Du Bois* (Albany: SUNY Press, 2009).

74. Valethia Watkins, "Votes for Women: Race, Gender, and W. E. B. Du Bois's Advocacy of Woman Suffrage," *Phylon* 53 (Winter 2016): 3–19.

75. Lisa Tickner, *The Spectacle of Women: Imagery of the Suffrage Campaign 1907–14* (Chicago: University of Chicago Press, 1988).

76. Adams and Keene, "Parades and Other Events" (76–116) and "Reaching the Group through Words and Pictures," 42–75, in *Alice Paul.*

77. Alicia Sheppard, *Cartooning for Suffrage* (Albuquerque: University of New Mexico Press, 1994).

78. Elisabeth Israels Perry, "Introduction," in Sheppard, *Cartooning,* 12.

79. Katharina Hundhammer, *American Women in Cartoons 1890–1920: Female Representation and the Changing Concepts of Femininity during the American Woman Suffrage Movement: An Empirical Analysis* (Pieterlen, Switzerland: Peter Lang, 2012).

80. Catherine H. Palczewski, "The Male Madonna and the Feminine Uncle Sam: Visual Argument, Icons, and Ideographs in 1909 Anti-Woman Suffrage Postcards," *Quarterly Journal of Speech* 91, no. 4 (2005): 365–94.

81. Jaqueline McLeod Rogers, "Geopolitics in the Anti-Suffrage Cartoons of American John Tinney McCutcheon and Canadian Newton McConnell: Stopping Trans-Atlantic Flow," *Peitho: Journal of the Coalition of Feminist Scholars in the History of Rhetoric & Composition* 17, no. 1 (Fall–Winter 2014): 31–45.

82. Carolyn Kitch, *The Girl on the Magazine Cover: The Origins of Visual Stereotypes in American Mass Media* (Chapel Hill: University of North Carolina Press, 2001). See also Kitch, "Destructive Women and Little Men: Masculinity, the New Woman, and Power in 1910s Popular Media," *Journal of Magazine & New Media Research* 1, no. 1 (Spring 1999): 1–19.

83. E. Michele Ramsey, "Inventing Citizens during World War I: Suffrage Cartoons in the *Woman Citizen,*" *Western Journal of Communication* 64, no. 2 (Spring 2000): 113–47.

84. Rachel Schreiber, "She Will Spike War's Gun: Suffrage, Citizenship and War," in *Gender and Activism in a Little Magazine: The Modern Figures of The Masses,* ed. Rachel Schreiber (Farnham, UK: Ashgate Publishing, 2011), 124–58. See also Schreiber, "'She Will Spike War's Gun': The Anti-War Graphic Satire of the American Suffrage Press," in *Modern Print Activism in the United States* (Farnham, UK: Ashgate Publishing, 2013), 43–64.

85. Margaret Finnegan, *Selling Suffrage: Consumer Culture and Votes for Women* (New York: Columbia University Press, 1999).

86. Laura L. Behling, "'The Woman at the Wheel': Marketing Ideal Womanhood, 1915–1934," *Journal of American Culture* 20, no. 3 (1997): 13–30.

87. Kenneth Florey, *American Woman Suffrage Postcards: A Study and Catalog* (Jefferson, NC: McFarland & Company, 2012); and Florey, *Women's Suffrage Memorabilia: An Illustrated Historical Study* (Jefferson, NC: McFarland & Company, 2013).

88. Christina Elizabeth Dando, "'The Map Proves It': Map Use by the American Woman Suffrage Movement," *Cartographica: The International Journal for Geographic Information and Geovisualization* 45, no. 4 (2010): 221–40.

89. Katherine Feo Kelly, "Performing Prison: Dress, Modernity, and the Radical Suffrage Body," *Fashion Theory: The Journal of Dress, Body & Culture* 15, no. 3 (2011): 299–321.

90. Barbara A. Bardes and Suzanne Gossett, *Declarations of Independence: Women and Political Power in Nineteenth-Century American Fiction* (New Brunswick, NJ: Rutgers University Press, 1990).

91. Ann L. Ardis, *New Women, New Novels: Feminism and Early Modernism* (New Brunswick, NJ: Rutgers University Press, 1990).

92. Victoria Olwell, "Typewriters and the Vote," *Signs: A Journal of Women in Culture & Society* 29 (Autumn 2003): 55. See also Leslie Petty, *Romancing the Vote: Feminist Activism in American Fiction, 1870–1920* (Athens: University of Georgia Press, 2006); Jean Marie Lutes, "Beyond the Bounds of the Book: Periodical Studies and Women Writers of the Late Nineteenth and Early Twentieth Centuries," *Legacy* 2 (2010): 336–56.

93. Amy Easton-Flake, "Fiction and Poetry in *The Revolution* and the *Woman's Journal*: Clarifying History," *American Journalism* 36, no. 1 (April 2019): 32–50.

94. Mary Chapman and Angela Mills, eds., *Treacherous Texts: U.S. Suffrage Literature, 1846–1946* (New Brunswick, NJ: Rutgers University Press, 2011).

95. Bettina Friedl, *On to Victory: Propaganda Plays of the Woman Suffrage Movement* (Boston: Northeastern University Press, 1987); Karen J. Blair, "Pageantry for Women's Rights: The Career of Hazel MacKaye, 1913–1923," *Theatre Survey: The Journal of the American Society for Theatre Research* 31, no. 1 (May 1990): 23–46.

96. Angela V. John, *Elizabeth Robins: Staging a Life, 1862–1952* (New York: Routledge, 1995).

97. Susanne Aitsch, *Staging Separate Spheres: Theatrical Spaces as Sites of Antagonism in One-Act Plays by American Women, 1910–1930* (Frankfurt: Peter Lang, 2006).

98. Susan A. Glenn, *Female Spectacle: The Theatrical Roots of Modern Feminism* (Cambridge, MA: Harvard University Press, 2000).

99. Christine Woodworth, "'Equal Rights by All Means!': Beatrice Forbes-Robertson's 1910 Suffrage Matinee and the Onstage Junction of the US and UK Franchise Movements," *Theatre History Studies* 37 (2018): 209–22.

100. Gretchen Bataille, "Preliminary Investigations: Early Suffrage Films," *Women and Film* 1 (1973): 42–44.

101. Kay Sloan, "Sexual Warfare in the Silent Cinema: Comedies and Melodramas of Woman Suffragism," *American Quarterly* 33, no. 4 (1981): 412–36. Sloan also produced a thirty-five-minute documentary, which includes footage from including

A Lively Affair (1912); *A Busy Day* (1914), originally titled *The Militant Suffragette*, in which Charlie Chaplin portrays a woman suffragist; and the prosuffrage film *What 80 Million Women Want* (1913). *Suffragettes in the Silent Cinema* (New York: Women Make Movies, 2003).

102. Amy Shore, *Suffrage and the Silver Screen* (New York: Peter Lang, 2014). See also Shore, "Suffrage Stars," *Camera Obscura: Feminism, Culture, and Media Studies* 21, no. 3 (63) (2006): 1–35.

103. *One Woman, One Vote*, directed by Ruth Pollak (Boston: Educational Film Center/WGBH, 1995); and *Not for Ourselves Alone: The Story of Susan B. Anthony and Elizabeth Cady Stanton*, directed by Ken Burns (Alexandria, VA: PBS, 1999).

104. *California Women Win the Vote*, directed by Martha Wheelock (Studio City, CA: Wild West Women, Inc., 2011); *Inez Milholland: Forward into Light*, directed by Martha Wheelock (Studio City, CA: National Women's History Project and Wild West Women, Inc., 2016); *Votes for Women*, directed by Kay Weaver and Martha Wheelock (Studio City, CA: Wild West Women, Inc., 1996).

105. *The Perfect 36: When Women Won the Vote*, directed by Yoshie Lewis (N.p.: Pretzel Pictures, 2017).

106. Krista Cowman, "The Militant Suffrage Campaign on Screen," in *Screening Protest: Visual Narratives of Dissent across Time, Space, and Genre*, ed. Alexa Robertson (Abingdon, UK: Routledge, 2019), 209–29.

107. Kristy Maddux, "Winning the Right to Vote in 2004," *Feminist Media Studies* 9, no. 1 (2009): 73–94.

108. Suzanne Bouclin, "Women's Suffrage: A Cinematic Study," *Revue LISA/LISA e-journal* 12, no. 7 (2014), https://journals.openedition.org/lisa/6918.

109. Jill Lepore, *The Secret History of Wonder Woman* (New York: Alfred A. Knopf, 2014).

110. Adrienne LaFrance, "The Weird Familiarity of 100-Year-Old Feminism Memes," *Atlantic*, October 26, 2016, https://www.theatlantic.com/technology/archive/2016/10/pepe-the-anti-suffrage-frog/505406/.

111. Maria DiCenzo, Lucy Delap, and Leila Ryan, *Feminist Media History: Suffrage, Periodicals and the Public Sphere* (Basingstoke, UK: Palgrave Macmillan, 2011). The trio had earlier collected classic articles from key journals in the three-volume sourcebook they edited, *Feminism and the Periodical Press, 1900–1918* (London: Routledge, 2006).

112. Maria DiCenzo, "Gutter Politics: Women Newsies and the Suffrage Press," *Women's History Review* 12, no. 1 (2003): 16. See also Maria DiCenzo, "Militant Distribution: Votes for Women and the Public Sphere," *Media History* 6, no. 2 (2000): 115–28; DiCenzo, "Feminism, Theatre Criticism, and the Modern Drama," *South Central Review* 25, no. 1 (2008): 36–55; and DiCenzo, "Pressing the Public: Nineteenth-Century Feminist Periodicals and 'the Press,'" *Nineteenth Century Gender Studies* 6 (Summer 2010), http://www.ncgsjournal.com/issue62/dicenzo.htm.

113. Victoria Bazin and Melanie Waters, "Mediated and Mediating Feminisms: Periodical Culture from Suffrage to the Second Wave," *Women: A Cultural Review*

27, no. 4 (2016): 347–58. See also Simone Murray, "Deeds *and* Words: The Woman's Press and the Politics of Print," *Women: A Cultural Review* 11, no. 3 (2000): 197–222.

114. Barbara Green, "The Feel of the Feminist Network: *Votes for Women* after *The Suffragette*," *Women: A Cultural Review* 27, no. 4 (2016): 359–77. See also Barbara Green, *Spectacular Confessions: Autobiography, Performative Activism, and the Sites of Suffrage* (New York: St. Martin's and Palgrave Macmillan, 1997); Green, "Feminist Things," in *Transatlantic Print Culture, 1880–1940: Emerging Media, Emerging Modernisms*, ed. Ann L. Ardis and Patrick Collier (New York: Palgrave Macmillan, 2008), 66–79; Green, "Advertising Feminism: Ornamental Bodies/Docile Bodies and the Discourse of Suffrage," in *Marketing Modernism: Self-Promotion, Canonization, Rereading*, ed. Kevin J. H. Dettmar and Stephen Watt (Ann Arbor: University of Michigan Press, 1996), 191–220; and Green, "Introduction to *The Freewoman*," *Brown Modernist Journals Project*, n.d., www.dl.lib.brown.edu/mjp/render.php?id=mjp.2005.00.111&;view=mjp_object.

115. Barbara Green, *Feminist Periodicals and Daily Life: Women and Modernity in British Culture* (Cham, Switzerland: Springer, 2017).

116. John Mercer, "Making the News: Votes for Women and the Mainstream Press," *Media History* 10 (December 2004): 187–99.

117. Katherine E. Kelly, "Seeing through Spectacles: The Woman Suffrage Movement and London Newspapers, 1906–13," *European Journal of Women's Studies* 11 (August 2004): 327–53.

118. Miranda Garrett and Zoë Thomas, eds., *Suffrage and the Arts: Visual Culture, Politics, and Enterprise* (New York: Bloomsbury Visual Arts, 2018).

119. Ian McDonald, *Vindication! A Postcard History of the Women's Movement* (London: McDonald/Bellow, 1989); Sheila Stowell, *A Stage of Their Own: Feminist Playwrights of the Suffrage Era* (Manchester: Manchester University Press, 1992); and Irene Cockroft and Susan Croft, *Art, Theatre, and Women's Suffrage* (London: Aurora Metro, 2010). See also Katherine Cockin, *Women and Theatre in the Age of Suffrage: The Pioneer Suffrage Players, 1911–1925* (Houndmills, UK: Palgrave, 2001); Naomi Paxton, "Introduction," in *The Methuen Drama Book of Suffrage Plays: Taking the Stage*, ed. Naomi Paxton (Slingsby, UK: Methuen Drama, 2018); and Madeleine Bernstorff, "From the Past to the Future: Suffragettes—Extremists of Visibility in Berlin," in *Early Cinema Today: The Art of Programming and Live Performance*, ed. Martin Loiperdinger (Bloomington: Indiana University Press, 2012), 43–51.

120. Carol Barash, "Dora Marsden's Feminism, *The Freewoman*, and the Gender Politics of Early Modernism," *Princeton University Library Chronicle* 49, no. 1 (1987): 31–56.

121. Mary Chapman, *Making Noise, Making News: Suffrage Print Culture and U.S. Modernism* (New York: Oxford University Press, 2014).

122. Barbara Green, "Feminist Periodical Culture," *Literature Compass* 6, no. 1 (2009): 191–205; Green, "Complaints of Everyday Life: Feminist Periodical Culture and Correspondence Columns in the *Woman Worker* and the *Freewoman*," *Modern-*

ism/modernity 19 (September 2012): 461–85; and Green, "Mediating Women: Evelyn Sharp and the Modern Media Fictions of Suffrage," in *The History of British Women's Writing, 1880–1920*, ed. Holly Laird (London: Palgrave Macmillan, 2016).

123. Chapman, *Making Noise*, 12.

124. Sara Egge, "'Strewn Knee Deep in Literature': A Material Analysis of Print Propaganda and Woman Suffrage," *Agricultural History* 88, no. 4 (Fall 2014): 591–605. See also Egge, *Woman Suffrage and Citizenship in the Midwest, 1870–1920* (Iowa City: University of Iowa Press, 2018).

2

Nineteenth-Century Suffrage Journals

Inventing and Defending New Women

LINDA STEINER

Nineteenth-century US suffragists used their periodicals to invent and advocate a new political woman who deserved prestige, esteem, and respect. As the editor of *The Lily* asserted in 1849, "There is a demand now for a new type of womanhood."[1] In the pages of the suffrage papers, women who were otherwise isolated and marginalized found ways of being that gave their lives coherence, purpose, and meaning. Suffragists disagreed on the precise features of these new women, and their papers rationalized differing versions of what it meant to be a member of the suffrage community. Nevertheless, having articulated, dramatized, and celebrated new identities for women, these papers taught participants how to argue for the legitimacy and value of their lives. They challenged suffragists to demand the status they deserved: the right to enter the public sphere, including access to the ballot box.

Suffrage newspapers generated new words and new definitions for the new women they dramatized and celebrated. They encouraged women to re-name themselves—or, sometimes, not change their names. If women wanted respect, they should not adopt their husbands' names, diminutives, or pet names. Although she did not invent "bifurcated trowsers," Amelia Bloomer so vigorously promoted them in *The Lily* (as appropriate for physically active, busy women liberated from tight corsets and other unhealthy, unsafe fashion dictates) that they became known as "bloomers."[2] Not surprisingly, these new women insisted that women manage, own, produce, and even distribute suffrage papers so that they addressed women's sex-specific[3] interests, recognized women's accomplishments, and advertised products appropriate for women, if they carried ads at all. Suffrage editors adamantly argued that "Ladies' Magazines" would misunderstand their political interests and the "ordinary papers" would either misrepresent or bury their stories.[4] The editor of the *Woman's Era*, for black women, complained that no men editors had found space for speeches given at a Congress of Women in 1896:

> Their columns are "so crowded" with patent matter, ghastly jokes on women, by would-be male wits with women's front names, lists of tin dippers and pie plates received at tin weddings, etc. Sometime our women will come to realize that only through the columns of a paper controlled by themselves will the hard and beneficent work they are doing all the time be made known to the world, and so bring to them the respect and dignity they so richly deserve.[5]

This chapter begins by summarizing how major economic, cultural, political, and social changes in the United States challenged and undermined the symbolic standing of nineteenth-century women. The suffrage movement was a plausible response to this status upheaval. Then I show why mid- to late-nineteenth-century suffrage periodicals were crucial to sustaining the movement, beginning with pre–Civil War suffrage periodicals that proposed a specific kind of new woman, essentially a "sensible woman" who deserved respect and esteem. I explain the rift among suffragists not in terms of arguments over the strategies most effective in winning enfranchisement, but rather in terms of arguments over what kind of woman was to be advocated and celebrated. I focus on the competition between the "strong-minded" women aggressively defended in *The Revolution* and the more moderate "responsible women" advocated by the *Woman's Journal*. Also significant is the "earnest" new black woman dramatized in the *Woman's Era*, which called for women's suffrage in more muted ways.

The Relationship between Status Politics and Social Movements

Profound upheavals in US society, politics, the economy, family, and technology dramatically changed the lives of mid-nineteenth-century middle-class women. Industrialization and the resulting separation of workplace and home enforced a new and wider division of spheres, making informal training and nondomestic work more difficult for women to get. Urbanization largely relegated women as a class to the domestic sphere, where they lived in increasingly smaller households; the birthrate decreased as large families became more a burden than a resource in cities. Once immigration reduced labor shortages, women were pushed out of the paid workforce. Moreover, monetary reward was widely heralded as the mark of success in the emergent "modern" American culture, so women's unpaid domestic duties became more decorative (or symbolic) than valued. The egalitarian rhetoric about extension of the ballot certainly did not apply to women. In sum, the cumulative and intersecting impact of these changes meant that the activities and responsibilities that once were the grounds for a meaningful, satisfying womanly identity became superfluous. Women were excluded from the activities and achievements that society then most celebrated and glorified. Relative to men, all women experienced status disruption, losing responsibility and prestige. Women living on farms and in rural areas experienced different disruptions than urban women and factory workers. Women of color and poor or working-class women experienced change differently from white middle-class women, who apparently never considered how their complaints about "enslavement" and "bondage" might alienate the former.[6] Yet, suffrage newspapers and journals addressed women's cultural, social, and political marginalization by helping women redefine themselves as people whose lives were meaningful and who deserved important political rights.

Most historians treat the suffrage movement's ideology and politics as if the aim were solely enfranchisement per se and the internal arguments turned entirely on the best strategies for winning the vote.[7] Drawing on Max Weber's attention to how status groups command different degrees of prestige, honor, respect, and esteem, I treat the ultimate goal of "new women" as status elevation.[8] Humans not only make and use symbols to give order and coherence to individual and shared experience, but they also want social recognition and affirmation of their identity and community.[9] The suffrage press was a critical arena for staging the conflict, experimenting with different versions of new women, and explaining how to advocate for enfranchisement but also other needs and interests. I use Joseph Gusfield's notion of status politics to suggest that especially in the United States, where class distinctions are weak, people essentially *must* act "to preserve, defend, or enhance the dominance and prestige" of their own group's way of being in the larger society.[10] Material or political resources are useful in preserving status boundaries (wealth and political power, although separate kinds of goods, may facilitate the acquisition of cultural capital). But the conflict resides in the symbolic or cultural realm. Notably, Gusfield suspected, losses to social esteem are probably felt most keenly by those who have less compensation in other dimensions.

A US constitutional amendment enfranchising women would unambiguously, definitively, and nationally symbolize the prestige and public standing of new women, regardless of whether women voted in particular ways, or even voted at all.[11] But many suffrage periodicals adopted additional agendas and issues. They used news articles, fiction, poems, editorials, anecdotes, biographies, essays, advertising, cartoons, and graphics to define women's interests broadly.[12] Typical of early suffrage editors, Paulina Wright Davis, for example, reminded readers each month that *The Una*, whose slogan was "Devoted to the Elevation of Women," tackled "The Rights, Relations, Duties, Destiny and Sphere of Woman: Her Education—Literary, Scientific, and Artistic; Her Avocation—Industrial, Commercial, and Professional; Her Interests—Pecuniary, Civil, and Political." *The Revolution* confronted questions of work, coeducation, money and wages, child-rearing, physical exercise, dress reform, marriage, divorce, sexual politics, partisan party politics, women's role in religion, cooperation with other reform movements, economics, and class conflict. Such breadth is consistent with the way that status politics plays out as a zero-sum game. Whether they focused narrowly on enfranchisement or social issues broadly, suffrage editors apparently understood that increases in their status subtracted from adversaries' prestige.[13] Even Davis, known for her lofty, mild-mannered literary tone, once claimed: "To refuse to consider a cause actively was not simply neutrality, but was to oppose reform and to support the status quo. When the blood-stained heroism of the battlefield demands the homage of our admiration, we must either bravely rebuke the ruffian crime or partake its guilt."[14]

Notably, both pro- and antisuffrage women faced the same status disruptions. Both groups launched movements that relied on periodicals that crystallized unease over change, promoted group identification and shared beliefs, unambiguously differentiated members from adversaries and decentered the role of those adversaries, clarified the means of achieving desired goals, and mobilized support. Antisuffragists chose a different solution, of course, celebrating the so-called "true woman" who deserved prestige in her role as nurturer, homemaker, and agent of moral and cultural socialization. Gusfield points out that unlike human limbs, norms do not necessarily atrophy through disuse. Standards of charity, purity, fidelity, or womanliness may be consistently ignored in practice yet remain important statements of what is publicly approved as virtue. So, antisuffragist periodicals articulated ideological support for separate spheres, recognizing that suffragists' efforts to integrate public and private spheres reduced the social distance on which bestowal of status privileges to women depended. Like other countermovements, antisuffragists invoked established social myths of the time, most prominently that women enjoyed, derived prestige from, and belonged exclusively to a special domestic sphere.[15]

Antisuffragists proposed to elevate the status of a fundamentally conservative woman. The major antisuffragist newspaper the *Woman's Protest* insisted:

"Our aim is to conserve the home, to conserve motherhood, to conserve womanhood."[16] But other antisuffragists articulated the debate over women's status in manifestly symbolic terms—and in precisely the way that suffragists did: "The whole question of Woman's Suffrage rests on something deeper than the point at issue. No suffragist is really fighting heart and body for the doubtful advantage of going to the voting booth; she is fighting for the ideal which that act symbolizes, the new ideal of womanhood."[17]

Versions of the New Woman

Different women's suffrage periodicals responded to shared problems in different ways. The definition of the new woman and her worldview was neither static nor monolithic but varied across space and over time. Each group supported its own organ in the effort to make claims for the moral authority of its style and thereby attract converts. Editors experimented with several versions of the new woman, with writers and readers proposing, rejecting, amending, and refining various conceptions of how new women talked, dressed, and conducted domestic and public life. The publications tried out different rituals and symbols, different histories and futures, different villains and heroines, different political and personal strategies. One writer aptly described suffrage periodicals as "our own camping ground . . . where we may indulge in private rehearsals and scan our own mistakes with a critical eye, the truest wisdom being not to 'pass our imperfections by.'"[18]

Many of the earliest suffrage papers advocated "sensible" women who were smart, self-reliant, practical, energetic, healthy, and capable. This sensible type was dramatized in Elizabeth Aldrich's *Genius of Liberty* (1851–53), published in Cincinnati; *The Una* (1853–55), begun in Providence, Rhode Island; the Indiana-based *Mayflower* (1861–65), the only suffrage paper published during the Civil War; and especially *The Lily* (1848–56). *The Lily* was proposed by Seneca Falls, New York, temperance ladies who resented their subservience to men temperance leaders.[19] The temperance society soon abandoned the project. But Amelia Bloomer, who had attended the Seneca Falls Convention but did not sign the Declaration of Sentiments, decided to put out the paper and soon pushed suffrage to the forefront, explaining: "It was a needed instrument to spread abroad the truth of a new gospel to woman, and I could not withhold my hand to stay the work I had begun."[20]

Especially at the early stages of its publication, *The Lily* offered no clear-cut definition of new women. But in a March 1850 editorial Bloomer argued that it was "high time that women should open their eyes and look where they stand." As *The Lily*'s focus shifted from temperance to woman's rights, its image of the ideal woman changed from one whose primary virtues were benevolence, piety, and nurturance to one capable of responsible action and intelligent analysis. Bloomer emphasized the importance of emancipating women "from cruel enactment of Unjust Laws by which her rights and inalienable claims to equality have been subverted, from the blighting influence of Prejudice by which she has been denied the privilege of being heard in self-defense, and from the blind, soul-destroying Bigotry by which she has been taught to look upon herself."[21]

The most radical and controversial suffrage journal was *The Revolution* (1868–70), edited and published in New York City by Elizabeth Cady Stanton and Susan B. Anthony, with an abolitionist friend, Parker Pillsbury. Its first masthead asserted: "Principle, not policy; Justice, not favors." This was soon amended to add: "Men, their rights and nothing more; Women, their rights and nothing less." Initially bankrolled by an eccentric man whose other political interests were inimical to women reformers, *The Revolution* abandoned flowery philosophical treatises and abstract descriptions of the cause; it explicitly extended and broadened the conception of women's interests. *The Revolution*'s title and credos, as well as other rhetorical strategies, vigorously proclaimed a breed of women who were always assertive, sometimes willful, often dogmatic. Both advocates and critics explicitly used the term "strong-minded women."

Alienated by *The Revolution*'s highly politicized militancy, as suggested by references to an army of women ready to fall into rank and file, the more conservative weekly the *Woman's Journal* prescribed a more "responsible" woman. The *Journal* was established in 1870 in Boston by Lucy Stone, her husband Henry Blackwell, and some of their reform-minded friends, including Julia Ward Howe, William Lloyd Garrison, and T. W. Higginson. Stone and Blackwell had already in 1866 sent out a prospectus for a paper they intended to call *Universal Suffrage*, to signal their interest in enfranchisement and "complete recognition of the industrial and social and political equality of women and Negroes."[22] Mary Ashton Livermore merged her two-year-old Chicago suffrage paper *The Agitator* into the *Journal* so that she could take on the editorship. The *Journal* quickly surpassed *The Revolution* in subscriptions, advertising, and other forms of support; the debt-ridden Anthony soon sold *The Revolution* (for a dollar). The *Woman's Journal* was the longest-running suffrage paper, having occasionally changed its name and picked up the subscription lists of smaller outlets that couldn't sustain themselves. By the time the *Journal* ended in 1931, it was advocating an equal rights amendment.

Suffrage Sisterhood

The papers invariably reflected the politics of their individual editors, especially in the early years when they were not part of some overarching organization. Even so, the papers were regarded—by editors and readers—not simply as communications to women, but as communications *of* and *for* women. Bloomer declared that *The Lily* "is edited and published by Ladies, and to Ladies it will mainly appeal for her support. It is woman that speaks."[23] Aldridge promised subscribers that *Genius of Liberty* "belongs to All; every one will be heard in her own style, principle, and want; 'tis the common property of Woman."[24] At least early on, face-to-face contact was difficult for far-flung suffragists. Paulina Wright Davis boasted that *The Una* reached women who never attended suffrage conventions or lectures: "It has been a voice to many who could not have uttered their thoughts through any other channel—and we have abundant evidence that it has been a source of consolation, looked for every month with anxious expectation, to those who are in solitary places."[25]

Consensus held that women should produce suffrage papers, but suffragists had different opinions on the extent to which and ways in which men should be involved. This principle was tested when the men who printed both *The Lily* and a paper edited by Amelia's husband Dexter (who was neither involved in *The Lily* nor supportive of it) refused to help a woman typesetter hired by Amelia. The Bloomers fired the uncooperative printers, Amelia noting that the resulting delays were "nothing compared with what had been gained on the side of justice and right."[26] Responsible women largely accepted men, perhaps philosophically consistent with their attempts to integrate their special landscape into the larger world. The *Journal* deplored hypocrisy, domination, tyranny by men. But *Journal* editors Blackwell and Higginson demanded men's participation, for "an anti-woman society cannot be reformed by an anti-man affair." In his editorial "Truth Knows No Sex," Blackwell added, "Henceforth let it be understood that the Woman Suffrage movement is not a woman's movement, but a movement of men and women for the common benefit."[27] Higginson opposed all women's institutions (including women's colleges): "What women need is not a separate repast, however choicely served; they need only their fair share in the daily family dinner."[28]

Unanimity was only rarely achieved. Most editors expressed worry that jealousy and backbiting would stymie reform. Elizabeth Aldrich complained, "As a class we have been uncollected, unmarshalled, and destitute of a cementing spirit; no general duty has awakened us; no common effort has ever brought us together."[29] Nevertheless, each suffrage paper regularly reported the successes and problems of other women editors, and often quoted or reprinted news from other reform-minded women's periodicals. Especially in the 1890s, the *Journal* publicized black women's clubs and organizations, as well as the Boston-based monthly *Woman's Era*. In its final issue (December 15, 1856), *The Lily* noted: "When one woman strikes a blow for the elevation of her sex, it redounds to the interests of the whole; and wherever one fails in her purposed plans all feel the calamity and contend against increased odds in maintaining their individual enterprise. We are bound together."

Indeed, suffrage editors formed their own sub-community, publicizing and even writing for other suffrage papers. One Vermont editor testified that Bloomer and other woman editors "contribute largely to our social and intellectual enjoyment and . . . with such and so many associates as our exchanges furnish, we feel no vacuum in our sympathies—are conscious of no social privations."[30] Helen Gougar compared the sale of her *Our Herald* (1881–85) to Elizabeth Boynton Harbert, who renamed it the *New Era*, to turning over a favored child to a stepmother.[31] Some suffrage-minded women also wrote for general periodicals. Having the experience of helping her husband with his *Seneca County Courier*, Bloomer continued *The Lily* even after moving to Ohio, where he purchased a local paper. In Ohio, as the *Western Home Visitor's* assistant editor, Amelia Bloomer again expressed her women's rights views, although these drew considerable criticism.

Born in 1855 to a prominent Philadelphia family, Gertrude E. H. Bustill Mossell wrote about African American women's issues for many white newspapers as well as white magazines such as the *Ladies' Home Journal*, and she was famous for writing for black magazines and newspapers around the country: She was the *Woman's Era* Philadelphia correspondent; the women's editor for the *New York Age*, 1885–89, where her very first column advocated women's suffrage; and the women's editor for the *Indianapolis World*, 1891–92.[32] Her 1894 book *The Work of Afro-American Women* celebrated suffrage heroines and urged women to take up careers. In the section on journalism, Mossell encouraged women: "Have an intelligent comprehension of every department of work on the paper. As a reporter I believe a lady has the advantage of the masculine reporter in many aspects. She can gain more readily as an interviewer access to both sexes."[33]

For their part, readers described the reading experience as if they were neighbors chatting over the fence. *Lily* correspondents often began letters by confiding that they needed to put down the broom and pick up the pen to write "dear Lily before she forgets me." But the more important point was the act of reading it. An Ohio subscriber wrote *The Mayflower*, "How dear your little paper has become to me—how it cheers and strengthens me, even as the voice of a friend. . . . It seems endowed with almost human sympathy, perhaps because the writers do not write coldly from the head alone, but warm their glowing thoughts by the pure light of a true and earnest purpose that emanates from the heart."[34] A Michigan woman wrote that in the *Journal*, "I read over the names of the brave women till I feel as proud of them as if they were my own sisters and dearest friends."[35] Among several claiming to have been radically transformed as a result of a suffrage paper, one enthusiastic reader testified, "Since *The Revolution* has removed the bandages from our eyes and the scales have fallen also, we begin to see women 'as trees walking.'"[36] Another asserted, "Who takes up a copy of the *Woman's Journal* and reads what women are doing all the world over, but feels a glow, a hearty cheer, in looking on the fields where these reapers are toiling. . . . What Woman's heart is not stirred by the thought of this sisterhood . . . this holy order."[37]

Internal Cleavages

Disunity is manifest in the rivalry between *The Revolution* and the *Woman's Journal*. The former articulated a peculiarly politicized worldview by which converts could understand, judge, and act on the very real and problematic issues of the day. Although *Revolution* writers often used religious language, it specifically justified rebellion and exploited militaristic vocabulary to encourage "soldiers" to help wage the war of *The Revolution*. This was indeed different from Paulina Davis's dictum that "victory won by persuasion and argument is more certain of good results than a triumph wrung from weakness or extorted from fear."[38] The choice of *The Revolution*'s name was hardly accidental: the time had passed, Stanton insisted, for Lilys, Unas, and Mayflowers.[39] For Anthony, Stanton, and their followers, speaking out authoritatively was more important than whether suffragists' messages were coherent or consistent. *The Revolution*'s model of and for strong-minded women was often contradictory. They never apologized for the fact that new women needed to experiment with their identity, their style, and their politics. Indeed, *The Revolution* invited and thrived on controversy: the suffrage movement needed opposition just as vegetation needs winds and storms to drive its roots down into the earth.

Complicating this process, however, was the fact that a larger but not necessarily sympathetic audience also witnessed this highly charged drama. *The Revolution* wished to attract a national audience. To the extent that it achieved this scope, however, it sacrificed opportunities for private rehearsal, for backstage revisions in script and direction, and for costume changes.

Hostile critics gleefully pounced on each indication of inconsistency and internal discord. A small group of suffragists admired the "revolutionary" image and tried to live up to the reputation of the new "strong-minded" woman who was energetic, politicized, and aggressive. Some readers congratulated *Revolution*'s belligerence, "so different from the namby-pamby milk-and-water journals that dare not publish the truth."[40]

A greater percentage of suffragists, however, apparently regarded strong-minded women as repugnantly unfeminine, if not "mannish," and as arrogant and vulgar, if not immoral. Lucy Stone and her followers were highly uncomfortable with Stanton's militancy, especially her endorsement of Victoria Woodhull and her sister Tennessee Claflin, who advocated "free love" and other radical ideas in their *Woodhull & Claflin's Weekly*.[41] Stone was horrified that Stanton's organization, the National Woman Suffrage Association, claimed to speak for suffragists and asserted national legitimacy. She believed that a more dignified and responsible version of the new woman was "better"—and more likely to attract support. Jettisoning the causes and values that proved alienating, Stone successfully established the American Woman Suffrage Association, said to be a more widely representative organization dedicated to "the orderly and efficient prosecution of the woman suffrage movement." Soon after, Stone launched the *Woman's Journal* to symbolize and give voice to the organization's version of the reasonable, calm, responsible new woman. For twenty years, Stone's group rejected peace offers from Stanton's faction because "peace, at the expense of principle, and union, at the sacrifice of individual freedom, are never worth having."[42] And although the *Journal* refused to condone overt racism on the part of southern suffrage organizations, it did what it could to recruit "new" southern women, including reprinting articles from southern women's suffrage organs, such as the *Women's Chronicle*, published 1888–93 in Arkansas.

The *Journal*'s neat, tight layout, its graphics, and its editorial board of well-known national leaders likewise proclaimed its essential commitment to progressive women who worked alongside men for the benefit of all humanity. Indeed, the *Journal* once responded to a new subscriber's question that being mannish and defiant was unnecessary; one could advocate equality and still advocate for and appeal to "a genuine woman, gentle, tender, refined and quiet."[43] So decorous was its vocabulary that even Harriet Beecher Stowe, while approving of the *Journal*'s conservatism and respectful attention to domesticity, once objected to its "high-falutin'" descriptions of a "reformeress' marble brows."[44]

The *Woman's Journal* managed a difficult feat: to articulate an alternative "responsible" style that was both intellectually plausible and affectively satisfying to its adherents and eventually respected by the larger society, yet exciting enough to sustain women over the long run. That is, its studious avoidance of anything that would alienate potential suffrage supporters required it to ignore or downplay radical ideas. Nevertheless, the *Journal* understood dignified good will and decorum did not themselves necessarily rally a community into action, and its mission was to spur supporters. Thus, the *Journal* also indulged in satire, vented anger and frustration, complained and protested. It vigorously reminded women to eschew false pedestals and to focus on self-respect: "Fetters are none the less such, nor do they symbolize any less degraded conditions . . . because, instead of being rough and ragged, they are smooth and wreathed in roses."[45]

The ability of the Boston-based weekly to attract subscribers, stockholders, and advertisers was a sign not simply of the publishers' business acumen but also the growing acknowledgment of the legitimacy of a particular kind of new woman. The issue was again self-esteem, mutual esteem, and national esteem. While not entirely neglecting the justice of enfranchisement, the *Journal* claimed that suffragists' interests were identical to humanity's; it stressed the social benefit of enfranchisement. The very act of participating in the suffrage movement would morally transform women into one universal community. Julia Ward Howe, who regularly invoked peace and cooperation, wrote with no small amount of idealism and optimism, that now that women were working together, "envy, petty jealousy, and unfounded dislike will now give way, and women will regard each other with the largeness and liberty of reasonable beings."[46] When Stanton's and Stone's rival organizations finally merged to become the National American Woman Suffrage Association in 1890, the *Woman's Journal* became NAWSA's official newspaper.

The Earnest Suffragists of the *Woman's Era*

Having written for a black paper in Boston, Josephine St. Pierre Ruffin was a member of the New England Woman's Press Association and a friend of Lucy Stone, Julia Ward Howe, and other Boston suffragists. Ruffin launched both the *Woman's Era* (1894–97), the first newspaper published by and for African American women, and the Woman's Era Club, likewise for black middle-class "new" women.[47] Ruffin was editor and publisher, her daughter Florida was the assistant editor, and her husband George, a prosuffrage state legislator, was also involved in what Ruffin called her "high class paper."

The *Woman's Era*'s debut issue insisted that "women of all races and conditions" had long needed "such a journal as a medium of intercourse and sympathy"; the *Era* would promote both a keener appreciation of the hindrances constricting educated, refined black women and a better understanding among all classes.[48] Historian Wilson Moses describes the *Woman's Era* as a tasteful publication representing "the 'civilizationist' imperatives and domestic feminism of its founder," as its chief mission was encouraging respectability and uplift among black women, especially by articulating conservative ideals of sexual morality.[49] Most of the pages were filled with club news and reports of the activities and plans of black women's groups around the country. The magazine also included articles on health, exercise, and the "social laws" of etiquette (having a visiting card, dressing neatly), as well as gossip, fiction, and poetry. The "style" that Ruffin promoted is clearly evident in features about individual heroines, such as Victoria Matthews, who, as Victoria Earle, wrote for both the white and black press. The *Woman's Era* emphasized that Matthews was a prominent progressive woman "desirous of doing what she can for her race."[50] Indeed, in 1896 Matthews wrote in the *Era* about working as an organizer for the newly formed National Association of Colored Women, with Mary Church Terrell as president and Ruffin as vice president.

The *Woman's Era* also promoted women's suffrage from its first issue, when it carried tributes to Lucy Stone, describing her as an "ardent, consistent, and persistent abolitionist" who "consecrated" herself to suffrage only after blacks were emancipated and to whom all women owed a significant debt.[51] One article noted that Stone's last public appearance in Boston, shortly before her death in 1893, had been at the Woman's Era Club; that is, according to Ellen Battelle Deitrick, Stone's first and last speeches were "in the interests of colored people." An 1895 editorial insisted, "There is no class in the United States that suffers under such disadvantages as the colored women. This class has everything to gain and nothing to lose by endorsing the woman suffrage movement."[52] The editorial explained that black women were prepared and eager for jobs as clerks and stenographers, and might be hired if enfranchised. Regarding two elderly black women who supported suffrage, Ruffin noted: "With the suffragists the colored woman is in good company."[53]

That said, Ruffin was notably willing to attack individual white women, particularly Frances Willard, national president of Woman's Christian Temperance Union. Notwithstanding Willard's "splendid" temperance work, Ruffin denounced Willard as an apologist for lynching.[54]

Local and Regional Efforts

Gradual expansion of the railroad, as well as advantageous postal rates and improved mail delivery enabled suffrage editors to bring their papers with them when they moved to another state and to distribute to both close-by and distant readers, thus nationalizing the movement to a degree. This was limited, however. When Amelia and Dexter Bloomer moved again, to Iowa, she calculated that the state was "too sparsely settled to make it safe for us to rely on it to support the paper; and the distance is too great and facilities for carrying mail too insufficient for us to calculate on a large eastern circulation."[55] Meanwhile, local efforts were assisted by developments in printing and distribution technologies as well as a gradual lowering of printing costs; this permitted relatively easy access to publishing for women, as long as they were uninterested in commercial profit. In the late nineteenth century and especially after the turn of the century, state and regional suffrage organizations launched their own outreach and organizational tools.

Some of the most colorful efforts appeared on the West Coast. Emily Pitts Stevens fearlessly advocated women's political and social equality with men, including the right to vote and earn equal pay, in *The Pioneer*, whose motto was "Liberty, Justice, Fraternity." Stevens was associated with the Women's Cooperative Printing Union, which successfully printed legal briefs, annual reports, business materials, and books, among other things. Abigail Scott Duniway was the *Pioneer*'s Oregon editor before establishing her own strong-minded weekly paper in Portland, the *New Northwest*, with the motto "Free Speech, Free Press, Free People." The indefatigable Duniway ran the paper 1871–87 with the help of her six children. Duniway also published the *Coming Century*, "Journal of Progress and Reform" (1891–92) and edited the *Pacific Empire* (1895–97), a Portland suffrage weekly. Duniway's feisty denunciations of antisuffragists and other opponents were even more extreme and zealous than Stanton's. Unlike some suffrage editors, such as Stevens, Duniway opposed prohibition not merely for strategic reasons but also on philosophical grounds, given the importance for men and women to exercise moral responsibility and self-control.

Often an individual's pet project, these more particularized communications could address a community's specific interests and mobilize and sustain their more local constituencies, especially in rural areas, where women could not attend rallies and meetings. For example, from 1891 to 1894, when the Kansas equal suffrage amendment of 1894 was roundly defeated, Emma Pack edited the *Farmer's Wife*; it was published by her husband, a Populist Party partisan and former newspaper publisher. Under the motto "Equal Rights to All, Special Privilege to None," the paper promoted women's suffrage, temperance, and populism, as well as addressing farm women's specific interests. In 1882, Caroline Churchill turned her paper the *Colorado Antelope* into *Queen Bee*, which lasted to 1895. The weekly claimed to be the only paper in Colorado "advocating Women's Political Equality and Individuality."

From 1871 to 1875, *Balance*, one of several Chicago papers, advocated for responsible women, as evident in its motto, "Impelled by Zeal; Restrained by Principle." Every month, *Balance* promised "to weigh measures and men (and women) in a fair and impartial manner . . . ; we do not intend to run into any wild extremes but preserve an 'even balance.'" *Balance* explicitly accused "strong-minded women" of antagonizing too many people. Toledo's strong-minded suffragists launched the *Ballot Box* in 1875; three years later, Matilda Joslyn Gage moved the paper to Syracuse, renaming it the *National Citizen and Ballot Box*, with the slogan "Self-Government is a Natural Right, and the Ballot is the Method of Exercising that Right." A former NWSA president, Gage ran excerpts of the first volume of the *History of Woman Suffrage* and abandoned the newspaper in 1881 to work with Anthony and Stanton to complete the *History's* second volume.

Clara Bewick Colby, to take one final example, launched the *Woman's Tribune* in 1883 to serve western and midwestern rural women, including frontier women not yet converted to reform and committed "new women" suffragists. Colby took up the slack left by the suspension of the *Western Woman's Journal* (1881–83), "Devoted to Woman and her Home, Industrial, Educational, and Legal Interests, especially advocating Woman Suffrage." Both papers had also used the Nebraska state motto ("Equality Before the Law"). The vice president of the Nebraska Woman Suffrage Association, Colby originally published the *Tribune* in her home state.[56] For three years, she published from Washington, DC, when Congress was in session and otherwise from Nebraska; during the 1888 International Council of Women meeting in Washington, DC, the paper, otherwise a weekly or monthly, appeared daily. In 1893 Colby moved the newspaper to Washington year-round and in 1904 she published from Portland, Oregon, ending in 1909 for lack of money and support.[57] The *Tribune* was associated with the National Woman Suffrage Association, and Stanton often wrote for it. However, it also carried news of Stone's group, along with local, state, national, and international suffrage organizations, as well as clubs serving other reforms, even ones Colby disliked, such as the Women's Christian Temperance Union.

Conclusion

No national movement—or countermovement, for that matter—can survive, much less succeed, without publicly shared discourse, without "media." In the case of the suffrage movement, its organs scripted, auditioned, rehearsed, and dramatized the new women. Through their periodicals, nineteenth-century suffragists produced and transformed a new social reality in which new women enjoyed a meaningful identity. As Elizabeth Aldrich, editor of the *Genius of Liberty*, said: "We want a common nervous circulation, we want a general excitement, a common sensibility, a universal will, and a concordant action."[58] This is precisely what suffrage journals provided, although not without a certain amount of friction. Although the proportionate emphases shifted, the suffrage papers always managed a necessary and crucial double role: they encouraged converts by celebrating their accomplishments and victories, and stirred them by warning against apathy and reminding them of oppression. Suffrage papers persuasively illustrated alternative versions of a satisfying, meaningful, important life for women and brought suffragists into a new and exhilarating world in which their lives had special purpose. Over time, the suffragists cultivated intellectually and emotionally satisfying models for acting, thinking, judging, and feeling.

Establishing the new woman and consolidating support around her also required distinguishing her from "conventional" women, clarifying what she was *not*. She was not submissive, dwarfed, or silenced by a powerful husband. *Lily* writers somewhat exaggerated old-style women to repudiate silly, frivolous, simpering gossips. Using the pseudonym Sunflower, Stanton wrote in *The Lily*, "I do hate a sickly, sentimental, half-developed, timid needle-loving woman." Stanton was even more vociferous on the distinction in *The Revolution*, recasting as odious what enemies regarded as virtuous. For Stanton, antisuffrage women were "driveling, dependent imbeciles" whose crowning achievement was physical degeneracy, and whose "chief delight is to believe themselves born to cling to whatever is nearest, in a droopy, like the ivy-to-the-oak way, and to be viney, and twiney, and whiney throughout."[59] Stanton clearly enjoyed refuting the image of suffragists as bearded Amazons, presenting herself and her children as proof that strong-minded women were also attentive neighbors, thrifty housekeepers, helpful daughters, and contented and even stylish wives.

According to social movement theorists, movement leaders must alter the target audiences' self-perceptions so that supporters and potential supporters believe in their self-worth and ability to bring about urgent change. I argue that for suffragists, esteem, a sense of agency, and self-worth were the point. And just as antisuffragists recast suffragist demands for political integration as evidence that suffragists were "anti-female, anti-family, and anti-American,"[60] so suffragists (at least the "responsible" ones) redefined themselves as feminine, working for change that would strengthen families and the entire country. They judged antisuffragists as too physically and mentally weak to provide genuine support to family and country.

Pre-1900 suffrage papers sought to explain the slow, faltering quality of the cause. Suffrage editors used religious vocabulary to assure converts that "all important truths are at first rejected, and their ministers despised, persecuted, and often crucified."[61] But women who tried to follow *The Revolution's* often-contradictory prescriptions for the strong-minded style may not have been as confident as Stanton was about this aggressive identity. With some exceptions, most post-1900 suffragists and suffrage periodicals, following the lead of the *Woman's Journal*, emphasized organizational, tactical, and procedural matters, narrowing their focus to strategies for winning the vote. They neatly pivoted away from disputes over marriage, divorce law, education, careers, and the nature and relationship of women and men. Perhaps having at least temporarily accepted a tamer vision of womanhood, post-1900 new women could settle down in earnest to fight for status.

In any case, women continued to redefine themselves and their places in the world. Status conflict is never-ending and dynamic. Arrangements of esteem are never static, never complete: inevitably, new contenders emerge and demand status. In their newspapers and magazines, nineteenth-century suffragists managed to construct only provisional definitions. That said, their rhetorical passion and sincerity brought forth an alternative identity that conferred on their daily lives a vital, exciting sense of significance. They dramatized this transformed woman in a way that was satisfying to them, appropriate to the emerging modern culture, and warranting political authority.

Notes

1. Amelia Bloomer, "*The Lily*," *Lily*, November 1, 1849, 88.

2. Linda M. Scott denounces nineteenth-century feminists such as Elizabeth Cady Stanton for prudish hypocritical judgmentalism about fashion, but notes that both feminists and antifeminists have used "style" to signal their politics. Scott, *Fresh Lipstick: Redressing Fashion and Feminism* (New York: Macmillan, 2006).

3. The notion of gender was invented a century later; suffragists discussed women as a "sex."

4. Paulina Wright Davis, "Special Notice," *Una*, February 1855, 25.

5. "Two to Our Correspondents and Subscribers," *Woman's Era*, January 1896. All references to the *Woman's Era* are from the Emory Women Writers Resource Project's electronic version (which lacks page numbers), http://womenwriters.digitalscholarship.emory.edu/advocacy/search.php?doctitle=Woman.

6. As many contemporary historians acknowledge, the latter largely ignored the former. See, e.g., Ellen C. Dubois, *Feminism and Suffrage: The Emergence of an Independent Women's Movement in America, 1848–1869* (Ithaca, NY: Cornell University

Press, 1978; 2nd ed., 1999). Her second edition acknowledged that racism was endemic in white women suffragists.

7. See Eleanor Flexner, *Century of Struggle: The Woman's Rights Movement in the United States* (Cambridge, MA: Belknap Press of Harvard University Press, 1975); and Aileen S. Kraditor, *The Ideas of the Woman Suffrage Movement: 1890–1920* (New York: Columbia University Press, 1965).

8. See also Pierre Bourdieu's notion of symbolic capital (referring to honor and prestige), in *Distinction: A Social Critique of the Judgement of Taste* (1979; reprint, Abingdon, UK: Routledge Classics, 2010).

9. In *The Feminization of American Culture* (New York: Alfred A. Knopf, 1977) Ann Douglas mocks newly leisured middle-class white women and disestablished Protestant clergymen for using popular sentimental literature to console women about their political and economic marginalization by putting them on a moral pedestal. But this dismissive psychological approach ignores the importance of cultural affirmation to humans.

10. Joseph R. Gusfield, *Symbolic Crusade: Status Politics and the American Temperance Movement* (Urbana: University of Illinois Press, 1963), 3. Gusfield analyzes the temperance movement in terms of status conflicts between long-established Protestants and urban immigrant Catholics.

11. Whether courts explicitly recognize this or not, they constantly face the problem of social/status hierarchy in cases involving group conflict. Jack M. Balkin says Supreme Court justices understood that a battle over the constitutionality of protections of homosexuals from discrimination symbolized an important cultural struggle over gay rights and the national status of homosexuals. Balkin, "The Constitution of Status," *Yale Law Journal* 106 (1997): 2313–74, https://digitalcommons.law.yale.edu /fss_papers/262.

12. Dubois (*Feminism and Suffrage*) likewise sees the movement as radical in offering a multifaceted understanding of women's subordination and not being single-issue; she disputes the idea that it was fundamentally conservative or unconnected to other ideas about women's rights and social justice. Her second edition, however, acknowledges not only a conservative side disconnected from other issues about subordination that focused exclusively on the vote, but also that this more conservative dimension won out.

13. Gusfield notes that social movements want to confer "respect upon the norms of the victor and disrespect upon the norms of the vanquished" (*Symbolic Crusade*, 174).

14. Paulina Wright Davis, "The Influence of Opinions on the Character," *Una*, November 1853, 168–69.

15. Susan Marshall, "In Defense of Separate Spheres: Class and Status Politics in the Antisuffrage Movement," *Social Forces* 65, no. 2 (1986): 327–51. Marshall argues that antisuffragists feared that free intermingling of the sexes removed social distance and women's domination of certain cultural resources, such as modesty and spirituality, from which they derived considerable social prestige.

16. Marshall, "In Defense of Separate Spheres," 336.

17. Marshall, "In Defense of Separate Spheres," 337.

18. *Woman's Journal*, February 4, 1882, 35.

19. The *Seneca County Courier* praised Lucretia Mott's "eminently beautiful and instructive" speech at the 1848 "Woman's Rights Convention" held in Seneca Falls and commended the Declaration of Sentiments as "succinct." But the *Courier* was unenthusiastic about its "radical" resolutions; it emphasized that the doctrines "are startling to those who are wedded to the present usages and laws of society."

20. Amelia Bloomer, "Why We Publish," *Lily*, January 1853, 12.

21. Amelia Bloomer, "Prospectus for 1852," *Lily*, December 1851, 93.

22. Qtd. in Louise R. Noun, *Strong-Minded Women: The Emergence of the Woman Suffrage Movement in Iowa* (Ames: Iowa State University Press, 1969), 79. Hoping to provide an alternative to *The Revolution*, from January 1869 to May 1870, Stone and Blackwell wrote for the *Woman's Advocate*, a "responsible minded" periodical run by William Tomlinson, in New York City.

23. Bloomer, "*The Lily*," 88.

24. Elizabeth Aldridge, "The Last Year's Subscribers," *Genius of Liberty*, October 1852, 1.

25. Paulina Wright Davis, "To Our Readers," *Una*, December 1854, 376.

26. Amelia Bloomer, "Why Don't *The Lily* Come?" [*sic*], *Lily*, April 15, 1854, 59.

27. Henry B. Blackwell, "Truth Knows No Sex," *Woman's Journal*, May 28, 1870, 164–65.

28. Thomas W. Higginson, "Lectures for Women," *Woman's Journal*, September 14, 1872, 290.

29. Elizabeth Aldrich, "Strength in Union," *Genius of Liberty*, November 15, 1852, 12.

30. Clarinda Nichols, "Lady Editors," *Lily*, March 1850, 23, reprinted from the *Brattleboro (VT) Democrat*.

31. "Hail and Farewell," *New Era*, January 1885, 25.

32. Rodger Streitmatter, *Raising Her Voice: African-American Women Journalists Who Changed History* (Lexington: University Press of Kentucky, 1994), 40.

33. Mrs. N. F. Mossell, *The Work of the Afro-American Woman* (1894; reprint, New York: Oxford University Press, 1988), 101.

34. "Letters," *Mayflower*, November 15, 1861, 168.

35. "Letters," *Woman's Journal*, January 22, 1870, 18.

36. "Papillion," Editorial, *Revolution*, October 29, 1868, 260.

37. S.C.H., "Compensation," *Woman's Journal*, December 28, 1872, 412.

38. Paulina Wright Davis, "Endings and Beginnings," *Una*, December 1853, 182.

39. Davis saw her paper, like the heroine of Spencer's *Faerie Queene*, as embarked on a dangerous pilgrimage through the wilderness of ignorance and bigotry.

40. "What People Say to Us," *Revolution*, October 29, 1868, 260.

41. In 1872 Woodhull ran for president as a member of the Equal Rights Party, supporting women's suffrage and equal rights; her running mate was the abolitionist Frederick Douglass.

42. Hannah Clark, "Union Not Strength," *Woman's Journal*, January 7, 1871, 2.

43. "Letters," *Woman's Journal*, July 29, 1871, 236.

44. *Woman's Journal*, January 22, 1870, 27.

45. "Lack of Self-Respect," Editorial, *Woman's Journal*, September 14, 1870, 116.

46. Julia Ward Howe, "Woman in the Presidential Canvas," *Woman's Journal*, October 13, 1872, 324.

47. "The Honorees," Massachusetts Foundation for the Humanities, http://mass humanities.org/programs/shwlp/honorees/. In 1895, Ruffin and other women helped organize the National Federation of Afro-American Women.

48. "Greeting," *Woman's Era*, March 24, 1894.

49. Wilson J. Moses, "The Lost World of the Negro, 1895–1919: Black Literary and Intellectual Life before the 'Renaissance,'" *Black American Literature Forum* 21, no. 1/2 (1987): 73. Moses argues that ignoring this more "traditionalist" strain in black intellectual and literary life erases from literary history, among others, Ruffin, Mary Church Terrell, and the Grimké sisters.

50. S. Elizabeth Frazier, "Mrs. Wm. E. Matthews," *Woman's Era*, May 1, 1894.

51. "Lucy Stone," *Woman's Era*, March 24, 1894.

52. "Colored Women and Suffrage," *Woman's Era*, November 1895.

53. "Colored Women and Suffrage."

54. "Miss Willard and the Colored People," *Woman's Era*, July 1895.

55. Amelia Bloomer, "Farewell," *Lily*, December 15, 1854, 181.

56. Bewick was valedictorian of the University of Wisconsin–Madison's first co-educational class, in 1869; she later quit as a University of Wisconsin instructor over pay inequity.

57. Duniway denounced the "untimely invasion of Mrs. Clara B. Colby and other self-imported Eastern Suffragists," *Pathbreaking: An Autobiographical History of the Equal Suffrage Movement in Pacific Coast States* (1914; reprint, New York: Kraus, 1971), 95.

58. Aldrich, "Strength in Union."

59. Elizabeth Cady Stanton, "Home Truths," *Revolution*, January 15, 1868, 1.

60. Marshall, "In Defense of Separate Spheres," 336.

61. "Straws," Editorial, *Revolution*, May 7, 1868, 280–81.

3

The *Woman's Exponent*

A Utah Case Study in the Campaign for Women's Suffrage

SHERILYN COX BENNION

A prospectus for the *Woman's Exponent*, to be published twice monthly and intended primarily for women members of the Church of Jesus Christ of Latter-day Saints,[1] promised to discuss "every subject interesting and valuable to women."[2] It predicted that, since the women of the Territory of Deseret already enjoyed the privilege of voting, the *Exponent* would not need to make "a specialty of that pet subject with most woman's papers."[3] Over the forty-two years of its existence, the paper proved the prospectus wrong: while it did indeed contain material that ran the gamut from poetry to household hints, its two editors consistently defended and supported women's right to vote—or "woman suffrage" as it was commonly called. Already on page one of the first number, dated June 1, 1872, the "News and Views" column agreed with a writer who claimed that "if it is an advantage to vote, women ought to have it; if a disadvantage men ought not to be obliged to bear it alone."[4] An editorial included suffrage in a list of topics that would interest women of both Utah and the world.[5]

The *Exponent* sought to inform the women of Utah about suffrage campaign developments, encourage their support, help them to organize for more effective influence, publish their writing, and, during periods when they were allowed to vote, become informed and go to the polls. Within the borders of the territory, the *Exponent* tried to counteract the influence of those who opposed suffrage. Antisuffragists generally believed women voters would help perpetuate polygamy,[6] a church practice with which women's suffrage was intricately connected until polygamy was officially discontinued in 1890.

Moreover, the paper aimed to extend its influence beyond Utah, defending Mormon women as independent, progressive, and satisfied with their lot. It joined eastern suffragists and their publications in attempting to make women's suffrage a national reality and, through exchanges with the eastern publications and participation in committees and conventions of the national organizations, became a part of the national movement.

The women of Utah were the first in the nation to go to the polls. Although Wyoming's legislature had enacted women's suffrage in December 1869, the first election in which women legally voted came in February 1870 in a Salt Lake City municipal contest held just two days after the territorial legislature approved suffrage for them.[7] The *Exponent* survived four distinct periods in the saga of Utah women's battles to maintain or regain their right to vote. The first lasted from its founding in 1872 until 1882, when federal legislation took suffrage away from women and men living in polygamous relationships. The second, from 1882 to 1887, when Utah's nonpolygamous women and men could continue to vote, ended with passage of federal legislation disenfranchising all Utah women. The third lasted from 1887 to 1896, with federal acceptance of a Utah constitution giving women the vote. By the time of the *Exponent*'s demise in 1914, women in Utah were again voting, but that right had not been extended nationally.

Louisa Lula Greene became the *Exponent*'s first editor at age twenty-three, after the editor of the *Salt Lake Herald*, who had published some of her poetry, invited her to edit the new paper. The *Herald* published the *Exponent* prospectus and its first few numbers, but the women's paper was editorially independent. Greene agreed to be editor only after encouragement from Eliza R. Snow, widow of both Joseph Smith and Brigham Young and probably the most influential woman in the church.[8] A year after taking on the editorship, Greene married Levi Willard Richards, a well-connected church leader. She edited the paper for five years, during which time she bore two children, neither of whom survived. In 1877 she explained to the paper's readers that rearing a family was now the most important branch of "Home Industry" for her; but she added that her interest in the public weal had not diminished nor did she think "the best season of a woman's life should be completely absorbed in her domestic duties."[9] She continued to contribute to the *Exponent* and other church publications and to fill church assignments, as well as to publish poetry. She bore seven children; four sons survived.

In the meantime, Emmeline Blanche Woodward Harris Whitney Wells became coeditor in December 1875, having published articles in the *Exponent* as early as 1873. In 1877, at forty-nine years of age, she took over sole editorial control. Wells's personal life had been difficult; after one marriage ended in divorce and another with the death of her husband, she married Daniel H. Wells, a prominent figure in church and civic affairs. The youngest of her five daughters was fifteen when Wells became editor; all five assisted her at various times in the *Exponent* office.

Wells owned, published, and edited the paper for the thirty-seven years, while also traveling extensively for both church and suffrage organizations, often as an officer. She spearheaded a wheat storage program instituted by church leaders, chaired the Utah Woman's Republican League, served as regent of the Utah Daughters of the Revolution, founded the Utah Woman's Press Club and was vice president of the National Woman's Press Association, and started the Reapers' Club, a women's literary group. She also published a book of poetry and wrote hymns. At eighty-two she was named general president of the Relief Society, the Mormon women's organization.

Although the twice-monthly *Woman's Exponent* did not cover *everything* of interest to women, it did include a great variety of items intended to ensure its appeal to women readers. In addition to the poetry and household hints, there were articles on education and health, correspondence, editorials, fiction, poetry, news notes, biographies of notable women, encouragement of home industry, exchanges from other publications, and news of a variety of organizations, including those sponsored by the church and those devoted to promoting women's suffrage. Some form of support for women's rights appeared in most issues. The paper also announced birthdays, anniversaries, and deaths of women throughout the territory.

Salt Lake City's daily newspapers greeted the new publication favorably. The *Herald* contributed advice and moral support. The *Salt Lake Tribune*, which became under new owners more stridently anti-Mormon a year later, called it "the greatest stride the Mormons have yet made in literature, being well edited and quite newsy" and suggested it would likely do well among "Mormon ladies," since it was "much more modern in style and contains less of priestly cant than most other Mormon publications."[10] The *Deseret News*, official newspaper organ of the church, called it "a very creditable addition to the Journalistic literature of the Territory" and wished it "long life and success."[11]

Arguments for Women's Suffrage

From the beginning, the *Exponent*'s prosuffrage position focused on the two major kinds of arguments generally used by news outlets that supported women's suffrage—the contributions that women voters could make to society, known as the social utility argument, and the inherent justice of allowing them to vote, usually called the equal rights argument.

The idea that voting women would have a refining influence on the electoral process and on society in general was the *Exponent*'s most frequently asserted benefit of suffrage. An 1872 plea for women to vote expressed this: "Not that they may teach men wisdom by their superior intelligence, but that they may exert their more beneficent and chaste influence in endeavoring to purify the social atmosphere."[12] A petition to the Massachusetts legislature, reprinted in the paper in full, summarized the equal rights argument: "Woman has the same right to life, liberty and the pursuit of happiness as a man. . . . They are equal stockholders, as citizens, in the great political corporation called Government, and it is unjust to deprive them of their equal expression, since they are equally interested in its safety and prosperity."[13]

In an 1895 interview with Wells, the *Salt Lake Tribune* noted two reasons for women's suffrage specific to Utah that she had included in a report to a National Woman's Suffrage Association convention and also often used in the *Exponent*. First, women had successfully voted in state elections for seventeen years after they had been extended suffrage by the Utah legislature in 1870, and, second, the state undoubtedly had a higher percentage of women owning their own homes and paying taxes than any other state, because of congressional enactments making them virtual heads of families.[14] Another qualification of Utah's Mormon women appeared in the *Exponent*: suffrage had been earned "by peril, by toil, and by sacrifice offered up with bleeding hearts:—murdered prophets, starved and ill-clad children, plundered homes, untimely deaths of fathers, mothers, bothers, sisters, babes and friends."[15] Generally, the *Exponent* used both equal rights and social utility arguments, without attempting to marshal them in any particular order. Its aim was to gather and present all possible justifications for suffrage. Editorials and articles rarely mentioned only one idea.

Utah's women could vote, but this had begun seriously to be threatened by 1872, when the *Exponent* was founded. At least four federal bills proposed between 1872 and 1882 would have ended suffrage for most Mormon women. The paper responded to these efforts, sometimes at length but usually as a relatively small part of its total content. A study of *Exponent* editorials by historian Carol Cornwall Madsen found thirty-three that focused on suffrage during its first ten years, the period when all Utah women could vote. Editorials emphasizing "women's rights," some of which mentioned suffrage, constituted a separate category in this study.[16] But these numbers obscure numerous other mentions of suffrage in the paper. In reports of meetings and activities of national suffrage organizations, in articles, exchanges, news notes about developments in other states and nations, and letters, the *Exponent* kept the topic continually before its readers. An *Exponent* index notes 205 mentions of suffrage during its first ten years.[17]

The *Anti-Polygamy Standard*

Sentiment against polygamy had intensified in both Utah and nationally; the Ladies' Anti-Polygamy Society of Utah was formed in 1878 at a mass meeting attended by 300 women. In 1880 an eight-page monthly antipolygamy periodical became the society's mouthpiece, and for the two years of its existence the state had a woman's periodical that opposed Utah women's suffrage, as well as one that supported it. The *Anti-Polygamy Standard* used on its first page a biblical motto from 1 Corinthians 7:2: "Let every Man have his own Wife, and Let every Woman have her own Husband." Its "Salutatory" in the first number defined its objective as promoting the work of the society: "to plan and execute such measures as shall in the judgment of its members tend to suppress polygamy in Utah and other Territories of the United States."[18] Opposing women's suffrage in the territory was one such measure. Objections to polygamy and the conviction that women in polygamous relationships were controlled completely by their husbands and would never vote against the practice were the basis of the *Standard*'s expressed opposition.

Jennie Anderson Froiseth, the *Standard*'s editor, had been instrumental in the organization of the Anti-Polygamy Society and used the *Standard* to promote both the society and legislation to end polygamy. Born in Ireland in 1849, she moved with her family to New York, and studied in Berlin and Florence before marrying. She had come to Utah with her husband, B. A. M. Froiseth, a surveyor and mapmaker, who had been assigned to Salt Lake City's Fort Douglas by the US government.

Froiseth's publication reflected wide-ranging interests, including news of non-Mormon religious congregations, advice on home and family matters, mining news, and sketches of notable female benefactors, as well as reports on activities of the Anti-Polygamy Society, of which she was an officer, and exposés of life in polygamy, a continuing staple of *Standard* content. Utah women's suffrage was a secondary concern but was intertwined with opposition to polygamy, since Froiseth was convinced, and tried to convince readers, that as long as Utah women voted their support for plural marriage would ensure its perpetuation. She avoided involvement with the national campaign for women's suffrage.

The *Standard*'s position opposing women's suffrage in Utah was most clearly explained in an editorial in June 1880 that attempted to refute the points made in a letter from *Exponent* editor Wells to the *National Citizen and Ballot Box* and concluded, "Suffrage, as it exists in Utah, is an entirely different matter from what the suffragists in the East are working for. . . . There it represents a principle, here it was established to place greater power in the hands of the men, and instead of representing the sentiments of the women, it is only a reflex of the opinions of the priesthood. . . . We venture to assert that the suffrage movement has received a blow from which it will not recover for years, in virtually recognizing Mormon polygamy."[19]

The *Exponent*, although it reprinted material from eastern suffrage publications, resolutely ignored the existence of the *Anti-Polygamy Standard*, and the *Standard* never referred directly to the *Exponent*, although an *Exponent* report of Wells's remarks at a mass meeting the month following organization of the Anti-Polygamy Society perhaps referred to the Utah women who opposed polygamy and suffrage. Wells lamented attacks: "We never thought that woman could rise up against woman. . . . [Still] we intend to meet it with all the energy and fortitude we possess, and it will be 'diamond cut diamond' rest assured."[20] However, in campaigning for their respective positions on local and national issues, both papers answered the arguments advanced by their antagonists. Writers for the *Standard* admitted that although "the ballot in the hands of intelligent educated American women would tend to suppress many forms of vice, and purify the social atmosphere," they could not close their eyes "to the truth that Utah is a hot bed of immorality and shameless crime."[21] A follow-up article claimed that allowing woman suffrage to continue in Utah would uphold "polygamy, the union of Church and State, and obeying the vile behests of priestly leaders."[22] The *Exponent* insisted that, on the contrary, "Mormon women, as a class, are eminently qualified to vote intelligently . . . and the most perfect liberty is accorded them for the expression of their opinions upon subjects connected with the nominations to be made, or of their views in securing the most excellent methods of government."[23]

As conflict escalated, both papers devoted attention to the continuing controversy and events that unfolded both locally and nationally. In April 1882 a Utah Constitutional Convention convened, in one of seven attempts at statehood over a period of fifty years. Three of the seventy-two delegates were women, including Wells. The document that the convention and Utah voters approved gave women the right to vote, to hold most political offices, and to have equal property rights with men. By this time, however, President Chester A. Arthur had signed a federal act that deprived many Utah women of the right to vote and the constitution was not accepted by the US Congress.

Passage of the Edmunds Act, sponsored by Senator John F. Edmunds, in 1882 initiated the second phase of the *Exponent*'s—and Mormon women's—relationship with suffrage, when only nonpolygamous Utahns could vote, hold office, or serve on a jury. This attempt to thwart one of the "twin relics of barbarism"[24] ended suffrage for many Utah women who had voted during the twelve years since the territorial legislature had given them that right. The *Standard* hailed the act with an article titled "The Morning Dawns," approving its strong provisions but insisting that it could and should have gone further, denying all Mormons the right to vote,[25] since, as it later pointed out, "all Mormons are polygamists in belief."[26] The *Exponent* published the complete text of the act after condemning its passage, asking how it was possible "thus to deprive American citizens of the birthright of freedom."[27]

The *Anti-Polygamy Standard* lasted for another year, continuing its condemnation of polygamy and polygamists and its criticism of eastern suffragists who supported Utah women's right to vote. Although the final issue, which combined numbers for February and March of 1883, promised a fourth volume "enlarged and improved and otherwise better adapted to accomplish the end desired" and appealed for renewals and new subscribers, no new volume was forthcoming, and no explanation for the paper's demise was given. A statement included in the announcement of the fourth volume might serve as its epitaph: "All through the existence of the *Standard* it has been struggling against fearful odds, right in the midst of the enemy's camp. . . . Notwithstanding, the *Standard* feels that it has done good work."[28]

The 1882 elimination of voting for women in polygamous relationships changed the emphasis of the *Exponent*'s suffrage content. From 1882 to 1887 it maintained its concern for women's equal rights but lamented the loss of suffrage occasioned by the Edmunds Act and fought against the further erosion of Utah women's suffrage contemplated by the federal government. One correspondent charged Senator Edmunds with having "no conception of the influence of women even without the ballot." The writer continued, "They are a power in the land, and the name of Senator Edmunds will become a hiss and a byword among all nations."[29]

According to Madsen, the *Exponent* published seventeen editorials focused principally on suffrage from 1882 to 1887. However, the index lists more than fifty mentions of suffrage and suffrage associations, apart from its separate mentions of bills that threatened Utah women's right to vote as one of their provisions. An 1883 editorial sounded familiar themes of social utility, Utah women's independence, and their appreciation for equal rights and added a religious note—another common characteristic of *Exponent* content: the essential role of the mother in forming the character of her sons as well as her daughters would be enhanced by the important responsibilities of the ballot, and through the advancement of women "a broader plane might be reached for all humanity." The people of Utah were not all disenfranchised and still had some power, the editorial added. Voting Utahns were undoubtedly capable of maintaining the rights of women. "They know they have right on their side, and God and the right are a great majority."[30]

The *Exponent* celebrated small victories, such as a territorial district court's upholding of the 1870 law that gave Utah women suffrage, which had been challenged once again. The paper published the complete opinion in 1882.[31] However, such victories were rare, and as Senator Edmunds introduced new, more drastic legislation in December 1885, concern that Utah women might lose even the limited voting rights that had been left them in 1882 became a major theme of the paper's suffrage coverage. It also continued to publish reports about suffrage efforts in other states and foreign countries and activities of the national suffrage organizations.

Before the new bill was introduced, the *Exponent* noted the upholding of the 1882 Act by the US Supreme Court, confident that "the reverence [Utahns] have for the country which they love and honor, will give them grace and courage to submit to the enforcement of the law," although they had a right to protest against "the one-sided administration of it, and against the wicked and unjust proceedings of officials sent here to administer it." It predicted that trials suffered by Utahns would be "salutary and beneficial in their effects," however hard they might seem and stated that "many who were faint-hearted before, and especially among the young people, are growing stronger in defense of the principles of the Gospel, and this is something most desirable and gratifying."[32]

Upon introduction of the 1885 Edmunds Bill, the *Exponent* published the complete text. Ending suffrage for all Utah women was only one part of the bill, which also outlawed polygamy, dissolved the corporation of the church, and forfeited church properties to the federal government. A March 1886 mass meeting of Utah women filled the Salt Lake Theatre and featured a brass band, several speeches, and the passage of protest resolutions. The resulting petition to the president and Congress, published by the *Exponent* in April, cited abuses of congressional action and examples of offenses and sought relief, without success. After the Senate passed the new bill in January 1886, it moved to the House, where it became the Edmunds-Tucker Bill, in honor of the chair of the House Judiciary Committee, John Randolph Tucker, who recommended passage. The House complied. Members of the National Woman Suffrage Association presented a petition to President Grover Cleveland asking him to veto the section of the act that disenfranchised Utah women, but the complete bill became law in March 1887, although without the signature of the president. He objected to its harsh provisions and hesitated to jeopardize his relationship with the church by signing it, but a veto would antagonize both political parties.[33] From then until Utah statehood in 1896, no woman could vote in any Utah election. The *Exponent*'s reaction to the act was predictably negative, but restrained. Looking toward the bill's seemingly inevitable passage, it reminded readers that "Trials Tend to Strengthen and Purify."[34]

Utah Connections with National Suffrage Movement

The third period of the *Exponent*'s career as champion of women's suffrage began in 1887 with passage of the Edmunds-Tucker Act and ended in 1896, when Utah was admitted to the Union as a state, with a constitution that included women's suffrage. Madsen's study listed forty-one suffrage editorials during this time, but the *Exponent*'s index includes 401 mentions of suffrage and suffrage associations, many more in comparison with other periods. This reflects a time of transition for the national suffrage associations and for Utah's relationship with them. The *Exponent* recorded this at length, including not only minutes of meetings and the resulting resolutions, but also progress toward unification of the National Woman Suffrage Association (NWSA, the organization that represented the more "strong-minded" Elizabeth Cady Stanton) and the American Woman Suffrage Association (AWSA, led by Lucy Stone), as well as efforts in Utah to maintain membership qualifications that included the formation of both state and local associations. Nineteen of Utah's twenty-nine counties had societies by 1895, and reports of their meetings, along with lists of speakers—and sometimes summaries of their speeches—occupied considerable space in the paper.

Before the founding of the *Exponent*, leading women of the Mormon Church, spearheaded by editor Wells, had connected with NWSA officers and cultivated a friendship, along with support for Utah women's suffrage and the *Exponent*'s efforts to maintain it, that continued throughout the paper's life. Wells served as vice president of the NWSA for Utah and held other offices over the next twenty years. She reported NWSA activities regularly in the *Exponent*, corresponded with prominent figures in the suffrage movement, and contributed letters and articles to eastern suffrage publications, including the Boston-based *Woman's Journal*, the Philadelphia-based *Woman's Words*, and the Syracuse-based *National Citizen and Ballot Box*. At the time of the

1879 convention, the *Woman's Journal*, the organ of the more conservative American Woman Suffrage Association, ridiculed the NWSA for admitting two Mormon women. Elizabeth Cady Stanton retorted in the *National Citizen and Ballot Box*, which largely sided with the NWSA: "I should think Mormon women might sit on our platform without making us responsible for their religious faith.... When the women of a whole Territory are threatened with disfranchisement where should they go to make their complaint but to the platform of the National Suffrage Association?" [35]

Through speeches, resolutions, and conventions, and especially various suffrage or suffrage-leaning newspapers, the NWSA championed the cause of women's suffrage, even for the beleaguered women of Utah, although it did not endorse the Mormon practice of polygamy. It campaigned for retaining Utah women's suffrage whenever Congress attempted to eliminate it, as a means toward the end of abolishing plural marriage. As its 1890 merger with the more conservative AWSA approached, however, the strong antipolygamy position of the AWSA and the broadening of membership in the new National American Woman Suffrage Association (NAWSA) meant that admission of Mormon women's organizations became more problematic. In order to comply with new requirements for membership, Mormon women in 1889 organized the Utah Territorial Suffrage Association, with county affiliates. Encouraging cooperation with non-Mormons, the association chose as officers only women who had not been involved in plural marriage. The Utah women were accepted, despite opposition; official church renunciation of polygamy later that same year reduced animosity. The NAWSA convened a National Conference in Utah in 1895, and the following year, after Utah's admission to the Union as the third state allowing women to vote, it sponsored a celebration of Utah women's restored suffrage in Washington, DC, in connection with its national convention. The *Exponent* continued to report activities of the National and International Councils of Women, which grew out of the NAWSA and of which Mormon women's organizations were members. Women's suffrage was only one of the social concerns of these organizations, and *Exponent* coverage of their activities reflected their broadened interests.

Even with changes in emphasis, an *Exponent* report that included excerpts from speeches given at a meeting of the Woman's Suffrage Association of Utah in 1889 provides evidence that social utility and equal rights arguments for women's suffrage remained constant refrains. One speaker pointed out that "when woman gains the ballot, her vote, given intelligently and wisely, will offset the vote of ignorance and fraud. God speed the day," while James E. Talmage, prominent Mormon theologian, was quoted stating that his greatest regret was that "woman has to plead and beg for that which rightly belongs to her. She is affected by the laws equally with man, and it is just that her voice should be as willingly heard as his."[36]

A "Utah Woman Suffrage Songbook," published in 1891 and available for purchase at the *Exponent* office, sold very few copies, "not half enough to pay for printing."[37] But poetry published in the paper still supported women's right to vote. A poem titled "Woman's Suffrage" began:

> We're a band of valiant women
> In a cause both true and just;
> Have started on a mission
> And in God we put our trust.
> We aim not at pomp and grandeur
> But ours is the call for right—
> And it has a beacon burning—
> To cheer us with its light.[38]

Statehood and Women's Suffrage

Utah's final constitutional convention convened in March 1895. Throughout 1895 the *Exponent* campaigned for inclusion of women's suffrage in the proposed constitution. As the convention began, it became apparent that the issue of women's suffrage would be contentious. Opponents suggested that the constitution should be submitted to Congress without the suffrage provision, which might well hurt its chances for acceptance, since most states had not yet seen fit to give women the vote. They maintained that Utahns could vote for suffrage at some point after the constitution had been accepted. When Wells returned from the NAWSA convention in Atlanta, she learned that opponents of a constitutional provision for women's suffrage were gathering signatures on a petition to submit to the Utah convention. As president of the Utah Woman Suffrage Association, Wells mobilized members to present a "memorial" (petition) to the convention that summarized why they wanted equality with Utah men, who had regained the franchise through a federal amnesty act in 1893.

The memorial, published in the *Exponent*, included arguments made in editorials, articles, and letters. It pointed out the injustice of taxation without representation and quoted Abraham Lincoln as believing that women would someday wield the ballot "to purify and ennoble politics." It reminded delegates that both political parties had pledged to support women's suffrage, asking them to end "the injustice and prejudice of the past, strike off the bonds that have heretofore enthralled woman, and open the doors that will usher her into free and full emancipation."[39] When the committee's majority report approving suffrage was delivered, a *Salt Lake City Tribune* editorial lamented that its adoption of suffrage would place Utah in a "small group of freak states." It asserted that, if proposed at all, women's suffrage should be submitted separately.[40] The debate continued after the committee's report, but, weary of the arguments and with their funds depleted, the delegates finally agreed to the women's suffrage provision. Four-fifths of Utah's voters approved the constitution that included it. The *Exponent* observed "great rejoicing" at the victory gained in Utah, which encouraged "all those who are working for the enfranchisement of womankind and the betterment of all mankind."[41]

Until its demise in 1914, the paper continued to support women's suffrage, although the emphasis changed from reacting to events that directly affected Utah women to urging national and international acceptance of women's suffrage and reporting on the organizations working toward that goal. The proportion of its content devoted to suffrage declined. Its last seventeen volumes contained, according to Madsen, twenty editorials focused on women's suffrage. The index listed ninety-one entries under the suffrage heading, but this included thirty-two for 1896–97, before the paper discontinued reports of county suffrage organizations and lists of speakers at their meetings.

Between 1879 and 1897 the paper used a one-line motto under its front-page title: "The Rights of the Women of Zion, and the Rights of the Women of all Nations." With Utah accepted as a state and women's suffrage restored, the motto became "The Ballot in the Hands of the Women of Utah Should Be a Power to Better the Home, the State and the Nation," which ran until the final volume.

The *Exponent* continued to stress the importance of women's exercising their right to vote and urged the formation of study sessions to help them become informed. It advised in 1896 that it behooved "every man and woman who can exert an influence or cast a vote, to stand upon principle and maintain the right according to conviction and one's conscience," pointing out that women had come into "possession of the privilege of equal suffrage at a time when the nation is in such a state of doubt and uncertainty on such grave problems as are now imminent" and emphasizing the importance of women's registering to vote and, for noncitizens, becoming naturalized "that they may have the privilege accorded them under the law of the grand new State."[42] Celebrating each state and nation that accepted women's suffrage, it noted in 1912 the "sudden popularity of the suffrage cause" and hailed the adoption of suffrage in Kansas, Michigan, Oregon, and Arizona.[43]

Articles arguing for women's suffrage continued to appear, if in smaller numbers. The contention that women's voting would improve society predominated: "When the franchise has been extended over more space, and embraces more people and peoples, . . . then we may be able to see what a powerful factor for the amelioration and purification of society it will become."[44] In 1911 an exchange titled "Because" listed fifteen reasons why women should vote. Among the variety of justifications were women's obligations and rights—all equal to men's—to obey the laws, to pay taxes, to improve their children's environment, to be represented in politics as consumers, and to participate equally as citizens of a democracy.[45]

As time went on and more states and municipalities granted voting rights to women, antisuffragists complained that suffrage was a failure, that it was business as usual in places where women voted, and that the promised social gains had not materialized. The *Exponent* refuted these complaints. It reprinted a letter that Utah governor John C. Cutler had written to the *Woman's Journal* in which he stated, "Woman suffrage has been most successful as a practical expedient in Utah"; he went on to point out that not only had women been "broadened and bettered intellectually and socially," but their participation had been "on the side of peace at the polls and the selection of better officials." The governor concluded by recommending that every state adopt women's suffrage.[46] In 1912 editor Wells's daughter, Annie Wells Cannon, who in 1905 had been named assistant editor of the *Exponent* and had assumed much of the responsibility for it, rebutted a *Ladies' Home Journal* article that said women voters hadn't passed progressive laws. Cannon listed significant positive changes in Utah that had occurred when women voted.[47]

The *Exponent*'s Decline

As both the *Exponent* and its editor aged, it began to show signs of decline. Wells's position as general president of the Relief Society undoubtedly occupied much of her time. Circulation decreased, although exact numbers are impossible to determine, and estimates vary widely. The paper's first editor, Lula Greene Richards, wrote that she thought the subscription list never exceeded 1,000 during her five years at the helm.[48] Its earliest listing in a national directory of periodicals credited it with a circulation of between 500 and 1,000 in 1885. Later figures, listed as estimates, peaked at 700 in 1902 and dropped to 500 in 1909.[49] In 1881 the paper printed statistics that listed 754 subscribers, although some local church entities failed to submit figures.[50] It may well have represented "fifty thousand organized women," as claimed in an 1881 magazine article, but actual circulation figures certainly never approached that number.[51]

The *Exponent* abandoned its twice-monthly status and become a monthly in January 1903, after having occasionally combined numbers since the turn of the century. No issues appeared between May and September 1912, while Wells worked in vain to obtain funding for an expanded and improved paper. Its final volume ran from September 1912 to February 1914 and contained fourteen numbers. The paper had struggled to remain profitable over its entire existence, with periodic announcements of plans to expand and improve it but insufficient funds to carry them out. Wells's appeals for support continued to the end of the *Exponent*'s life without increasing subscriptions. In 1911 she wrote, "As a people we should sustain our own publications." The paper was entering its fortieth year, she continued, and this was a good time to give "a little encouragement and patronage. Let the sisters try what can be done in the several stakes to increase the number who will take it and pay in advance, and give it support by voice and by soliciting among those who should be its patrons."[52]

The *Exponent* had been an unofficial organ of the Relief Society since its early years. With its final volume, the legend under the paper's front-page title became "The Organ of the Latter-day Saints' Woman's Relief Society." Wells wished to transfer ownership to that organization, retaining her position as editor, but other Relief Society board members preferred a new, modernized magazine, and, seeing that her proposal would be declined, Wells announced in January 1914 that she would discontinue the paper. Its successor, the *Relief Society Magazine*, appeared from 1914 to 1970. It reported women's accomplishments and in 1920 cheered passage of the Nineteenth Amendment but never made achieving women's suffrage a significant goal.

Over the years, the *Exponent* had made substantial contributions of many different kinds. In its final number, Wells listed those she considered most important: assisting those who needed help; providing a medium through which many successful writers first appeared in print; standing for high ideals in home, state, and church; proclaiming the worth and just claims of women; teaching Latter-day Saints; having a positive influence in the mission field; and serving as the organ of the Relief Society.[53] It fulfilled its early commitment to bring interesting and valuable information to its readers, report Relief Society news, and provide an outlet for the work of both new and established women writers. Its contents were read and discussed in Relief Society meetings throughout the territory. Wells saw to it that copies were distributed at national and international women's meetings and at world's fairs. She told readers that they did not realize "what a power in the hands of women of this Church a newspaper is."[54] The office was a stopping place for "hundreds of tourists" who came each year "to inquire concerning the 'peculiar people' and especially the 'Mormon' women." [55]

In one of her regular end-of-the-volume editorials, Wells called the *Exponent* "instrumental in removing much of the prejudice which has existed in regard to the conduct of women in this Church." She added: "Through its columns the sisters old and young have spoken to the world, as they could not have done in any other way, [giving] evidence of their liberty of thought and action. . . . They have also told the story of their hardships and persecutions suffered in consequence of the bigotry and superstition that is always opposed to the dawn of new light."[56] The effort to present themselves favorably to women of the world undoubtedly also gave them more confidence in themselves and reinforced their religious commitment. Even the *Salt Lake Tribune* referred to the *Exponent* as a "powerful organ."[57] Magazine editor Edward W. Tullidge claimed, "It wields more real power in our politics than all the newspapers in Utah put together."[58]

An editorial in 1911 looked toward the future to recognize the value of the paper to historians, who would have "a fountain of material in the lives of the veterans of Mormonism" whose biographies the paper had published.[59] The editorial might have added that the *Exponent* would leave a rich archive of the lives of Utah women who worked for many different causes, wrote about their struggles and successes, and joined the crusade for women's suffrage. It remained a valiant voice in that campaign.

Notes

1. The Church of Jesus Christ of Latter-day Saints is the official name of the church, although it is more often referred to as the Latter-day Saint or the Mormon Church. The more common names will be used here. Among the especially useful works consulted were Carol Cornwall Madsen's biographies of Emmeline B. Wells, *An Advocate for Women: The Public Life of Emmeline B. Wells 1870–1920* (Provo, UT: Brigham Young University, 2006) and *Emmeline B. Wells: An Intimate History* (Salt Lake City: University of Utah Press, 2017), as well as essays included in Carol Cornwall Madsen, ed., *Battle for the Ballot: Essays on Woman Suffrage in Utah, 1870–1896* (Logan: Utah State University Press, 1997).

2. "Woman's Exponent," *Salt Lake Daily Herald*, April 9, 1872, 3.

3. "The New Woman's Journal," *Salt Lake Daily Herald*, April 10, 1872, 3. Some people continued to use Brigham Young's early designation, the Territory of Deseret, even though Congress had approved the smaller Utah Territory in 1850.

4. "News and Views," *Woman's Exponent* 1 (June 1, 1872): 1.

5. "Our Position," *Woman's Exponent* 1 (June 1, 1872): 4.

6. I have used the more common "polygamy," which describes multiple mates of either sex, in preference to "polygyny," the correct term for one man having multiple wives. "Plural marriage" is synonymous.

7. Women had voted shortly after the Mormon exodus to the West, from July 1847 to March 1849. Much earlier, New Jersey had allowed women to vote from 1790 to 1807.

8. Lula Greene Richards, "How 'The Exponent' Was Started," *Relief Society Magazine* 14 (December 1927): 605–8.

9. "Valedictory," *Woman's Exponent* 6 (August 1, 1877): 36.

10. "The *Woman's Exponent*," *Salt Lake Daily Tribune*, June 10, 1872, 542. After 1873, the *Tribune* advocated disenfranchising Mormon women.

11. "Local and Other Matters," *Deseret News* (weekly edition), June 12, 1872, 9.

12. "Why Women Should Vote," *Woman's Exponent* 1 (August 1, 1872): 36.

13. "The Woman Suffrage Hearing," *Woman's Exponent* 6 (March 1, 1878): 145.

14. "Utah's Woman Suffragists," *Salt Lake Tribune*, March 15, 1895, 5. With polygamy outlawed, many polygamous men were in prison or hiding, thereby rendered their wives as heads of households.

15. "The Christiancy Bill," *Woman's Exponent* 6 (January 1, 1878): 113.

16. Carol Cornwall Madsen, "Remember the Women of Zion" (Master's thesis, University of Utah, 1977), 156. Madsen calculated that 7.25 percent of 1,502 total editorials focused on suffrage but did not calculate percentages for individual volumes or time periods. The category "Women and Woman's Sphere" constituted 21.57 percent.

17. "The *Woman's Exponent*, Index," Church History Library, Church of Jesus Christ of Latter-day Saints, Salt Lake City, Utah.

18. "Salutatory," *Anti-Polygamy Standard* 1 (April 1880): 4.

19. "Polygamy and Woman Suffrage," *Anti-Polygamy Standard* 1 (June 1880): 20.

20. "Women's Mass Meeting," *Woman's Exponent* 7 (December 1, 1878): 103.

21. "An Open Letter to the Suffragists of the United States," *Anti-Polygamy Standard* 3 (April 1882): 1.

22. "Woman Suffrage in Utah," *Anti-Polygamy Standard* 3 (October 1882): 49.

23. "Woman Suffrage in Utah," *Woman's Exponent* 10 (November 15, 1881): 92.

24. This phrase, used in the Republican Party platform in 1856, became widely popular. The other relic of barbarism was slavery.

25. "The Morning Dawns," *Anti-Polygamy Standard* 3 (April 1882): 4.

26. "More Legislation for Utah," *Anti-Polygamy Standard* 3 (December 1882): 76.

27. "Some Things for Reflection," *Woman's Exponent* 10 (March 15, 1882): 156.

28. "To Our Friends," *Anti-Polygamy Standard* 3 (February–March 1883): 85.

29. "Stirring Sentiments," *Woman's Exponent* 14 (May 15, 1886): 185.

30. "Sweet Is Liberty," *Woman's Exponent* 11 (March 1, 1883): 148.

31. "The Test Case," *Woman's Exponent* 11 (October 1, 1882): 65.

32. "The Topic of the Day," *Woman's Exponent* 14 (June 1, 1885): 4.

33. James B. Allen and Glen M. Leonard, *The Story of the Latter-day Saints* (Salt Lake City: Deseret Book Company, 1992), 412–13.

34. "Trials Tend to Strengthen and Purify," *Woman's Exponent* 15 (November 1, 1886): 84.

35. Elizabeth Cady Stanton, "The Brand of the Slave," *National Citizen and Ballot Box* 4 (May 1879): 2.

36. "Woman's Suffrage Meeting," *Woman's Exponent* 17 (February 15, 1889): 138.

37. "Editorial Notes," *Woman's Exponent* 20 (January 15 and February 1, 1892): 108.

38. "Woman's Suffrage," *Woman's Exponent* 18 (June 15, 1889): 11.

39. "Convention and Woman Suffrage," *Woman's Exponent* 23 (April 1, 1895): 241.

40. "The Article on Elections," *Salt Lake Tribune*, March 23, 1895, 4.

41. "Equal Suffrage in the Constitution," *Woman's Exponent* 23 (May 1, 1895): 260.

42. "'Vote Wisely,'" *Woman's Exponent* 25 (July 1896): 12.

43. "Four More States for Suffrage," *Woman's Exponent* 41 (November 1912): 21.

44. "Thoughts," *Woman's Exponent* 27 (December 15, 1898): 76.

45. "Because," *Woman's Exponent* 40 (July 1911): 7–8.

46. "Notes and News," *Woman's Exponent* 37 (January 1909): 40.

47. "Suffrage No Failure in Utah," *Woman's Exponent* 40 (May 1912): 69.

48. Lula Greene Richards, "How 'The Exponent' Was Started," *Relief Society Magazine* 14 (December 1927): 607.

49. George P. Rowell, *American Newspaper Directory* (New York 1885), 579; and *American Newspaper Annual* (Philadelphia: N. W. Ayer and Sons, 1902 and 1909), 850 and 887.

50. "Relief Society Report," *Woman's Exponent* 10 (November 1881): 85.

51. "Emeline [*sic*] B. Wells," *Tullidge's Quarterly Magazine* 1 (January 1881): 252.

52. "The Fortieth Volume," *Woman's Exponent* 40 (July 1911): 4.

53. "Heartfelt Farewell," *Woman's Exponent* 41 (February 1914): 100.

54. "Our Little Paper," *Woman's Exponent* 14 (May 15, 1886): 188.

55. "A Happy New Year," *Woman's Exponent* 16 (January 1, 1888): 116.

56. "Our Little Paper," *Woman's Exponent* 8 (May 15, 1880): 188.

57. "Surplus Women," *Salt Lake Daily Tribune*, February 11, 1877, 2.

58. "Emeline [*sic*] B. Wells," *Tullidge's Quarterly Magazine* 1 (January 1881): 252.

59. "The Fortieth Volume," *Woman's Exponent* 40 (July 1911): 4.

4

Writing and "Righting"

African American Women Seek the Vote

ROBIN MAZYCK SUNDARAMOORTHY
AND JINX COLEMAN BROUSSARD

The black press has always been a leading voice in race issues, from abolition to Reconstruction, lynching and Jim Crow to racial uplift and other topics. From California to Iowa to Washington, DC, the black press "distributed a written record of the complexities of black humanity to thousands of subscribers throughout the country."[1] This approach extended to this influential medium's coverage of the women's suffrage movement—through articles, editorials, marriage and death announcements, poems, novel excerpts and reviews,[2] gossip columns, graphics, and photographs. The contributions of the black press were set against the backdrop of rampant segregation and other issues that caused black women to consider both their gender and their race.[3]

Journalists such as Ida B. Wells, Mary Church Terrell, and Frances Ellen Watkins Harper frequently advocated—in word and deed—African American women's right to vote and universal suffrage.[4] For many decades, historians paid scant attention to these and other prominent African American suffragists, but a more robust picture has come into view in recent years; the women are being written about with new vigor, in histories of their suffrage and social justice work and in individual biographies.[5] This chapter broadly examines the role of these women in the suffrage movement and the black press's treatment of them and this seminal issue. We examine how Wells was covered by black periodicals, especially in the *Broad Ax* and the *Chicago Defender*, briefly explore the relevant works of Terrell and Harper, and introduce writer Bettiola Fortson, a virtually unknown suffragist. The black press celebrated these women for their fearless determination, assiduousness, and excellent oratory and writing skills, yet provided lackluster support for the cause they so passionately fought for. Last, we take a cursory glance at what women and men (white and black) wrote about women's suffrage in a variety of black publications including the *Afro-American Sentinel* (Omaha), the *Christian Recorder* (Philadelphia), the *Kansas Blackman* (Topeka), and *The Appeal* (St. Paul and Minneapolis).

Ida B. Wells and the Alpha Suffrage Club

While the suffrage movement was once viewed largely through the lens of (especially middle-class) white women fighting for the vote, African American women were very much a part of the struggle. Just as some white suffrage leaders restricted African American women in the movement, so they also restricted their place in the history of the movement. Writing in *African American Women in the Struggle for the Vote*, Rosalyn Terborg-Penn blames white female suffragists for the invisibility of black women: "White women leaders of the movement constructed the history and determined the value of black women to the movement. . . . They determined which of the African American spokespersons, male and female, were notable, and whether the woman suffrage movement was broad enough to be inclusive of black suffragists."[6]

Thanks to the coverage in black periodicals throughout the country of the women's speeches, meetings, fundraisers, and a wide variety of events held by and for black suffragists, we can resurrect a truer representation of their role and contribution. An excellent example of this coverage can be seen in the way these outlets covered the Alpha Suffrage Club. Wells and white suffragist Belle Squire organized the Alpha Suffrage Club in 1913.[7] Its goal was to teach black women in Chicago about the political process and encourage them to work for change in their communities, in part by voting.[8] Wells wrote in her autobiography that the Alpha Suffrage Club showed black women that their vote could be to the "advantage of ourselves and our race."[9] Following her lead, thousands of black women registered to vote.[10] The organization also published the *Alpha Suffrage Record*, a community newsletter.[11]

In 1913 the *Afro-American* (Baltimore) ran a front-page above-the-fold article about Chicago suffragists; subheadings read, "White Seekers for Votes Invite Colored Women to Join in the Fight," "NEGRO WOMAN'S PROBLEMS SAME AS WHITES," and "'We Need Them and They Need Us,' Says White Suffragist."[12] The article discussed the meeting of "the first colored woman's club in the city," when white suffragist Belle Squire joined Ida B. Wells to

FIGURE 4.1. Ida B.
Wells. Schomburg
Center for Research
in Black Culture,
Manuscripts, Archives,
and Rare Books
Division, The New York
Public Library. "Ida B.
Wells" New York
Public Library Digital
Collections, http://
digitalcollections.nypl
.org/items/510d47da
-732f-a3d9-e040-e00a
18064a99.

give "stirring addresses." According to the newspaper, Squire said suffragists
"must broaden our views and enlist all women to our cause, regardless of
race or color, if we are to be successful. . . . We want every colored woman
in Chicago to become a suffragist. We need them and they need us." The
article continues: "We have been too narrow. We have been too prudish. But
we realize now that we must broaden out for our mutual good. The Negro
woman has exactly the same interests at stake as her white sister. She has
property and her children to protect. She has the same vital interest in the
creation and enforcement of laws." Squire was mentioned in subsequent
pieces about the Alpha Suffrage Club published in the *Broad Ax*, which has
been called "the most controversial newspaper in Chicago in the late nineteenth century."[13] Julius F. Taylor began the weekly newspaper in 1895 in Salt
Lake City, Utah; soon, after conflicts with the Latter-day Saints, he moved it

to Chicago, where it lasted until 1931.[14] A *Broad Ax* article promoting a suffrage fundraiser hailed Squire, white suffragist Virginia Brooks, and Wells as "heroines."[15] Squire and Brooks were praised for "loyally"[16] standing by Wells during the 1913 Woman's Suffrage March when she was told to march with other black women.

The *Broad Ax* and the *Chicago Defender* printed regular updates about the Alpha Suffrage Club. Some of these pieces were word-for-word reprints. Others were often published as unattributed quick blurbs about the happenings of the organization. This included invitations to "ladies in doubt as to whether women should vote or not,"[17] efforts to register women to vote, speeches by guests, agenda items as well as time and place notifications. Wells, on occasion, wrote these pieces. Known for her civic and political involvement, she was often busy working with various groups throughout Chicago. A famously crusading journalist, Wells wrote about lynching in her *Free Speech* newspaper and in the *New York Age* before moving to Chicago in 1895; she continued to write about lynching for black and white newspapers.

When the Alpha Suffrage Club celebrated its one-year anniversary, Wells noted some of its accomplishments in a *Broad Ax* article saying it enabled women to study political and civic questions for themselves and was "making a strong effort to get hold of every Colored woman in the city of Chicago."[18] The *Broad Ax* and the *Chicago Defender* both covered the banquet celebrating the 100-member club's anniversary. In his November 22, 1913, piece for the *Broad Ax* titled "Women Voters," reporter J. Hockley Smiley wrote: "The ladies became enthused over instruction in the art of voting. A voting machine occupied one corner of the room and its intricate operation was demonstrated by Miss Nina T. Curtis, assistant to County Judge Owens. This practical feature pleased the ladies, many wishing that the next day was election." Smiley quoted Wells explaining why the club intentionally held the event on the fiftieth anniversary of Abraham Lincoln's Gettysburg Address: "the world knows how dearly we love to commemorate any event with which Lincoln has to do." The *Chicago Defender* quoted the prosuffrage US Representative Maj. John R. Lynch asserting, "no person should be governed against their will."[19] It noted that Wells "in her usual happy manner introduced the speakers and incidentally interjected some good, strong, logical advice. Mrs. [Wells-] Barnett for a great many years has devoted her life to the uplift of her race and has been instrumental in securing justice and fair pay for many."[20]

When Judge Mary Bartelme, known for her efforts with young people, spoke to the Alpha Suffrage Club in 1914 about working in Chicago's juvenile court system, the *Broad Ax* covered the event, noting that Bartelme showed women "how they could use their newfound power in helping to remedy the awful conditions which have brought 600 girls of this tender age to her courtroom."[21] The same blurb announced a white suffragist's appearance at the club's next meeting, saying she "made such a splendid protest against barring Colored women out of white clubs." After Illinois women gained the right to vote in 1913, the *Chicago Defender* covered the parade that celebrated the bill's passage and listed twenty women affiliated with the Alpha Suffrage Club who participated, including Wells.[22] The black suffragists carried flags and banners "and together with the elaborate costumes of the women, made quite a gala appearance."[23]

In 1915, during the mayoral race in Chicago, candidate William Hale Thompson sought Wells's support. Thompson's supporters knew the African American journalist, antilynching activist, and suffragist wielded tremendous influence and so would be the ideal person to convince blacks to get behind him. That support was not a foregone conclusion, however, because Wells was determined to secure benefits for African Americans in exchange, saying, "I was sure we needed a greater interest taken in our welfare; that we needed a better chance for employment in city work; and that we especially desired that representation given us commensurate with our voting strength."[24] Wells wanted equal opportunity and treatment for African Americans in all aspects of life.

She and the Alpha Suffrage Club were instrumental in securing thousands of pledges from blacks to support Thompson. The *Broad Ax* and the *Chicago Defender* covered a club meeting where Thompson discussed plans "to get to work for Colored people."[25] Both newspapers also mentioned a public reception that Wells, Thompson, and others attended for an Illinois congressman who was being recognized "for his splendid defense of Negro womanhood."[26] After Thompson won the general election by a large margin, he, like other politicians who courted African Americans during campaigns, ignored them and their plight once he gained office.[27] The largely nonpartisan[28] Alpha Suffrage Club also endorsed Oscar De Priest, a black contender for alderman in that same 1915 election. The club wanted a candidate who would "be elected to represent the Negro in the city council."[29] When De Priest won, the *Broad Ax* reported that "joy reigned" among its members.[30]

Frances Ellen Watkins Harper: An Early Advocate

After Harper's parents died in 1828, her uncle, William Watkins, a Methodist minister, educator, and abolitionist assumed responsibility for her upbringing, ensuring Harper would learn while still young about political leadership and social service.[31] Like her uncle, Harper became a reformer, author, and agent of the secret Underground Railroad network. Over the years, Harper also became a prolific and noted poet, author, and lecturer.[32] When the Reverend Watkins and his family moved to Canada in 1850 to escape the growing precarity of blacks in Baltimore following passage of the Fugitive Slave Act, Harper chose to take a teaching job at Union Seminary, now Wilberforce University, in Ohio.[33] She eventually moved to Philadelphia to continue the abolitionist and reform activities she began while with her uncle.

Harper was active in such predominantly white organizations as the Women's Christian Temperance Union and the National Council of Women, venues in which she was accepted and came to win influential national leadership positions. Another such organization was the American Equal Rights Association (AERA), founded in 1866 to champion equal voting rights.[34] Harper was keenly aware that white suffragists prioritized women's rights over the franchise for black men and was not deterred by "the often subtle and sometimes blatant racism of her fellow feminists."[35] Instead, she remained committed to campaigning "for mutual recognition of their shared interests." Harper tried to advance race and gender equity simultaneously and, when speaking to predominantly white women's groups, diplomatically emphasized their obligation to create a just society for everyone. As a speaker at the eleventh annual Woman's Rights Convention in New York in 1866, Harper told the group why she joined the fight for woman's rights: following her husband's death, an administrator seized the property she had purchased. "I say then that justice is not fulfilled so long as woman is unequal before the law."[36] Because of their precarious station in life, black women need the franchise even more than white women, Harper declared at the American Woman Suffrage Association convention in 1873.[37]

Harper used poetry to promote woman suffrage. "John and Jacob—A Dialogue on Woman's Rights" portrays a conversation between two African American men with opposing views about whether women should vote. Jacob objects to his wife, and women in general, "running to the polls," and wonders who would stay home and handle domestic responsibilities if women voted. John, on the other hand, argues that his wife and women in general should have "a good right to vote / As you or any man." John convinces Jacob that a right or wrong carries equal weight for men and women.[38]

Harper's 1891 speech at the National Council of Women, titled "Our Duty to Dependent Races," countered the argument that blacks were not ready to exercise the vote. She argued that African Americans "who were deemed so inferior as to be only fitted for slavery, and social and political ostracism" had made tremendous progress and posed no threat to the social order. She refuted charges that African Americans were unfit for the franchise because they were "ignorant and easily deluded," "easily led," "clannish," lacking "po-

FIGURE 4.2. Frances Ellen Watkins Harper, LC-USZ62-118946,
Library of Congress, Washington, D.C.

litical convictions," "passionate," and "easily excited," who could be "easily bought" and "controlled by desperate and unscrupulous white men and made to hold the balance of power when white men are divided."[39]

Mary Church Terrell: Suffrage and Diplomacy

Born in 1863, decades after Harper, Terrell became a suffragist as a freshman at Oberlin College, announcing her independence in an essay titled "Resolved, There Should Be a Sixteenth Amendment to the Constitution Granting Suffrage to Women."[40] After earning her master's degree, Terrell taught college for two years in Ohio and one year at the leading black high school in Washington, DC, before spending two years studying in Europe.

Following her marriage in 1891, Terrell continued teaching while writing for such African American periodicals as the *Woman's Era*, whose editor was fellow African American suffragist Josephine St. Pierre Ruffin; *National Association Notes*, the official organ of the National Association of Colored Women (NACW); the *Voice of the Negro*, the *Norfolk Journal and Guide*, and the *Chicago Defender*. Her speeches sometimes became articles in some of those periodicals.

Terrell believed the route to gender and racial equality could be accomplished through diplomacy. She welcomed the opportunity to take her message to white female suffragists. Terrell had "a delightful, helpful friendship" with Susan B. Anthony that began in 1890, when she first attended a meeting of the National American Woman Suffrage Association (NAWSA).[41] At that Washington, DC, event, Terrell stood up and asked the association to officially consider "the various kinds of injustices" that victimized African Americans. According to Terrell, although she was not a member, she thought the attendees "might be willing to listen to a plea for justice from an outsider."[42] Anthony then asked her to write the resolution.

The accomplishments of black women despite obstacles, and their worthiness of suffrage and equality, were major themes in Terrell's speeches and writing. In her famous 1898 speech to the NAWSA titled "The Progress and Problems of Colored Women," Terrell highlighted the strides blacks had made after slavery ended and listed the social services that black clubwomen were utilizing to better the lives of women and children. She concluded: "Seeking no favors because of our color, no patronage because of our needs, we knock at the bar of justice, asking for an equal chance."[43]

Terrell worked with white suffragists' organizations despite their racism. As her profile rose in the suffragist ranks, some movement leaders asked her to speak more frequently. At its convention in 1900, the General Federation of Women's Clubs deferred to southern white suffragists and refused to allow Terrell to deliver welcoming remarks on behalf of the NACW. When Terrell was allowed a platform, she continued her message of progress, and she chastised white women for their "prejudice and lack of sympathy" toward blacks and their failure to assist African Americans who shared their goals.[44] Terrell's diplomacy was evident as she faced the same discrimination that other black women encountered in the 1913 suffrage parade, forced to march in the section for African American women. While Wells was considered militant and combative, Terrell was a mediator who could serve as the "unofficial ambassador to predominantly white organizations."[45]

Terrell continued to write about suffrage periodically in the first two decades of the twentieth century. Some of her articles ran in the general media, as was the case with a *Washington Post* piece in 1900. She compared the current "cultured, womanly woman" suffragist with those of a "quarter of a century ago" who was "mannishly-attired, short-skirted, short-haired," and a much-ridiculed "agitator."[46] The article repeated some of the criticisms Terrell used in recent NAWSA convention speech "Justice of Colored Women." Terrell condemned powerful people trying to withhold the franchise from black women. She argued it was nonsensical to enfranchise half the US population, "some of whom are illiterate, debauched, and vicious," merely because they "were shrewd and wise enough to have themselves born boys instead of girls, or who took the trouble to be born white instead of black." Even if women were "ignorant" of or apathetic about their "disenfranchisement," that was not an excuse to perpetuate an unjust system.[47]

Terrell criticized both black men and women who opposed suffrage in a 1912 article in *The Crisis*, the official magazine of the NAACP:

> It is queer and curious enough to hear an intelligent colored woman argue against granting suffrage to her sex, but for an intelligent colored man to oppose woman suffrage is the most preposterous and ridiculous thing in the world. What could be more absurd than to see one group of human beings who are denied rights which they are trying to secure for themselves working to prevent another group from obtaining the same rights?[48]

In *The Crisis*, Terrell wrote that for blacks to use their influence against woman suffrage was "inconsistent." She reasoned they were aligning themselves with the same people who denied the black man the vote.[49] Arguing for woman suffrage in the black newspaper, the *Norfolk Journal and Guide*, Terrell used verifiable facts to illustrate how women were at the mercy of discriminatory laws because they lacked the franchise.[50]

Even after passage of the Nineteenth Amendment, Terrell continued the fight for women's suffrage, noting in a 1928 *Chicago Defender* article that Republicans had recognized white women's rights but erected "outrageous" obstacles to prevent black women from voting. When African Americans tried to qualify to vote, she asserted, registrars posed "all sorts of ridiculous questions" and "did everything in their power to prevent and discourage them." Continued exclusion from the franchise prevented black women from "improving their condition."[51]

Balanced Perspectives

These women suffragists faced racial and sexual oppression when participating in the suffrage and club movements.[52] African American women "flaunted the prescribed roles for wives and mothers and supported a wide range of feminist activities," writes historian Dorothy Sterling, adding that, even if black women primarily emphasized "the struggle for racial equality," women such as Wells and Terrell typified "a strong tradition of black feminism."[53] Black newspapers described black suffragists with reverence and respect, lauding their accomplishments.

The July 7, 1900, issue of the *Colored American* reprinted (from *Leslie's Weekly*) "An Honored Tribute: America's Leading Weekly Tells of Mrs. Terrell's Worth and Sterling Qualities." The article called Terrell "a woman of exceptional natural ability" who "has proved herself to be an orator among orators" with "fine presence, and strong magnetic power; graceful, eloquent, logical." In 1904 the *Broad Ax* similarly indicated its esteem by headlining an article "Mrs. Mary Church-Terrell was the Most Brilliant Woman at the Women's Congress, Berlin, Germany."[54] Likewise, the *Broad Ax* reported a 1912 speech by Terrell in Muskogee, Oklahoma, under the headline, "Race Has a Bright Future: People of Muskogee Pleased with Mrs. M. C. Terrell's Work."[55] The unsigned article said, "The citizens of this far western town will not soon forget the masterly, eloquent and instructive address. . . . [Terrell's] plea for justice and equality of opportunity for her race . . . moved many persons . . . to tears." Charlotta Bass's *California Eagle* ran African American writer Eloise Bibb-Thompson's article tracing black women's path from slavery to freedom, hailing the sacrifices and accomplishments of Sojourner Truth, Mrs. Booker T. Washington, and a host of others. According to Bibb-Thompson, "as a platform orator, the colored woman has stirred the souls of men in Europe and America, for the names of Ida B. Wells-Barnett, and Mary Church Terrell are signals of justice and reform."[56]

The black press often described Wells in equally eloquent terms. One mainstream newspaper mentioned her reputation "as an earnest and conscientious woman who has devoted her life to her people."[57] When Wells defied instructions to march at the back of the 1913 Woman Suffrage Parade in Washington, DC, the *Chicago Defender* likened her to Joan of Arc. It proclaimed:

> The race has no greater leader among the feminine sex than that of Mrs. Ida B. Wells-Barnett. . . . Mrs. Barnett not only braved the scorn of her Southern sisters (white), but she enjoyed a period of publicity not to her liking. . . . All praise to Mrs. Barnett for her firm stand against the bitter prejudice of the women of the South. They tried to [relegate] her to the "Jim Crow" section of the procession, but she refused and a few of her loyal friends supported her. . . . Mrs. Barnett represents the highest type of womanhood in Illinois . . . and is always to be found along the firing line in any battle where the rights of the race are at stake.[58]

For the *Broad Ax*, James C. Waters wrote that Wells-Barnett proudly marched with the head officials of the Illinois delegation "showing that no Color line existed in any part of the first national parade of the noble women who are in favor of equal suffrage."[59] The paper mentioned other African American parade participants including Terrell, suffragist Carrie Clifford, and Library of Congress librarian Daniel Murray. Julius F. Taylor, editor and publisher of the *Broad Ax*, noted that the College section[60] included "a very pleasing bevy of Colored girls . . . [who] were greeted with hearty applause all along the line."[61]

Bettiola Fortson: Ardent Suffragist and Poetess

The glowing language the black press used to describe Wells and Terrell extended to other black suffragists such as Bettiola Heloise Fortson. A 1914 *Broad Ax* report called Fortson, who was born in 1890 and moved to Chicago as a child, "the new Afro-American poetess of the middle west" and an "ardent suffragist."[62] Articles culled from the *Broad Ax* and the *Chicago Defender* describe an enterprising, active woman who saw value in the black press. According to a *Broad Ax* report, Fortson was paid a nominal fee for items she submitted to the paper each week.[63] When Fortson decided to publish a book of original poetry, she asked the editor/publisher of the *Broad Ax* to help her raise money by producing a "pamphlet"[64] to sell at the National Federation of Colored Women's Clubs at Wilberforce, Ohio, where she was a delegate. Taylor instead printed five of her poems in his August 1, 1914, issue and gave Fortson 500 copies of the issue to sell during the conference; he let her keep all the money to help fund her book. The poems published in the paper included "Brothers," written in memory of two brothers in Mississippi who died defending a black woman's honor;[65] poems honoring Booker T. Washington and the poet Paul Laurence Dunbar; and "Quo Jure? (By What Right?)," a stirring poem about racial inequality and racial discrimination. The second stanza is:

> You class me as being inferior
>   And By What Right?
> We breathe the self-same air,
> We have given the sense of smell,
> We, too, have some ways unfair,
> And here we all must dwell.[66]

When *Original Poems and Essays of Bettiola Heloise Fortson* was published in 1915, Taylor introduced Fortson, providing a sketch of her life. She con-

FIGURE 4.3. Bettiola
Heloise Fortson

tinued to attract steady coverage in the *Broad Ax* and the *Chicago Defender*,
including for her acting and for her poetry readings in Illinois, Kentucky,
Iowa, and Nebraska. She placed second in a popularity contest sponsored by
the *Chicago Defender*.[67] Fortson was sickly and during one period of confine-
ment, Taylor wrote, "No one holds Miss Fortson in any higher esteem than
the writer, for we have always regarded her, as an excellent sensible young
woman, who possess a large amount of dramatic talent and literary ability."[68]
When Fortson recited poems at a Bethel A.M.E. Church despite a bad bout
of rheumatism, the *Chicago Defender* wrote she "delighted" audiences and
"deserved credit for being present . . . rather than disappoint her audience."[69]
She died at the age of twenty-six in 1917 after contracting tuberculosis.[70]
Wells-Barnett spoke at her funeral.

Fortson, who had served as second vice president of the Alpha Suffrage
Club, clearly held Wells in high esteem. Fortson's poem titled "Queen of our
Race" described Wells's fearless actions during the women's suffrage parade.
The first stanza reads

Side by side with whites she walked,
Step after step the Southerners balked,
But Illinois, fond of order and grace,
Stuck to the black Queen of our race.[71]

Speaking Out

From the antebellum period through passage of the Nineteenth Amendment and, in some cases, beyond, black women—including journalists—worked to secure universal suffrage because they viewed the vote as a means of elevating their race.[72] Despite the discrimination from white suffragists,[73] however, black women carved out their own space, often using newspaper articles to eloquently challenge their white counterparts to treat them as equals. In a piece in *The Bystander* (Des Moines), a suffragist and corresponding secretary for the Iowa State Federation Colored Women's Club, Mrs. G. L. Johnson[74] described the double discrimination that race women faced in the fight for suffrage. Johnson wrote, "We as a race have been made to feel that this is our country, because we have served it—and served it well—and have a right to partake of all things that have a tendency to develop our intellect and become more citizenized."[75] Meanwhile, she added: "The reason the southern states could not come to a national settlement on the question of suffrage was because they knew that if they asked for 'woman suffrage,' that would include the Negro woman.... They haven't decided how ... to grant the white woman the vote and exclude the Negro woman at the same time."[76] Ultimately, Johnson argued that suffragists wanted men "to understand that we don't want the vote to take full charge of the government, but we want to help them"; she was confident that women would be "wide-awake" to certain issues that men would neglect.[77] The Des Moines Suffrage Club, an African American organization, endorsed her piece. *The Bystander* also published Johnson's poem, "An Appeal to Woman," which urged women to "get yourself ready, and fight with all your might."[78] In another example of black women fighting two battles simultaneously, her comments and poem were published during the height of tensions surrounding the release of the infamous silent movie *The Birth of a Nation*, which her editorial also addressed.[79]

Writing in her *Afro-American*'s "Women's Column" out of Baltimore, Margaret Black noted that "the editor allows us only a short space and being women, of course, we must bow to the inevitable."[80] Those limitations did not prevent her from writing a fiery article, warning readers that if they participated in the fight for the right to vote, they should expect something more than "a little praise and a few dollars."[81] Acknowledging that African

American women "are willing to work," Black stressed, "we want the benefit of our work." Black then asked white suffragists: "If we fight for you and help you win, are you going to help us to fight segregation and all forms of Jim Crowism?" To Black, "the World's Greatest Battle today is the Negroes' battle against prejudice. Instead of diminishing it seems to be increasing, and with us there must be no discharge, not retreat, not armistice, it is a battle to be fought to the bitter end."[82]

White suffragists did in fact help their black sisters. The *Appeal* reprinted a 1918 editorial by Nellie Francis, a prominent black suffragist, that first appeared in the *Minneapolis Pioneer Press*, a white newspaper. Francis, who was also the leading figure for black women's clubs in Minnesota, praised white suffragists: "Personally, I am not surprised at the high ground taken by the suffragists. It's exactly what I would have expected of suffragists, as I know them and keen would have been my disappointment if they had failed to make this sacrifice."[83] She predicted the unity shown by the white suffragists "will win for the cause of suffrage many sympathizers who would otherwise have been indifferent to its success."

Black Press: The Many Voices on Women's Suffrage

Diametrically opposed positions appeared in the black press, including within a particular newspaper. The *Broad Ax* reprinted a piece from an unknown editor who lamented the difficulties of his job; one problem was that readers criticized him regardless of what position he took. Regarding a woman's right to vote, he wrote that some readers demanded the editor to be "a militant suffragist," while others "demanded that he rail against women voting."[84]

While black publications admired what suffragists were doing, they were conflicted. One issue was the role (and power) of women once they obtained the vote. In 1868, the *Christian Recorder*, the official newspaper of the AME Church, published "A Glance at Three of the Minor Objections to Female Suffrage." The author, identified only as "Schuyler," passionately opposed women's suffrage, saying that by attending canvasses and voting, women would lose their refinement. Moreover, "Schuyler" asserted that women lacked the mental capacity to vote and were incapable of judging of the fitness of political candidates. "Her knowledge is intuitive," he asserted.[85]

An 1894 *Kansas Blackman* article "Woman Suffrage" admitted that "women make the world better, purer, nobler and more grand" but then almost immediately asked if women are "broad enough in the political sense to fully comprehend the great problems of national government affairs?"[86] The *Chi-*

cago Defender likewise speculated that universal suffrage might cause women to shirk their familial responsibilities: "Which is of greater importance, the home or the government? Is not the home the cradle of the government?"[87]

Conversely, several articles and poems upended arguments against women's suffrage by noting the irony that an illiterate and corrupt man could vote but a virtuous, smart woman could not. In 1898 the *Afro-American Sentinel* (Omaha) included an article on successes in the global fight for women's suffrage.[88] The Rev. R. Z. Roberts, an AME pastor, published "Shall Our Women Vote?" in the *Christian Recorder* in 1887. Roberts extolled a woman's intellect and supported the right for African American women and women around the world to vote. Roberts wrote:

> Women think, write and reason with undisputed correctness of judgement. Yet the saying is "her place is in the family circle." If women have that refining influence, why not let it go where it is needed? A man who would not respect a woman at the polls, would have but little or no respect for her at home or any other place of personal contact. Our women should vote.[89]

In sum, late nineteenth-century and early twentieth-century black women journalists used their voices to advocate, including on behalf of the voiceless.[90] They knew what the vote meant: the vote would remedy the exploitation of women and children and would enable them to positively influence legislation that would guarantee "full citizenship economically, socially, politically."[91] From the antebellum period through passage of the Nineteenth Amendment and in some cases beyond, they worked to secure universal suffrage. Besides the lecture circuit and active participation in suffragist associations and black organizations, they also used black and white publications to communicate about the need for suffrage. African American women still work for equal rights. They head to the voting booth in droves—not taking that privilege for granted and understanding that black women's battle for the right to vote 100 years ago was hard-fought.

This chapter is dedicated to Rosalyn Terborg-Penn for her groundbreaking work on black women suffragists.

Notes

1. Hollis Robbins and Henry Louis Gates Jr., eds., *The Portable Nineteenth-Century African American Women Writers* (New York: Penguin Books, 2017), xxvii.

2. Robbins and Gates, eds., *African American Women Writers*, xxvii.

3. See, for example, Rayford W. Logan, *The Betrayal of the Negro: From Rutherford B. Hayes to Woodrow Wilson* (New York: Collier Books, 1965).

4. Rosalyn Terborg-Penn, *African American Women in the Struggle for the Vote, 1850–1920* (Bloomington: Indiana University Press, 1998), 58.

5. Kate C. Lemay and Martha S. Jones suggested the need for more history in their "The Bold Accomplishments of Women of Color Need to Be a Bigger Part of Suffrage History," *Smithsonianmag.com*, March 19, 2019, https://www.smithsonianmag.com/smithsonian-institution/bold-accomplishments-women-color-need-be-bigger-part-suffrage-history-180971756/. See also Kate Clarke Lemay, with Susan Goodier, Martha S. Jones, and Lisa Tetrault, *Votes for Women! A Portrait of Persistence* (Princeton, NJ: Princeton University Press; and Washington, DC: National Portrait Gallery, 2019). See also Lori Amber Roessner and Jodi Rightler-McDaniels, eds., *Political Pioneer of the Press: Ida B. Wells-Barnett and Her Transnational Crusade for Social Justice*, Women in American Political History (Lanham, MD: Lexington Books, 2018); and Joan Quigley, *Just Another Southern Town: Mary Church Terrell and the Struggle for Racial Justice in the Nation's Capital* (New York: Oxford University Press, 2016).

6. Terborg-Penn, *African American Women in the Struggle for the Vote*, 164.

7. Katherine E. Williams, "The Alpha Suffrage Club," *Half-Century Magazine*, September 1916, 12.

8. Terborg-Penn, *African American Women in the Struggle for the Vote*, 99.

9. Ida B. Wells-Barnett and Alfreda Duster, *Crusade for Justice: The Autobiography of Ida B. Wells, Negro American Biographies and Autobiographies* (Chicago: University of Chicago Press, 1972), 345.

10. Wells-Barnett and Duster, *Crusade for Justice*, 347; Mildred Thompson, *Ida B. Wells-Barnett: An Exploratory Study of an American Black Woman, 1893–1930*, Black Women in United States History 15 (Brooklyn, NY: Carlson Pub., 1990), 105–6; Paula Giddings, *When and Where I Enter: The Impact of Black Women on Race and Sex in America* (New York: William Morrow, 1984), 130.

11. Terborg-Penn, *African American Women in the Struggle for the Vote*, 99. A copy of the *Alpha Suffrage Record* can be found at https://www.lib.uchicago.edu/ead/pdf/ibwells-0008-009-07.pdf.

12. "Chicago Women Join Suffragettes," *Afro-American*, January 11, 1913, 1.

13. Juliete E. K. Walker, "The Promised Land: The *Chicago Defender* and the Black Press in Illinois, 1862–1970," in *The Black Press in the Middle West, 1865–1985*, ed. Henry Lewis Suggs (Westport, CT: Greenwood Press, 1996), 21.

14. Taylor was a staunch Democrat, which was very rare at the time. Most blacks were Republicans due to the party's role in ending slavery. That, combined with his criticisms of Booker T. Washington and a variety of Chicago ministers, made him very unpopular. See Allan H. Spear, *Black Chicago: The Making of a Negro Ghetto, 1890–1920* (Chicago: University of Chicago Press, 1967), 82; Michael S. Sweeney, "Julius F. Taylor and the *Broad Ax* of Salt Lake City," *Utah Historical Quarterly* 77, no. 3 (Summer 2009): 204–5.

15. "The Alpha Suffrage Club," *Broad Ax*, March 29, 1913, 3.

16. "The Alpha Suffrage Club," 3.

17. "Alpha Suffrage Club," *Broad Ax*, September 1, 1914, 4.

18. Ida B. Wells, "The Alpha Suffrage Club to Give a Banquet," *Broad Ax*, November 15, 1913, 2.

19. "Alpha Suffrage Club Banquet," *Chicago Defender*, November 22, 1913, 4.

20. "Alpha Suffrage Club Banquet," 4.

21. "Alpha Suffrage Club," *Broad Ax*, May 30, 1914, 2.

22. "Alpha Suffrage Club," *Chicago Defender*, July 5, 1913, 1.

23. "Alpha Suffrage Club," 1.

24. Wells-Barnett and Duster, *Crusade for Justice*, 350.

25. "Alpha Suffrage Club," *Broad Ax*, November 7, 1914, 4; "Alpha Suffrage Club," *Chicago Defender*, November 7, 1914, 3.

26. "Alpha Suffrage Club," *Broad Ax*, March 20, 1915, 5; "Alpha Suffrage Club," *Chicago Defender*, March 20, 1915, 3.

27. Wells-Barnett and Duster, *Crusade for Justice*, 353.

28. The club began as a nonpartisan organization but evolved due to "a system fueled by fierce partisanship." See Patricia Ann Schechter, *Ida B. Wells-Barnett and American Reform, 1880–1930*, Gender and American Culture (Chapel Hill: University of North Carolina Press, 2001), 198.

29. "Alpha Suffrage Club," *Broad Ax*, November 28, 1914, 1.

30. "Alpha Suffrage Club," *Broad Ax*, April 10, 1915, 4.

31. Darlene Clark Hines, Elsa Barkley Brown, and Rosalyn Terborg-Penn, eds., *Black Women in America: An Historical Encyclopedia*, 2 vols. (Brooklyn, NY: Carlson Publishing, 1993), 2: 533.

32. Lydia Bjornlund, *Women of the Suffrage Movement*, Women in History Series (San Diego: Lucent Books, 2003), 68.

33. Bjornlund, *Women of the Suffrage Movement*, 68; See also David B. Sachsman, S. Kittrell Rushing, and Roy Morris Jr., *Seeking a Voice: Images of Race and Gender in the 19th Century Press* (West Lafayette, IN: Purdue University Press, 2009), 180.

34. The AERA split into two groups in 1869 because members disagreed on strategies and desired outcomes and had conflicting personalities. The American Woman Suffrage Association (AWSA) advocated for a state-by-state approach to secure the vote for women, while the newly formed National Woman Suffragist Association (NWSA) favored a federal amendment. The two organizations merged twenty years later and became the National American Woman Suffragist Association (NAWSA) and adopted the state-by-state strategy.

35. Valerie Lee, ed., *The Prentice Hall Anthology of African American Women's Literature* (Upper Saddle River, NJ: Pearson Prentice Hall, 2006), 26; Frances Smith Foster, ed., *A Brighter Coming Day: A Frances Ellen Watkins Harper Reader* (New York: Feminist Press at the City University of New York, 1990), 21.

36. Frances Ellen Watkins Harper, "Proceedings of the Eleventh National Woman's Rights Convention," held at the Church of the Puritans, New York, New York, May 10, 1866, 45–46, http://newsbank.com.

37. Edith Mayo, "African American Women Leaders in the Suffrage Movement,"

Turning Point Suffrage Museum, https://suffragistmemorial.org/African-american-women-leaders-in-the-suffragist-movement.

38. Foster, ed., *A Brighter Coming Day*, 240.

39. Rachel Foster Avery, ed., *Transactions of the National Council of Women of the United States* (Philadelphia: J. B. Lippincott, 1891), 86–91, http://www.digitalhistory.uh.edu/active_learning/explorations/lynching/harper.cfm.

40. In Mary Church Terrell, *The Progress of Colored Women* (Washington, DC: Smith Brothers, 1898), 144, Daniel Murray Pamphlet Collection, Library of Congress, https://hdl.loc.gov/loc.rbc/lcrbmrp.t0a13.

41. Debra Michals, "Mary Church Terrell," National Women's History Museum, https://biography/mary-church-terrell.

42. Michals, "Mary Church Terrell."

43. Terrell, *Progress*, 10, 13.

44. Rosalyn Terborg-Penn, "African American Women and the Woman Suffrage Movement," in *One Woman One Vote: Rediscovering the Woman Suffrage Movement*, ed. Marjorie Spruill Wheeler (Troutdale, OR: NewSage Press, 1995), 147.

45. Dorothy Sterling, *Black Foremothers: Three Lives*, 2nd ed. (New York: Feminist Press at the City University of New York, 1988), 131.

46. Mary Church Terrell, "What Women May Do: Suffragists Talk of the Work Which Is Open to Them," *Washington Post*, February 10, 1900, 2.

47. Terrell, "What Women May Do," 2.

48. Mary Church Terrell, "The Justice of Woman Suffrage," *Crisis*, September 1912, 243.

49. Mary Church Terrell, "Woman Suffrage and the Fifteenth Amendment," *Crisis*, August 1915, 191.

50. Mary Church Terrell, "Up-to-Date," *Norfolk Journal and Guide*, October 15, 1927, 16.

51. Mary Church Terrell, "Up-to-Date," *Chicago Defender*, December 1, 1928, A2.

52. Sterling, *Black Foremothers*, xxii.

53. Sterling, *Black Foremothers*, xxii.

54. Owen M. Waller, "Mrs. Mary Church-Terrell Was the Most Brilliant Woman at the Women's Congress, Berlin, Germany," *Broad Ax*, July 30, 1904, 1.

55. "Race Has a Bright Future," *Broad Ax*, May 25, 1912, 3.

56. Eloise Bibb-Thompson, "The Negro Woman in America," *California Eagle*, June 13, 1914, 1.

57. "Two Notable People Are Married: They Have Done a Great Deal in the Interest of Colored People," *Chicago Daily Tribune*, June 28, 1895, 4.

58. "Marches in Parade Despite Protests," *Chicago Defender*, March 8, 1913, 1.

59. James C. Waters, Jr., "The Equal Suffrage Parade Was Viewed by Many Thousand People from All Parts of the United States," *Broad Ax*, March 8, 1913, 1.

60. The twenty-two founding members of Delta Sigma Theta Sorority, Incorporated, marched in the parade to support the suffrage movement, according to

a C-Span interview with Gwendolyn Boyd, the DST Centennial Events chair. As undergraduates, they needed a chaperone to leave campus, so one of their Howard University professors walked with them. The event was the sorority's first official act. https://www.c-span.org/video/?c4394600/womens-suffrage-march.

61. Julius F. Taylor, "The Equal Suffrage Parade Was Viewed by Many Thousand People from All Parts of the United States," *Broad Ax*, March 8, 1913, 1.

62. "Miss Bettiola Fortson," *Broad Ax*, August 1, 1914, 2.

63. "Miss Bettiola Heloise Fortson Is Still Confined to Home with Illness," *Broad Ax*, April 7, 1917, 4.

64. "Miss Bettiola Heloise Fortson Is Still Confined to Home with Illness," 4.

65. "Poems and Sonnets—by Miss Bettiola Fortson the New Afro-American Poetess of the Middle West," *Broad Ax*, August 1, 1914, 2.

66. Bettiola Heloise Fortson, *Original Poems and Essays of Bettiola Heloise Fortson* ([Chicago]: N.p., 1915), 27.

67. "Who Is the Most Popular Girl in Chicago?," *Chicago Defender*, May 30, 1914, 4.

68. "Miss Bettiola Heloise Fortson Is Still Confined to Home with Illness," 4.

69. "A Quartet of Artists: Theodore P. Bryant, Wyatt Houston, Miss Bettiola Fortson, and Mrs. Estella Bond-Majors at Bethel Church," *Chicago Defender*, May 16, 1914, 6.

70. "The Passing Away of Miss Bettiola Heloise Fortson—Funeral Services Were Held over Her Remains Tuesday Morning from Olivet Baptist Church—Interment at Mt. Forest Cemetery," *Broad Ax*, April 21, 1917, 2.

71. Fortson, *Original Poems and Essays of Bettiola Heloise Fortson*, 27.

72. Terborg-Penn, "Woman Suffrage Movement," 137.

73. Marjorie Spruill Wheeler, "Introduction: A Short History of the Woman Suffrage Movement in America," in *One Woman, One Vote*, ed. Wheeler, 13; Terborg-Penn, "Woman Suffrage Movement," 135.

74. Mrs. G. L. Johnson was also identified as Mrs. Jennie Johnson, Johnie Johnson, and Mrs. Gibbs Lamar Johnson in various issues of *The Bystander*.

75. Mrs. G. L. Johnson, "Why the Negro Woman Should Vote," *Bystander*, May 12, 1916, 1.

76. Johnson, "Why the Negro Woman Should Vote," 1.

77. Johnson, "Why the Negro Woman Should Vote," 1.

78. Johnie Johnson, "An Appeal to Woman," *Bystander*, May 5, 1916, 1, https://chroniclingamerica-loc-gov.

79. Johnson, "Why the Negro Woman Should Vote," 1.

80. Margaret Black, "Women's Column," *Afro-American*, May 9, 1896, 2.

81. Margaret Black, "Our Duty," *Afro-American*, September 30, 1916, 6.

82. Black, "Women's Column," 2.

83. Mrs. W. T. Francis, "Mrs. W. T. Francis: Praises Stand Taken by the Woman Suffragists," *Appeal*, October 12, 1918, 3. W. T. Francis is Nellie's husband William Francis, an ambitious African American lawyer in Minnesota. Paul D. Nelson, "Wil-

liam T. Francis, at Home and Abroad," *Ramsey County History* 51, no. 4 (Winter 2017): 3–12, https://publishing.rchs.com/wp-content/uploads/2017/03/RCHS_Winter 2017_Nelson.pdf.

84. "Running the Paper," *Broad Ax*, February 12, 1916, 4.

85. Schuyler, "A Glance at Three of the Minor Objections to Female Suffrage," *Christian Recorder*, August 29, 1868, 1.

86. "Woman Suffrage," *Kansas Blackman*, May 11, 1894, 1.

87. "Home Duties," *Chicago Defender*, December 6, 1913, 4.

88. "Woman Suffrage in Ireland," *Afro-American Sentinel*, July 2, 1898, 3.

89. Rev. R. Z. Roberts, "Shall Our Women Vote?" *Christian Recorder*, April 21, 1887, 1.

90. Jinx Coleman Broussard, *Giving a Voice to the Voiceless: Four Pioneering Black Women Journalists* (New York: Routledge, 2004).

91. Giddings, *When and Where I Enter*, 121.

5

Woman Suffrage and the New Negro in the Black Public Sphere

JANE RHODES

In the fall of 1915, as the New York State legislature was about to decide whether to give women the right to vote, the esteemed African American writer, attorney, and activist James Weldon Johnson penned a defense of woman suffrage for the *New York Age*. His stinging argument, aimed at African American men's resistance, took on the oft-cited idea that the ballot would somehow compromise black women's femininity and respectability. Why, he suggested, was it acceptable for black women to work in public—often in demeaning positions—to help support their families, but not to engage in the public sphere? "If working for a living does not 'drag woman down from her lofty throne,' etc., we should like to know how taking an interest in good government and casting a vote once or twice a year is going to do it," he wrote. Johnson pointed out to his readers that "colored" votes would double in number if women had access to the ballot, effectively increasing African Americans' political influence. Perhaps more important, denying suffrage to women was unconscionable if one believed in the principles of equal rights. African American men trod on dangerous ground if they demanded their right to the franchise while arguing against women's suffrage: "The right to vote should not depend upon such qualifications as education, wealth, color or sex. Every honest, law-abiding citizen of sound mind and legal age should have the right to say how and by whom he is to be governed."[1]

The next week, Johnson continued his defense of the suffragists when he praised the October 23 Woman's Suffrage Parade in which tens of thousands marched down Fifth Avenue. He was particularly struck by the dignity and seriousness portrayed by the participants, noting black women's presence among the throngs. "The colored women in the parade showed up splendidly. . . . One body of colored women that marched together made a fine impression," he wrote, invoking both racial and gender pride.[2] Johnson's commentary attempted to shift African Americans' sense of the suffrage movement as racially divisive and discriminatory. Two years earlier, the National American Woman Suffrage Association had held a suffrage parade in Washington, DC, in which black women were asked to march separately behind their white counterparts. This event was reported in the black press and rankled even strong suffrage advocates. The New York march in 1915 was more fully integrated, which the *New York Age* took pains to point out. When the New York measure was defeated the following week, Johnson remained an unstinting advocate, noting that suffrage activists were regrouping for "a wider and more aggressive campaign." But, he argued, they needed money and greater support from black allies.[3] Two more years passed before New York State enfranchised women, capping off a long legacy of black women's suffrage activism.[4] Commentary across the black public sphere was a critical part of the debate over suffrage during a dramatic transformation of African American social and political thought.

This chapter examines the divergent perspectives on women's suffrage communicated through the black press of the New Negro era, particularly a group of radical newspapers and magazines that emerged to challenge the status quo. These publications, dating roughly from World War I to the Great Depression, coincide with the national fervor around the Nineteenth Amendment, and black Americans were actively engaged in this debate. The period—also associated with the Harlem Renaissance—was one of a proliferation of black media that captured the talents of a growing cadre of black intellectuals and activists. Philosopher Alain Locke and his peers coined the term "New Negro" to characterize the mood and aspirations of blacks, many having relocated from the Deep South as part of the Great Migration, who harbored a sense of discontent and an aching desire for change. "For the younger generation is vibrant with a new psychology; the new spirit is awake in the masses, and under the very eyes of the professional observers is transforming what has been a perennial problem into the progressive phases of contemporary Negro life," Locke wrote.[5] Locke and his colleagues distinguished "Old Negroes" crippled by their identity as a social problem, from "New Negroes" who were determined to stand up and use their intellectual and artistic capacities to the fullest. New Negro militancy is the term used to describe this activist generation shaped by the US entrance into World War I and the resulting pacifist movement, the Bolshevik revolution in Russia, and the stirrings of anticolonial revolution in Africa and Asia. Editors and writers called for a fundamental transformation of the world order. How did these New Negro militants respond to women's suffrage, and how did their periodicals help create a radical black public sphere that took up these questions?

The *New York Age*, where Johnson served as contributing editor, was then the city's oldest extant black newspaper (having been established in 1887). It was closely associated with the old guard, particularly Booker T. Washington, who was a silent owner until his death in 1915. In 1916, a year after writing his editorials on women's suffrage, Johnson joined the staff of the National Association for the Advancement of Colored People (NAACP), and his views on suffrage echoed those of his colleague W. E. B. Du Bois and the organization's influential periodical *The Crisis*, founded in 1910. Prior to World War I, activist political discourse in the black press was dominated by weekly newspapers such as the *New York Age*, the *Chicago Defender*, and the *Boston Guardian*, as well as *The Crisis*, a monthly magazine that merged serious intellectual engagement with advocacy. These race-based publications supported women's rights to varying degrees. For example, Robert Abbott, the powerful editor of the *Chicago Defender*, initially opposed suffrage, citing classic gender stereotypes purported to render black women incapable of political engagement. In 1912, he declared that women were "by nature and environment clannish" and that were they to vote "the colored race will suffer further ills in legislation."[6] But by 1913, when the state of Illinois approved suffrage, Abbott gradually endorsed the idea of black women as voters and political actors.[7] By the time the United States entered World War I, many black-owned and edited publications reflected diverse and increasingly dissident ideological positions. In 1919, the *Indianapolis Freeman* declared, "The Negro press was never more militant nor more wide awake for race progress than it is today. Our press is the people's natural spokesman. . . . It is sane without being timid—radical without being a firebrand."[8]

If Du Bois and Johnson's periodicals spoke for the established black elite, a cadre of new publications also entered in the black public sphere during the suffrage debates. Among them were the short-lived *Negro Voice*, founded by Hubert Harrison as the organ of his pacifist Afro-American Liberty League, and the socialist-inspired magazine *The Messenger*, published by A. Philip Randolph and Chandler Owen, both launched in 1917. The next year, two new newspapers began publication in the same month: the revolutionary *Crusader*, founded by Cyril Briggs, and the *Negro World*, established by Marcus Garvey as the organ of the Universal Negro Improvement Association (UNIA). Each periodical reflected a distinct political strain, and their views—

or lack thereof—regarding black women's suffrage highlight the ideological and cultural diversity among those identifying themselves as part of the New Negro crowd. *The Messenger, Crusader,* and *Negro World* are available for analysis and provide additional evidence for this discussion. Each opens a window into the rapidly changing gender politics in black America that were prompted by the campaign for and eventual passage of the Nineteenth Amendment.

Gender Politics and the New Negro

For many African Americans, women's suffrage was a direct threat to patriarchal authority, a dominant ideology that structured racial uplift and re-spectability norms. Men should dominate the public, that is, political sphere, while women were allowed to function behind the scenes. In hindsight we can view the romanticizing of patriarchy as a capitulation to the logic of white supremacist ideas that constructed black sexuality and black family structures as deviant, uncivilized, and ultimately threatening. Advocates of racial uplift, including black churches and black women's clubs, conveyed conflicting gender conventions by advocating for black women's educational attainment and leadership while also expecting that they focus their energies on marriage and the domestic sphere. Although women—particularly those among the black elite—played a critical role in racial advancement, how far their public presence should extend was much debated. African American and African Caribbean men with middle-class aspirations consistently de-veloped their ideas of self through "conceptions of production, patriarchy, and respectability," notes Martin Summers. He uses the term "bourgeois manliness" to capture how, in opposition to female subjectivity, black men saw themselves establishing status and authority in the world. The discourse of groups ranging from Masonic and fraternal organizations to the black na-tionalist Universal Negro Improvement Association all presented the protec-tion of black women as black men's greatest responsibility.[9] As a result, many believed that entering into the political domain would leave black women vulnerable and defenseless and would irrevocably harm their virtue. Some scholars assert that few black elites opposed woman suffrage, but commentary in the black press reveals major tensions among African Americans on this subject, and ambivalence and condescension toward women even among men considered suffrage advocates.[10]

The racism of white suffrage leaders shaped black Americans' varying views on the movement. By the dawn of the twentieth century, the pre-eminent suffrage organization, the National American Women's Suffrage

Association (NAWSA), embraced a "southern strategy" that tolerated racist appeals to win white southerners' support. African Americans invested in the suffrage cause roundly denounced this practice, and the antiblack rhetoric of some suffragists. At the turn of the century, for example, the black feminist scholar and educator Anna Julia Cooper scolded white suffragists on this point. Cooper asked: "Why should woman become plaintiff in a suit versus the Indian or the Negro, or any other race or class who have been crushed under the heel of Anglo-Saxon power or selfishness?"[11] She argued that suffrage was a universal right that must be respected, regardless of race. Ida B. Wells-Barnett, a distinguished journalist and editor and fierce antilynching activist, resorted to protest actions within the movement to battle its embedded racial antipathy. In her adopted hometown of Chicago Wells-Barnett founded the Alpha Suffrage Club in 1913; this was active in promoting passage of Illinois's women's suffrage bill, worked to register black voters, and aided in the election of black candidates, despite the complaints of some black men. At the 1913 NAWSA suffrage parade in Washington, DC, Wells-Barnett was among the black women who were asked to march in a segregated group at the rear. She refused to comply, initially dropping out of the parade and later joining two of her white counterparts in the Illinois delegation, much to the consternation of the organizers. Her act of resistance put the NAWSA on notice that black women would not accept their marginalization and that the struggle for the vote was theirs to wage.[12]

African Americans' conflicting views regarding women's suffrage were also pragmatic responses to the dangers and failures of black men's forays into politics after Reconstruction. Violence and structural barriers to African Americans' political voice pushed many black women to retreat into the domestic sphere, suggests Michele Mitchell, and "the turn toward domesticity" reflected the reality that electoral politics was beyond their reach. Thus, it was not only men who resisted suffrage; some of the most active and visible black women registered caution, particularly in the face of the racism of white suffragists.[13]

New Negro Journalism Promotes Suffrage

The Crisis, like the *New York Age*, took a strong stance in support of woman suffrage and offered a counternarrative to those black voices critical of the movement. W. E. B. Du Bois wrote more than twenty editorials and essays in *The Crisis* that challenged black Americans to change their views on suffrage while also opposing the movement's racist underpinnings. As early as 1912, in a special issue on the topic, Du Bois penned an editorial that framed suffrage as a human rights issue that blacks could not ignore. "Nothing human must be foreign, uninteresting, or unimportant to the colored citizens of the world," he wrote. ."Votes for women means votes for black women." [14] That year, Du Bois also published an NAACP resolution delivered to NAWSA, which made an explicit connection between racial justice and women's rights. The resolution attempted to forge a united front among African Americans and women and declared that both groups were "trying to lift themselves out of the class of the disfranchised."[15] In so doing, Du Bois both supported the suffrage campaign and sought to undermine the idea, circulated by some women's right's advocates, that African Americans were overwhelmingly opposed to the movement. In August 1915, during New York State's crucial debates on suffrage, *The Crisis* published a special forum on the subject (discussed at length by Linda Grasso in chapter 6 in this book) that featured the voices of black women—still a rarity for the black press beyond their "women's pages." These writers advanced the argument that the vote would enhance, rather than denigrate, black women's virtue and was not a threat to male authority.[16]

The Messenger magazine came on the scene with the intention of injecting a youthful, more radical voice into the already rich debates circulating in the black public sphere. The journal's founders and editors, A. Philip Randolph and Chandler Owen, fashioned themselves as pioneering black socialists and called their journal "The Only Radical Negro Magazine in America." Randolph and Owen epitomized the New Negro generation—each moved to New York's Harlem from the South as a young man, anxious to be part of the community's intellectual and cultural ferment and vitality. They became active in Socialist Party politics and hoped to bring the black masses into its fold. *The Messenger* has been recognized for its strong critiques of World War I and its campaign against lynching, while advancing trade unionism as a crucial tool for black liberation. In the first issue, which appeared in November 1917, Randolph and Owen issued a manifesto declaring, "Our aim is to appeal to reason, to lift our pens above the cringing demagogy of the times and above the cheap, peanut politics of the old, reactionary Negro leaders." They would later label Du Bois as an "old School Negro professor" and challenge the influence of *The Crisis* and other vestiges of the black establishment.[17] From the outset, *The Messenger* advanced the idea that class and gender, as well as race, must be part of a "new social order," putting them at odds with masculinist or race-first activists as well as with what they viewed as the bourgeois black elite.

The Messenger's inaugural issue carried an editorial titled "Woman Suffrage and the Negro" that warned its readers that suffrage was inevitable, noting that "women are tax payers, producers and consumers just the same as men are, and they are justly entitled to vote." The editorial chastised black men who remained resistant to black women's political and social equality, particularly "squeamish moralists." "Sex is no bar to woman's participating in the industrial world and it should be none to her participating in the political world," the editors asserted. The editorial's main purpose was to push black men to support suffrage legislation, using the same arguments advanced by Johnson and Du Bois, among others: "Remember that if the right to vote benefits the Negro man, the right to vote will also benefit the Negro woman." "Mr. Negro Voter, do your 'bit.'"[18]

But the women's rights issue was just one dimension of the editors' agenda of promoting the Socialist Party and denouncing what they viewed as blacks' slavish support for Republicans. A summer 1918 editorial titled "Negro Women in Politics" argued that if black women were given the vote they "will be largely influenced by their male companions," a position that did not signal great appreciation of women's equality. Instead, this assessment laid the groundwork for a diatribe about black men's alliance with the Republican Party: "It is discouraging and painful, however, to think that the Negro women will be led, like dum-driven cattle by the old, fossilized, ignorant, venal and discredited Negro leaders, to the Republican slaughter-house." It is difficult to identify the authors of unsigned commentary in the early issues of *The Messenger*, but there were clearly conflicting attitudes about gender among the editors and writers. In the same issue, another essay was far more sanguine about black women's potential to transform politics. They were encouraged to attend meetings of the Women's Political Association so that they could use their newly acquired political power "intelligently, in order to help liberate their people in the South, who are now in the bondage of political disenfranchisement." Yet, this essay—contrary to the journal's professed ideology—endorsed elitist ideas and respectability politics when it declared: "There is a crying need for young colored women of education and character to assume the reins of leadership in the political, economic and social life of their people."[19]

The Messenger's youthful hubris occasionally led its editors to make outlandish claims in their attempts to validate their place among the New Negro militants. An editorial in the magazine's second issue announced that "this publication was the only one published by Negroes in New York which supported woman suffrage. . . . All the other Negro publications either opposed it or ignored it, thinking that the question of woman suffrage was a minor consideration." In so doing, Randolph and Owen erased the early commentary of *The Crisis* and the *New York Age*, among others. Continuing the

FIGURE 5.1. Cover of *The Messenger*, Inaugural/Election Issue, November 1917. Courtesy of the Hathitrust (University of California).

self-congratulatory tone, the editors asserted that only socialist publications and socialist organizations campaigned on behalf of suffrage, and they took credit for the movement's success. "We have given the women their weapons. Forward now comrades for the greater victories which lie ahead!"[20]

Whether this assertion was made out of ignorance or arrogance, it attracted the attention of the NAACP, which was the object of the attack. The respondent was not *The Crisis* editor Du Bois, but rather a well-known suffragist in her own right, Mary White Ovington. She was a founding member of the NAACP and a long-time socialist, so she could not be presumed critical of *The Messenger*'s political stances. Nevertheless, she took Randolph and Owen to task for their contention that only they supported suffrage. Ovington chastised the upstart editors, telling them: "You have done excellent organizing work, I know, of which you may be proud; but Dr. Du Bois, and the NAACP, have been working along the same lines." Ovington was not going to sit by quietly as *The Messenger* overlooked her and her colleagues' labors on behalf of women's rights.[21] As a formidable white antiracism activist, journalist, and author, Ovington had a record of taking to task her sisters in the movement. In 1920, fresh from the final ratification of the Nineteenth Amendment, Ovington told her colleagues, "We must not rest until we have freed black as well as white of our sex." In particular, Ovington insisted that while the suffrage battle had been won, white women had to be "willing to aid the colored women of this country living in the Southern States to exercise the right of franchise."[22]

Making Women's Suffrage Invisible

Two additional black periodicals that emerged in 1918 articulated dramatically different visions of black resistance and civil rights. *The Crusader*, created by Caribbean-born activist Cyril Briggs, was a monthly magazine that blended black nationalism with Communist Party doctrine. Briggs and his family arrived in New York in 1905 amid a wave of West Indian immigration to the United States. As an editor of the black weekly *Amsterdam News*, Briggs became known for advocating a separate black nation within the boundaries of the United States, and the expulsion of white colonial powers in Africa. Briggs established *The Crusader* to "promote the idea of self-government for the Negro and Africa for the Africans," he wrote in an early issue. Notes Robert Hill, "*The Crusader* had the avowed purpose of spearheading a racial crusade, as Briggs told it, 'to help make the world safe for the Negro.'"[23] Briggs is best known for his leadership of the African Blood Brotherhood (ABB) founded in 1919, a quasi-secret society linked to the Communist Party that advocated armed self-defense. *The Crusader* would become the ABB's official organ in 1921. Early issues of the magazine proclaimed "Onward for Democracy" and "Upward with the Race," signaling Briggs's dual interests in national politics and racial autonomy. Despite this professed commitment to cultivating democratic processes, throughout the four years of the *Crusader*'s publication it barely mentioned women's suffrage as a social or political issue. This absence is particularly noticeable given that women's rights and the Nineteenth Amendment were regular topics in both the mainstream press and the black press. While *The Messenger* and

The Crisis, for example, exalted black women's voting power, the pages of *The Crusader* disavowed women as political actors.

Indeed, the magazine rarely commented on black male political figures, black male suffrage, or much of the national political discourse. In the first issue, *The Crusader* endorsed the black men running for statewide offices on the Socialist Party ticket, which included A. Philip Randolph. But Briggs and his colleagues expressed no party preference: "Now, while this magazine is neither pro-Socialist, pro-Republican nor, least of all, pro-Democratic, it is distinctly Pro-Negro! The Party that gives the Negro a square deal is the Party that the Crusader Magazine is going to support." In the same issue, and in a rare reference to women's suffrage, the editor published excerpts from an unnamed periodical that argued that women's enfranchisement was "a war question that must be settled and settled affirmatively in war time."[24] The insertion of this piece into *The Crusader*'s pages suggests that the editors tacitly agreed with granting women the vote, but subsequent issues offered no other confirmation of this position.

Suffrage may have been beyond the purview of *The Crusader*, but black women were quite visible, from the front-page illustrations, which frequently featured a studio photograph of an attractive young woman, to the monthly section "Helpful Hints for Women and the Home," to occasional articles praising women's deeds and accomplishments. One of the magazine's regular contributors, Gertrude E. Hall, wrote regularly on the needs and concerns of black communities. Perhaps much of the campaign fervor for women's suffrage had subsided by late 1918 and seemed to many black Americans a marginal issue. But the absence of commentary on suffrage also underscored the growth in black nationalist thought that registered discomfort with women's political voice. The rise of patriarchal politics in groups like the African Blood Brotherhood and the Universal Negro Improvement Association were fueled by assertions of black manhood rights and calls for a withdrawal from, rather than participation in, the national body politic. Black nationalism was predicated on a vision of an independent and autonomous black future. When black suffragists prepared to run for office and take their place in the public sphere, they had to alter their approach given the rising salience of these perspectives. Julie Gallagher notes that "black clubwomen, who had long worked for racial uplift through the politics of respectability and the elevation of women's status, were displaced as race leaders" as a more masculinist political project held sway.[25]

Nowhere was this more evident than in the *Negro World*, a weekly newspaper founded by Marcus Garvey as the organ of the UNIA in the summer of 1918. The *Negro World* is believed to be the first black newspaper to have a circulation of over 200,000; it became the most widely read black periodical in the nation and around the globe.[26] Garvey founded the UNIA in 1914 in his native Jamaica, where he was a master printer and journalist. He brought the organization in 1916 to the United States, where it attracted a huge following, particularly among working-class blacks—those southern black and West Indian migrants who felt alienated from the educated black elite. If *The Crisis* and the *New York Age* spoke the language of an integrationist Old Negro establishment, the *Negro World* reached the New Negro masses through appeals to racial pride and conventional gender norms. Rather than emphasizing black women's progress through political engagement, the focus was on protection of black women and racial purity.[27] Garvey often expressed these ideals by arguing for black self-defense. In October 1919, following a spate of white mob violence around the country, he predicted a race war in which black men would throw off their abject status: "No mercy, no respect, no justice will be shown the Negro until he forces all other men to respect him. . . . Therefore, the best thing the Negro of all countries can do is to prepare to match fire with hell fire."[28]

Each issue of the *Negro World* began with a full front-page editorial addressed to "Fellowmen of the Negro Race," and Garvey used the newspaper to encourage readers to support political independence in Africa and his unique brand of black capitalism. "I am exhorting the Negro peoples of the world to prepare for and enter into the titanic struggle for the survival of the fittest in the spheres of commerce and industry," Garvey wrote.[29] The content of the *Negro World*, which was edited by a diverse group of writers and intellectuals, presented a Pan-African, anticolonial perspective in which the US and European colonizers were the enemy of black liberation. The newspaper was global in its outlook and insular in its interests—paying close attention to Africa and the Caribbean as well as black America but encouraging members to focus their energies on building the organization. In the Garveyite imagination, black participation in politics was a worthless, foolhardy exercise. Editor Hubert Harrison, often considered the "dean" of radical activists of the era, wrote that blacks had been duped into believing in the political process and that "we Negroes have no faith in American democracy."[30]

As with *The Crusader*, this did not mean that women were rendered invisible in the pages of the *Negro World*. While the UNIA had a strictly gendered division of labor, women had diverse roles in it; many rose to key leadership positions. In her study of black nationalist women, Keisha N. Blain finds that the organization allowed black women alternative routes for political participation beyond the confines of home and family.[31] Each issue of the newspaper featured articles about black women's undertakings in education and business and reports of women UNIA representatives speaking around the nation. In 1924, Garvey's second wife, Amy Jacques Garvey, became associate editor and started a woman's page titled "Our Women and What They Think." She created a forum to open up a dialogue about gender and critiques of masculinity previously absent from the publication. Her biographer, Ula Y. Taylor, suggests that as the partner of the UNIA leader and an activist in her own right, Jacques Garvey had to tread a careful line between accepting and rejecting patriarchal ideals. Her nearly 200 editorials and essays for the *Negro World* "were the embodiment of the concept of community feminism, as they advocated all-encompassing roles for black women who sought participation in a Pan-African movement." Taylor explains that community feminists focus their energies on the uplift of both men and women in their orbit while working to undermine ideas of female inferiority and to bolster women's efforts. Jacques Garvey also argued strenuously that women's value was both in the domestic sphere and the public sphere, and that "family life had not been neglected by women's entry into politics but had benefited from it," notes Taylor. Rather than explicitly endorsing woman suffrage, Jacques Garvey's columns—along with other commentary in the newspaper—promoted black women's political engagement in the Pan-African movement, acquiring knowledge through education and developing leadership skills.[32]

Voting Rights, Voter Suppression

By the time the Nineteenth Amendment was passed by the US Senate in 1919, the black press was intensely focused on the upsurge in racial violence including lynching, race riots, and the intransigence of Jim Crow discrimination in jobs, housing, and education. The front pages of the *New York Age*, for example, were preoccupied with the demobilization of the troops, the experiences of black soldiers overseas, and the lynching crisis in the South. But the paper continued the drumbeat of support for suffrage with numerous articles that reported on the success of black women as electoral candidates and the growth of clubs focused on their political empowerment. In the aftermath of the suffrage amendment's ratification, Johnson returned to this subject with an editorial, "The Colored Woman Voter," which predicted that black women would have an immediate effect on black politics and would be "less easily intimidated" than black men had been in the past. Johnson struck a paternal tone as he exhorted women to educate themselves about the voting process, and encouraged the creation of study classes in black communities to "reach every colored woman possible." He suggested that women needed such instructions to be "as simple and understandable as possible," and argued that they should allow men to assist them in the process.[33] The *New York Age* also offered numerous examples of black women denied access to the ballot in states including Georgia, Alabama, and Florida. Mary White Ovington reported in *The Suffragist* the story of a black Republican official in Florida who was kidnapped and made to think he was about to be lynched because of his efforts to register black women voters.[34] This was an extension of the intransigent hold of Jim Crow policies across the nation, which remained the target of black activists and the black press.

For several months *The Messenger* temporarily halted publication after federal government surveillance and threats of prosecution for seditious activities, part of a national Red Scare. When the magazine reappeared, its editors quickly returned to the topic of women's suffrage. Once the amendment was ratified, Randolph and Owen celebrated the measure. Like its counterparts in the radical black press, *The Messenger* registered suspicion and anger toward conventional party politics: "Now Negro women have the right to vote everywhere. Let us hope they will not follow in the footsteps of Negro men who have voted like cattle by wicked, ignorant and corrupt Negro and white Republican ward heelers. Negro women must realize Republicans and Democrats represent their enemies—the exploiting landlords and employers."[35] *The Messenger* focused much of its attention on the southern strategies to deny both black men and black women access to the franchise in the immediate aftermath of the suffrage victory. In particular, the editors wanted to push black voters to not merely celebrate the success of the Nineteenth Amendment but question the larger premise of the political status quo. They condemned black women who entered politics via the Republican Party, arguing that this was the constituency "which has winked at the disfranchisement of Negro men in the South for the last 30 or 40 years."[36]

Determined to forge an alternative political path, *The Messenger* pleaded with readers to see the Socialist Party as a better representative of black people's interests. Shortly after ratification of the Nineteenth Amendment in 1920, *The Messenger* ran full-page advertisements for local Socialist Party candidates, including its editors Randolph and Owen, who were running for state comptroller and the State Assembly in New York, respectively, and a woman identified as Miss Grace Campbell, who was also on the ticket for the Assembly. The magazine celebrated Campbell's candidacy, revealing that they were not opposed to black women's engagement with the electoral process, but with what they saw as a broken and corrupt political system that failed black people. "We want Negro women to stand up and fight as the political, economic and social equals of their white sisters," said *The Messenger*.[37] Another woman candidate promoted by *The Messenger* was Randolph's wife,

Lucille, who also ran on the Socialist Party ticket. In an interview, Randolph recalled with pride that the famed Socialist leader and one-time presidential candidate Eugene Debs campaigned for Lucille at a rally in Harlem. "He was carried away with my wife," said Randolph, noting that Debs and his colleagues were surprised that a black woman would have such political aspirations.[38]

Once women's right to vote became law, however, the subject disappeared from the pages of the black press, particularly the radical journals that questioned black Americans' involvement in mainstream politics. By 1922 there was nary a mention of women voting or running for office in the pages of *The Messenger*, although the magazine reported on black women's organizing in arenas that were the editors' chief preoccupations, particularly the growing black labor movement. Even Old Guard publications like the *New York Age* and *The Crisis* moved on to other pressing issues. That year James Weldon Johnson wrote an editorial for the *Age* that argued against essentialist notions of gender—specifically, that not all women would seize the opportunity to enter the public sphere. In his pessimistic observation, the era's new woman "has achieved her economic independence and . . . is ready to compete with men in constructive and creative work," but many "sheltered women" were far from seizing the franchise.[39]

By the end of the decade the *Age* had been supplanted in readership and influence by the *Amsterdam News*, which became the most widely read black newspaper in New York City. The *News* covered black women's major and minor successes in politics, such as the activities of the New York State Colored Republican Women's League. But in a ten-year retrospective on women's suffrage written by Howard University professor and dean Kelly Miller, the *News* echoed Johnson's sentiments. Miller joked that despite men's fears, woman suffrage did not destroy the fabric of society and had succeeded in granting women new privileges and opportunities. Yet, he argued, "the gentler half of our citizenry has impressed no practical influence upon the governmental equation."[40] During a period of intense suppression of black voting in the South and the dominance of political machines in the urban North, Kelly saw little material change in the segregation of American politics and the dominance of white supremacist thought. Roslyn Terborg-Penn's landmark study of black women in the suffrage movement came to similar conclusions. She noted that in the North black women were abandoned by white feminists and the Republican Party in the aftermath of ratification. Meanwhile, "African Americans' hopes for political equality were dashed as the majority of black women who lived in the South were quickly disenfranchised," Terborg-Penn explained. The Nineteenth Amendment succeeded in extending the ballot to all women regardless of race and class, she concluded, but for black women "it was suffrage in name only."[41]

Many African American women who had roots in the suffrage struggle continued the quest to gain a political foothold—running for office, building clubs, and educating the next generation of activists. Others worked within black nationalist settings, focusing on the work of groups like the UNIA or community-based civic organizations. While black nationalism encouraged men to cling to Victorian patriarchal notions, there also was a new generation of black men whose ideas diverged from convention to view women as equal partners in the quest for racial justice. Women were in the forefront of this struggle—journalists/activists like Amy Jacques Garvey promoted an idea of community feminism that encouraged female engagement in the public sphere while refusing to seek acceptance by white America. Black women played an influential, though often behind-the-scenes, role in the radical black press. Thus, while Jacques Garvey helped to shape the content of the *Negro World* her name was relegated to the "women's page," and at *The Messenger*, A. Philip Randolph's wife, Lucille Green Randolph, provided crucial, yet unseen, financial support through her hair salon where she also distributed the paper.[42]

The radical black press was a crucial vehicle for the widely divergent ideological perspectives coursing through black communities in the era of woman suffrage. The question of the vote intersected with other critical aspects of black life—the quest for economic survival, the ever-present threats of violence and discrimination, and the desperate need for self-esteem and a sense of humanity. These were dark times for African Americans, and these debates underscore the sense of urgency and disarray that these editors and journalists, as well as their readers, faced. The fault lines between men and women, between New Negroes and the Old Guard, between race-first black nationalists and reformers promoting integration, all emerged within the campaign for passage of the Nineteenth Amendment. Some press leaders viewed women's enfranchisement as a marker of progress. Others had good reason to doubt that the vote would matter for black Americans, or denounced the concept of participating in mainstream politics entirely. The debates in the pages of early twentieth-century newspapers and periodicals also reveal how this generation of black men and women sought to embrace new ways of being—including gender relations—while navigating the daily assaults on their citizenship.

This chapter is dedicated to the memory of Dr. Rosalyn Terborg-Penn, whose groundbreaking study, *African American Women in the Struggle for the Vote, 1850–1920*, influenced every aspect of this discussion. A wonderful friend, colleague, and mentor, she will be greatly missed.

Notes

1. James Weldon Johnson, "Woman Suffrage," *New York Age*, October 21, 1915, in *The Selected Writings of James Weldon Johnson: The New York Age Editorials, 1914–1923*, ed. Sondra Kathryn Wilson (New York: Oxford University Press, 1995), 75–76. All Johnson's *New York Age* articles are quoted from this volume.

2. James Weldon Johnson, "The Suffrage Parade," *New York Age*, October 28, 1915, 76–77.

3. James Weldon Johnson, "A Comparison," *New York Age*, November 11, 1915, 77–79.

4. See Julie A. Gallagher, *Black Women and Politics in New York City* (Urbana: University of Illinois Press, 2012), 23–25.

5. Alain Locke, "The New Negro," in *The New Negro: An Interpretation* (New York: Albert and Charles Boni, 1925), 3.

6. *Chicago Defender*, March 30, 1912.

7. See discussion in Mary E. Stovall, "The 'Chicago Defender' in the Progressive Era," *Illinois Historical Journal* 83, no. 3 (Autumn 1990): 162–63.

8. *Indianapolis Freeman*, October 18, 1919, qtd. in Theodore G. Vincent, ed., *Voices of a Black Nation: Political Journalism in the Harlem Renaissance* (Trenton, NJ: Africa World Press, 1973), 24.

9. Martin Summers, *Manliness and Its Discontents: The Black Middle Class and the Transformation of Masculinity, 1900–1930* (Chapel Hill: University of North Carolina Press, 2004), 111.

10. See, for example Kevin K. Gaines, *Uplifting the Race: Black Leadership, Politics, and Culture in the Twentieth Century* (Chapel Hill: University of North Carolina Press, 1996), 138.

11. Cooper quoted in Gaines, *Uplifting the Race*, 144.

12. Wanda A. Hendricks, Paulette Pennington Jones, and Careda Rolland Taylor, "Ida Wells-Barnett Confronts Race and Gender Discrimination," Illinois Periodicals Online, https://www.lib.niu.edu/1996/iht319630.html; see also Adade Mitchell Wheeler, "Conflict in the Illinois Woman Suffrage Movement of 1913," *Journal of the Illinois State Historical Society* 76, no. 2 (Summer 1983): 95–114.

13. Michele Mitchell, *Righteous Propagation: African Americans and the Politics of Racial Destiny after Reconstruction* (Chapel Hill: University of North Carolina Press, 2004), 135–36.

14. *Crisis*, September 1912.

15. Du Bois quoted in Garth E. Pauley, "W. E. B. Du Bois on Woman Suffrage: A Critical Analysis of His *Crisis* Writings," *Journal of Black Studies* 20, no. 3 (January 2000): 397.

16. See Pauley, "W. E. B. Du Bois on Woman Suffrage"; and Valethia Watkins, "Votes for Women: Race, Gender, and W. E. B. Du Bois's Advocacy of Woman Suffrage," *Phylon* 53, no. 2 (Winter 2016): 3–19.

17. "Negro Women in Politics," *Messenger*, July 1919.

18. "Woman Suffrage and the Negro," *Messenger*, November 1917.

19. "Negro Women in Politics," *Messenger*, July 1918.

20. "Woman Suffrage and *The Messenger*," *Messenger*, January 1918.

21. "Negro Women's Vote," *Messenger*, July 1918.

22. Mary White Ovington, "Free Black as Well as White Women," *Suffragist* 8, no. 10 (November 1920): 279, Library of Congress, Nineteenth Century Collections Online.

23. Robert A. Hill, ed., "Introduction," *The Crusader: A Facsimile of the Periodical* (New York: Garland Publishing, 1987), ix.

24. "The Negro Candidates," *Crusader*, September 1918.

25. Gallagher, *Black Women and Politics in New York City*, 33.

26. On the size and influence of the *Negro World*, see Vincent, *Voices of a Black Nation*, 29; and D'Weston Haywood, *Let Us Make Men: The Twentieth-Century Black Press and a Manly Vision for Racial Advancement* (Chapel Hill: University of North Carolina Press, 2018), chap. 2.

27. See discussion in Summers, *Manliness and Its Discontents*, 125.

28. "Soldiers of Ethiopia," *Negro World*, October 11, 1919.

29. "Fellow Men of the Negro Race," *Negro World*, July 4, 1919.

30. "Fellow Men of the Negro Race," *Negro World*, October 8, 1921.

31. See Keisha N. Blain, *Set the World on Fire: Black Nationalist Women and the Global Struggle for Freedom* (Philadelphia: University of Pennsylvania Press, 2018), 19–25.

32. Ula Y. Taylor, "Negro Women Are Great Thinkers as Well as Doers: Amy Jacques Garvey and Community Feminism in the United States, 1924–1927," *Journal of Women's History* 12, no. 2 (Summer 2000): 108, 112. For a full biography see Ula Yvette Taylor, *Veiled Garvey: The Life and Times of Amy Jacques Garvey* (Chapel Hill: University of North Carolina Press, 2002).

33. James Weldon Johnson, "The Colored Woman Voter," *New York Age*, September 18, 1920, 82.

34. Ovington, "Free Black as Well as White Women."

35. "Woman Suffrage," *Messenger*, October 1920.

36. "Vote in Name Only," *Messenger*, November 1920.

37. "The Negro Woman Voter," *Messenger*, November 1920.

38. *Reminiscences of Asa Philip Randolph* (1972), 112–114, Oral History Archives, Rare Book & Manuscript Library, Columbia University, New York.

39. James Weldon Johnson, "Equality and Privileges for Women," *New York Age*, September 2, 1922, 86.

40. Kelly Miller, "Ten Years of Woman's Suffrage," *Amsterdam News*, August 27, 1930.

41. Rosalyn Terborg-Penn, *African American Women in the Struggle for the Vote, 1850–1920* (Bloomington: Indiana University Press, 1988), 151, 163.

42. Tiffany Gill, *Beauty Shop Politics: African American Women's Activism in the Beauty Industry* (Urbana: University of Illinois Press, 2010), 51–52.

6

Differently Radical

Suffrage Issues and Feminist Ideas
in *The Crisis* and *The Masses*

LINDA M. GRASSO

The Crisis and *The Masses* were united in supporting women's suffrage but divided by political imperatives. In 1915, *The Crisis: A Record of the Darker Races*, a "militant civil rights journal" published by the National Association for the Advancement of Colored People (NAACP), and *The Masses*, a self-described "revolutionary and not a Reform Magazine," operated in Greenwich Village.[1] Both appeared once a month, cost ten cents a copy, and charged one dollar for a yearly subscription. Yet neither geographical proximity in a bohemian New York City enclave nor the same publication rate meant a shared readership. In 1915, *The Crisis* had 34,000 subscribers across the country, most of whom were black. The estimated 14,000 to 40,000 readers of *The Masses* were undoubtedly white.[2]

This essay argues that radicalism was racialized in the 1910s. The women's movement, within which the suffrage campaign and feminism flourished, was riven by white supremacist structures and ideologies, as was every aspect of US society. Antiblack prejudice and bigotry were national phenomena, which is evident in the rhetoric and actions of those who supported as well as opposed women's suffrage. As the campaign to enfranchise women gained momentum, some southern white suffrage leaders argued for granting white women the vote to perpetuate white supremacy, while some northern white suffrage leaders insisted that race issues were irrelevant and the support of southern white women was essential to securing a federal amendment.[3] In the same way the women's movement was segregated because of racism, so too were the most progressive and influential periodicals of the era.

Neither *The Crisis* nor *The Masses* was exclusively aimed at women. *The Crisis* was the official organ of an interracial preeminent black social justice organization whose goal was "to stand for the highest ideals of American democracy, and for [the] reasonable but earnest and persistent attempt to gain these rights and realize these ideals."[4] *The Masses* was an irreverent expressive outlet for left-wing political eclecticism, which included idiosyncratic interpretations of socialism, communism, and anarchism. Yet both deemed advocating women's suffrage important to their projects and their audiences because "the meaning of citizenship had, by the 1910s, expanded to include aspects of social justice."[5] These "aspects" were inextricably bound to issues of gender and race: debates about suffrage were also debates about gender conventions and expectations as well as the logic of white supremacy in a democratic country. "The colored American believes in equal justice to all, regardless of race, color, creed or sex," suffragist and educator Adella Hunt Logan proclaimed in a 1912 "Woman's Suffrage Number" of *The Crisis*, "and longs for the day when the United States shall indeed have a government of the people, for the people and by the people—even including the colored people."[6]

In 1915, after a federal amendment that would have guaranteed women voting rights was defeated and New York was set to vote on a state referendum, *The Crisis* and *The Masses* published special issues promoting the cause. *The Crisis* highlighted a "Votes for Women" symposium in August 1915 and *The Masses* named its November issue the "Woman's Citizenship Number."[7] The advocacy of these two publications for this highly controversial campaign was part of their larger commitment to a transformed social order in which opportunities and resources were equally distributed, citizenship rights were guaranteed and protected, and prejudices based on "sex" and "race" were eliminated.

Comparing the 1915 suffrage issues of *The Crisis* and *The Masses* enables an analysis of how these two communities, one black and one white, addressed gender discrimination and disenfranchisement from different racial perspectives. This comparison also impels a redefinition of radicalism, especially regarding feminism. *The Masses*, a white periodical, is typically considered "radical." *The Crisis*, a black periodical, is typically considered "African American." Given, however, that a bedrock principle of 1910s US feminism was the valuing of all women and girls as human beings, thinkers, artists, activists, and culture-makers—then a radical claim—both periodicals circulated differently radical feminist messages in their suffrage issues. *The Crisis* insisted that both black and white women were equally entitled to voting rights. *The Masses* promoted white women's emancipation and regarded women's suffrage as part of that crusade.

Although ostensibly focused on women's voting rights, the 1915 suffrage issues of *The Crisis* and *The Masses* say much about the ways in which the quest for women's social justice was perceived, enacted, and racialized at a pivotal moment in women's political history. Both radical in their outlier status, these special issues advance feminist ideas that set them apart from the white suffrage movement. In *The Crisis*, for example, W. E. B. Du Bois "approved" of women's suffrage, but he emphatically disapproved of white women's racism; to them, he asserted, Votes for Women meant "Votes for White Women Only."[8] In *The Masses*, contributor Jeanette Eaton also approved of women's suffrage because "women ought to be citizens and they will," but she emphasized an ideological divide between advocates at *The Masses* and members of the New York–based Woman Suffrage Party. The divide, Eaton's article suggests, concerns the willingness of *The Masses* to transgress genteel, Christian propriety in order to excoriate southern white bigotry. Pointing out the irony of antisuffragists mistakenly believing that the "blasphemous" *Masses* was "the national organ of the Woman Suffrage Party," Eaton says "to suffragists": "*The Masses* approves of you, but you do not approve of us."[9] While denouncers of women's suffrage did not see distinctions among prosuffrage organizations, activists within those organizations most certainly did.

As differently radical magazines, *The Crisis* and *The Masses* simultaneously limited and expanded women's visibility and power to agitate for democratic rights and freedoms. Both publications were created for, and spoke to, gender-integrated audiences and included women as editors and contributors, but they were dominated by powerful men: W. E. B. Du Bois at *The Crisis* and Max Eastman and Floyd Dell at *The Masses*. In *The Crisis* symposium, although women are equal participants, men contributors are the first to speak. In *The Masses*, women contribute poetry, short stories, and visuals, but men author most of the articles and draw most of the illustrations. At the same time, however, both periodicals created public spaces that enabled women to join men in protest and outrage: *The Crisis* lambasted white supremacy and black women's subordination and *The Masses* denounced capitalist enterprise, racial bigotry, and conventional gender arrangements, though paying minimal attention to black women's rights and oppression.

The 1915 suffrage issues of *The Crisis* and *The Masses* acknowledge the importance of women as contributors and readers: women speak and are spoken about; they are visualized in photographs and drawings; and their gendered concerns are addressed in advertisements for books, products, and services. The work of seventeen women, two of them white, is featured in the fifty-two-

School Teachers Wanted

We can place 3000 school teachers who wish to be pleasantly and profitably employed during their vacation time.

Write us today for full information and free circular reproductions of our specialties.

We will appoint you our representative and show you how to make from $2.00 to $10.00 per day and be your own boss.

Agents wanted everywhere. Special offer for ministers.

DOUGLAS SPECIALTIES CO.
3548 Vernon Ave.   (Dept. K)   **Chicago, Ill.**

(Trade Mark)

FIGURE 6.1. Advertisement for schoolteachers in *The Crisis*, August 1915, 162.

page *Crisis*. Many other women appear in news reports, photographs, and advertisements promoting education and employment. In the issue's "Men of the Month," a regular column, all those included are distinguished women in the arts and community leadership. Moreover, several advertisements for single-sex or coeducational schools make clear that women are welcome. The half-page advertisement for "The Cheyney Training School for Teachers," for example, recruits "young colored men and women . . . who earnestly desire to become teachers."[10] "Votes for Women," therefore, is a claim situated among a matrix of others that asserts black women are modern new women who are intellectual, professional wage-earners, and a fundamental part of a black middle-class avant-garde.

The special issue of *The Masses* also emphasizes women's importance. Almost half the size of *The Crisis* at twenty-eight pages, *The Masses* features the writing and drawings of seven white women; the majority of illustrations depict women. The books for sale in "*The Masses* Bookstore" address women's physical, psychological, and economic emancipation. Books in the "Sex" section, for example, range from *Sexual Life of Woman* by Dr. E. Heinrich Kisch to *What Every Mother Should Know* by Margaret Sanger to *Functional Periodicity: An Experimental Study of the Mental and Motor Abilities of Women during Menstruation* by Leta Stetter Hollingworth. The issue's last page has advertisements for a woman-designed "child's dressing stand" and a detachable pledge form for the "Last, Biggest, and Best" "Banner Woman Suffrage Parade." In this context, "woman's citizenship" is another manifestation of modern new women's independence as artists, designers, activists, mothers, and sexually liberated consumers.

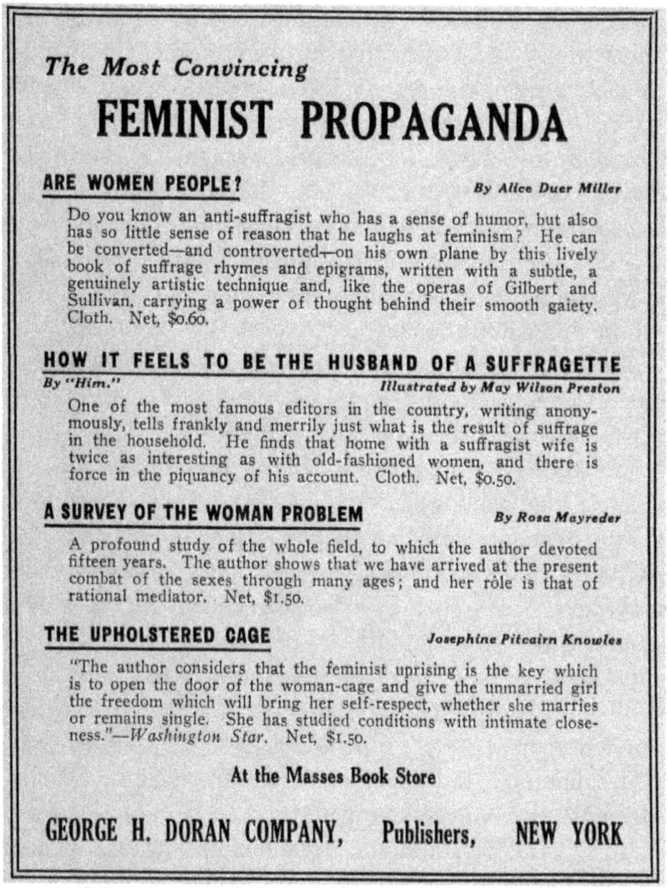

FIGURE 6.2. Advertisement for books in *The Masses*, November 1915, 22.

The specific contents of these similar features, however, signal the magazines' different imperatives, which affect the ways in which they advocate women's suffrage. For example, *The Crisis* advertised books such as histories and studies of race relations and black people, but no books about feminism or the women's movement. *The Masses* listed many books about feminism, the women's movement, psychology, sexuality, socialism, and class relations, but no race-related or black social justice books. Likewise, some of the distinguished clergy, educators, clubwomen, and legislators who address women's suffrage in *The Crisis* symposium stress how the vote will positively affect the black community, while the writers and artists in *The Masses* use feature stories and satire to underscore how nurturing women's individuality will positively affect the whole of society. Black people, however, as well as their history, struggles, and creative literature, are seemingly not part of this whole; they are virtually invisible in *The Masses*'s "Woman's Citizenship Number," with two exceptions: a short story by Mary White Ovington, discussed below, and an article by Inez Haynes Gillmore about the hypocrisy of a chivalric ideal in a country benefitting from an "industrial system" that makes "wage-slaves" of white children working in southern mills and "negro porters in the employ of the Pullman Company."[11]

Ironically, the interest of both periodicals in class issues also demonstrates their different agendas. In *The Masses*, women's participation in efforts to eradicate exploitive class inequities situates them as equal partners in a radical project of reconstructing economic hierarchies. In *The Crisis*, women's participation in a burgeoning black middle-class formation is decidedly radical for a group of people battling perpetual race and gender-based violence, dehumanization, and disenfranchisement. Thus, *The Masses* community envisions white women utilizing the ballot to deconstruct class boundaries and eviscerate constricting middle-class conventionality, while *The Crisis* community envisions black women utilizing the ballot to secure the privileges of middle-class status for themselves, their families, and their community.

The nonfiction prose about women's suffrage is another example of each special issue's differently radical imperatives. Although both contain single-authored expositions, *The Masses* includes three signed essays written by editors Eastman and Dell, and *The Crisis* includes twenty-six statements as part of a symposium in which "Leading Thinkers of Colored America" present a variety of affirmative views. This distinction reveals different ideas about leadership and organizational strategies. The symposium in *The Crisis*, which Du Bois pronounces as "one of the strongest cumulative attacks on sex and race discrimination in politics ever written," models community involvement, exchange, and reasoned argumentation and propounds the idea that debate is an effective form of persuasion.[12] The number of participants, coupled with their status as powerful change agents in law, education, civic organizations, politics, and the arts, authorizes and amplifies the pro–woman suffrage message. Equally significant, the symposium transmits the idea that leadership is shared. Convincing African American readers who may be apathetic, undecided, or opposed to women's suffrage that women's right to vote will ensure justice, progress, and political power cannot be entrusted to one individual and one way of arguing a position.

The polemics in *The Masses*, on the other hand, suggest that the two male editors are the vanguard of leadership. For Eastman and Dell, opposition to traditional gender norms takes precedence over debate about the advantages of women's suffrage for the nation and the community. Rather than seeking to change the minds of *Masses* readers, Eastman and Dell address the already converted and use rhetorical strategies that readers can then adopt when confronting "antis" themselves. They employ irreverence, satire, mockery, and scorn to protest women's lack of rights and freedoms. Dell, for example, in the lead essay "Adventures in Anti-Land," rails against "antis" who insist "woman's place is in the home." Women are "free and independent human being[s]," he proclaims, who are perfectly capable of participating "in political and intellectual life."[13] Taking a more temperate view, Max Eastman, in "Confessions of a Suffrage Organizer," focuses exclusively on argumentative strategy. Insisting that people are not rational about "questions involving sex," he advises that activists construct pro–woman suffrage arguments that affirm the "wishes" of adversaries rather than attempt to change their opinions. The best way to win converts, he argues, is to appeal to what people already believe and then to place the advantages of women's suffrage within that existing framework. "What our times respond to," he asserts, "is the propagandist who knows how to respect the wishes of other people, and yet show them in a sympathetic way that there is more fun for them, as well as for humanity in general, in the new direction."[14]

In the "Votes for Women" special issue of *The Crisis*, Du Bois also wants to lead readers in a "new direction," but he does so by orchestrating a symposium, an ancient Greek tradition that dignifies the proceedings. This format moves the women's suffrage debate out of the oral culture of churches and women's clubs and enables black women to speak publicly in print, alongside black men and in some instances directly to them. Moreover, it furthers the national circulation of pro–woman suffrage messages and creates a written record of advocacy. Participants ground their arguments for women's suffrage in beliefs about gender "that mesh with and appeal to society's discourses," a tactical necessity, social movement theorists posit, to effecting change in attitudes, customs, policies, and laws.[15]

Three discourses about gender undergird the pro–woman suffrage arguments in *The Crisis* symposium and sometimes they are all combined: women are the same as men; women are different from men; and women are both the same as and different from men. Those who believe women are the same as men argue that women and men should have the same civic entitlements. Others who believe women are different from men contend that women should have the vote because their perspectives as wives, mothers, and homemakers enable them to bring their unique skills, experiences, and "great mother-heart[s]" "to the building of an ideal country."[16] Reverend Francis J. Grimké's reasoning illustrates this position: "The average woman, in point of character, is superior to the average man and, in so far as she is, she is better fitted to share in the selection of public officials." At the same time, however, Grimké avers that women and men have equal interests in "the administration of laws" and to deprive women of the right to vote is to govern women without their consent, "which is contrary to the fundamental principle of democracy."[17]

Grimké, like many other participants, employs contradictory ideas about women's sameness and difference, thereby appealing to adherents of both convictions. What makes these arguments radical is the link between gender justice and racial justice. "Disfranchisement because of sex is curiously like disfranchisement because of color," District of Columbia Board of Education member Mrs. Coralie Franklin Cook declares. "It cripples the individual, it handicaps progress, it sets a limitation upon mental and spiritual development."[18]

The two issues also manifest different imperatives in their visual approaches: *The Masses* is illustrated with signed drawings that skewer illogic, discrimination, and bias or visually depict a political point about women's rightful place as equal world-building partners. For example, K. R. Chamberlain's drawing of a globe is captioned "Woman's Sphere," which succinctly summarizes the whole issue's ultimate point: "woman's sphere" is the whole world, not gender-segregated domains such as the kitchen and nursery. Other illustrations depict juxtapositions that highlight absurd hypocrisy, such as one drawing that excoriates white bourgeois women's complicity in capitalist exploitation: a standing woman dressed in fashionable clothes says to a kneeling woman with rolled-up sleeves and a scrub brush in her hand, "We've got other things to do, haven't we, Mary, besides interfere in politics!" Relying on laboring women permits such callous women to be oblivious "doll-babies" who believe they have nothing to do with politics.[19] Even though both women are seemingly connected by their close proximity in the female sphere of domesticity—an enclosed kitchen, complete with hanging laundry—they are clearly disconnected by class and privilege: the domestic laborer is a typical caricature of an Irish immigrant.

Employing stereotypes to denounce anti–woman suffrage opposition was a practice *The Crisis* chose to avoid. Instead, Du Bois used photographs to communicate positive, uplifting messages about the black community's pro–woman suffrage views. Except for a few drawings and photographs that accompany advertisements, and one photograph of a memorial tablet that honors freedom fighter Harriet Tubman, the visual content of the "Votes for Women" issue consists of unattributed photographs of people. These pictures, which are interspersed throughout each of the magazine's sections, are mostly conventionally posed individual portraits of dignified black men and women whose hairstyles, suits, dresses, and jewelry convey their refinement and gentility.

Other photographs highlight scenes of celebratory achievement, such as a picture of the "Banquet of the Federation of Colored Women's Clubs, Kansas City, Mo.," or the group of eight women captioned, "Votes for Women: A Symposium by Leading Thinkers of Colored America." The women in this photograph, seven of whom wear large roses pinned to their jackets, are a modern, cross-generational force for women's suffrage, part of the educated new woman vanguard who are also "leading thinkers of colored America."

Men and women who work and do, who excel and contribute, are visually present in *The Crisis*. Photographs humanize the speakers or those spoken about; they counteract stereotypes in print, song, film, and image of black men's debased criminality and black women's sexual impurity. They "furnish evidence" that a gender-integrated, united community advocates "Votes for Women" because, as Du Bois proclaims, "Half the governed, even in culture lands, have no voice in government. This is wrong. . . . Remember that one step toward the abolition of unjust Race discrimination is the abolition of unfair discrimination because of Sex."[20]

The front covers of these special issues also tellingly communicate each community's differently radical imperatives while advocating women's suffrage. As was typical of magazines during this period, the editors of *The Crisis* and *The Masses* used outside covers as visual introductions that are then followed by pages that advertise consumables, institutions, and services as well as other features, such as a table of contents or a preface-serving text, before the interior second cover appears. Both front covers of *The Crisis*'s "Votes for Women" and *The Masses*'s "Woman's Citizenship Number" strategically juxtapose images and words to convey historically resonant meanings about women's rights and freedoms.

The cover of *The Crisis*, for example, is dominated by a "composite photograph" of Abraham Lincoln and Sojourner Truth. Lincoln stands imposing and massive, touching a Bible given him by the "colored people of Baltimore."[21] An equally dignified Truth sits close to Lincoln, an upward-facing palm extended over the book, as if in sacred offering. This cover situates women's suffrage within historical African American struggles to achieve citizenship, literacy, and education; it also places an abolitionist and women's

FIGURE 6.3. Cover of *The Crisis*, August 1915.

rights black female crusader on par with a white, male president.[22] In this context, the suffrage campaign slogan, "Votes for Women," which appears under the photograph, means that black women have always been, and continue to be, engaged in social justice agitation; that black women are equally deserving of the rights and privileges the women's movement was seeking; and that securing the vote for black women is equivalent to actualizing democratic ideals for all citizens.

FIGURE 6.4. Cover of *The Masses*, November 1915. Illustration by Stuart Davis. Copyright © 2019 Estate of Stuart Davis / Licensed by VAGA at Artists Rights Society (ARS), NY.

In contrast, *The Masses* cover is cluttered with words and is less pronounced. The magazine's title is prominently displayed at the top of a framed illustration of a woman by artist Stuart Davis, the words "Woman's Citizenship Number," and the titles of four articles, accompanied by the names of three male authors, are also listed. Holding the "torch" of access, the woman's pose is reminiscent of the torch-bearing figure of the Statue of Liberty; her coat and fedora hat code her as a new woman representing the promise of democracy. The back of another woman walking briskly past emphasizes that this activist woman is in public. *The Masses* cover equates suffrage activism with modern progress and changing gender roles.

The differences between the two covers provide insight into how their designers made meaning of women's suffrage debates and also suggest how their audiences were persuaded to follow suit. The cover of *The Crisis* evokes the past and stresses the ways in which a history of murderous racism, segregation, and white supremacy shape the present; thus, suffrage is situated historically in a larger social justice struggle for African American women and men. Using the freighted symbol of Abraham Lincoln, who is twice invoked in *The Masses*'s "Woman's Citizenship Number" as a crusader of freedom, is also a response to a segregated "bohemia" in which "scant hospitality" was extended to "anyone black who sought admission."[23] The cover of *The Masses*, in contrast, invokes the present and gestures to the future, idealizing the idea that politically active, white women citizens will safeguard universal freedoms and democratic principles.

The Crisis and *The Masses* both feature women on the covers of their suffrage issues, conveying through visual representation how each periodical sees the women for whom they are advocating: in *The Crisis* the women are black and in *The Masses* the women are white. Whether any connection between black and white women is possible is contemplated only in the issues' short stories. Both authored by white women, the stories echo a dialogue that looks to the past, comments on the present, and attempts to imagine a future. It is a dialogue in which the themes of betrayal, protection, and democratic ideals, which are also major tropes in a variety of women's suffrage discourses, are reiterated and contemplated, explored and expounded upon, raising the question of whether there can be coalition and shared purpose between women and for women in justice-seeking communities.

The stories articulate the most radical feminist argument for suffrage that appears in either issue: women and black men need voting rights as a weapon against white men whose heinous behavior is empowered by an exploitive capitalist system. Their inclusion makes clear that both periodicals believe argumentation through logic, satire, and visual illustration is not enough; eliciting emotion through imaginative literature that could lead to direct action is equally important. Although the stories do not overtly relate voting rights to the characters' situations, they engage the issue by focusing on the suffrage tropes of betrayal and protection and their political message is unambiguous: women's and black men's oppression are violations of democratic ideals.

Mary White Ovington's story in *The Masses*, "The White Brute," presents a sparsely populated, segregated southern landscape inhabited by Sam and Melinda, a newly married black couple en route to their new home in Mississippi, and white men who range from indifferent, well-meaning but ineffectual, to terrorizing brutes. Sam and Melinda represent a new black family who embody the promise of a reconstructed South: Melinda is a cultured, educated, light-skinned woman and Sam is a hard-working, dark-skinned laborer. Ovington emphasizes this new union by referencing Melinda's status and having Sam speak in dialect. Melinda chose Sam, in his own words, "a black han' from de cotton fields," over the preacher who was "learned in books" because Sam is "big and strong" and makes her "feel safe."[24]

But the promise of security is violently snatched away from the couple before they reach their new home. Waiting for a train, Sam and Melinda are accosted by two white men "with coarse, somewhat bloated faces that betokened . . . too much drinking of crude whiskey" (17). They taunt Sam by saying his wife is too white for him. Knowing that a lynching had occurred in this town and that one of the men "carried a gun," Sam has few options. If he resists, the white "brutes" will kill him; if he does not, they will violate his wife. No one else intervenes because the assailants "own the town," wielding terror through murder, intimidation, and the law (18). The white men kidnap Melinda, rape her, and then return her to the train platform. Ovington does not describe the rape, only its devastating aftermath, which is figured as a shattered domestic idyll. Once in their new home, the couple is estranged from each other and trapped in despair.

Although both Sam and Melinda are victimized, the weight of the story concerns Sam's "inevitable helplessness" as a husband, provider, and protector.[25] His trauma and consciousness occupy more space, while Melinda's are communicated, if at all, in "whispered gasps" (18) and sobs. Unable to fulfill his manly role, Sam is tormented by shame that he failed to behave honorably. Ovington makes clear, however, that the real moral turpitude is a system of white supremacy that deprives black men and women of human and political rights. Without citizenship in humanity, Sam cannot make Melinda "safe" and Melinda cannot overcome her fear.

"The White Brute" is an aberration in *The Masses*, totally removed from the jaunty and hopeful messages about white new women's emancipation expressed in articles, illustrations, and woman-authored poetry. Moreover, the story's idealization of domesticity is strikingly at odds with the argument propounded in several articles that traditional gender roles are oppressive. Indeed, on the page directly following "The White Brute," Jeannette Eaton denounces women's magazines for glorifying "the work-basket and the egg-beater" and telling women that domestic accomplishments are their highest achievements.[26] Perhaps these contrasting conceptions of domesticity can be understood as representing different ideas of emancipation for different groups of new women. Ovington demonstrates that for black women like Melinda, who continue to suffer under white supremacy, self-chosen love and domesticity are exercises of freedom. Thus the shattered promise of domestic bliss and Sam's inability to perform a conventional manly role are symbolic of utter violation and betrayal. For the white feminist Eaton, in contrast, domesticity represents entrapment.

Another interpretation, however, is that the different meanings of domesticity and gender roles in Eaton's article and Ovington's story reveal a stark divide between black and white women in *The Masses*'s "Woman's Citizenship Number." Since no article, story, poem, or illustration engages the possibility of conversation or connection between black and white women, the implication is that their worlds are totally separate. In this context, Ovington's story is radical in its insistence that black women's oppression must be part of *The Masses*'s "revolutionary" perspective.

Kelsey Percival Kitchel's story in *The Crisis*, "The Rains: A Story of Jamaica," is populated by British white characters and the black laborers who serve them.[27] Like Ovington's "The White Brute," Kitchel's story includes a newly married couple and thematizes shattered domesticity and betrayal. Unlike Ovington's story, however, Kitchel's brings white and black women together in the same imaginative universe and thus sets up a potential staging ground for communication. "The Rains" concerns Teddy Barnaby, who goes to colonial Jamaica to manage an estate. Although betrothed to the "pink-and-white girl" he loves and leaves behind, he is lonely and begins a sexual relationship with Phema, a domestic servant, whom Kitchel portrays as an infatuated young woman who is desirous of the liaison (193). In the end, of course, the white master betrays her. As happens in so many nineteenth-century stories about slavery, Teddy brings home his new white wife, "a woman more than pretty and who is all—his" (195). But because the bride is bored, she does not keep to her prescribed role. Instead, she finds a sense of usefulness serving the "poor." When she learns that Phema is sick, she takes medicines to the hut in which Phema lies dying, holding her baby, whom Teddy, the wife's husband, has fathered.

The encounter between the two women is why this story is politically significant in *The Crisis*'s women's suffrage issue. Upon seeing the white mistress, Phema exclaims, "Why, Missus, hab yo' come? Yo' want my baby? . . . His baby? . . . Ah! You buckra will not even let us black people die in peace! Yo' use us fo' yo' work or fo' yo' pleasure like de mules, until we die—den yo' come to look an' laugh!" (197). The story ends when Phema's "red-brown eyes met the blue ones of Teddy's wife while over each face crept the grey of death—one of the body—one of the soul" (197). Thus, readers witness the deaths of both women and the white wife's realization that she has been victimized by her husband, a different kind of "white brute," but a white brute nevertheless.

Most important, however, is that what the women see when they finally look at each other is left unsaid. And herein lies a radical subterranean dialogue: Will white and black women, who are so often divided by a mutual "world-old race-hate" (196), ever be able to bond together in recognition of their shared gendered oppression at the hands of white men who indiscriminately crush them? "The Rains" makes clear that white women exert power over black women in a racist system of exploitation and peonage. But the story also makes clear that "Teddy's wife," who remains nameless, is victimized, like Phema, by a white male power structure in which all women are treated as sexual commodities and cast-off expenditures.

Many anti-racist advocates of women's suffrage, whether they based their arguments on the doctrine of universal equal rights, the belief that women were morally superior, or the conviction that women would apply their maternal instincts, skills, and experiences to mothering the nation, thought that women would utilize the ballot to "reckon with" such a system. The influential southern educator, clubwoman, and activist Nannie Helen Burroughs put it best: "The ballot, wisely used," she asserted in her *Crisis* symposium contribution, "will bring [the Negro woman] the respect and protection that she needs. It is her weapon of moral defence. . . . She needs the ballot to reckon with men who place no value upon her virtue, and to mould healthy public sentiment in favor of her own protection."[28]

A comparison of the 1915 suffrage issues of *The Crisis* and *The Masses* compels a reassessment of the definition of radicalism in suffrage media rhetoric. Women's claim to political power was undoubtedly radical. However, this label is often applied to white women's suffrage activities, such as picketing and parading, but not to African American women's activities in organizations, clubs, auxiliaries, and institutions. Radicalism was "the willingness to be more boldly public," Susan Goodier and Karen Pastorello assert in their study of women's efforts to achieve suffrage in New York State. But aren't African American women who advocate "Votes for Women" in the pages of *The Crisis* also displaying their "willingness to be more boldly public" when they present their positions in print? And given that many of their pro–woman suffrage arguments, with the one exception of linking race and gender oppression, are the same as white women's, why are they characterized as "not radical in their thinking"?[29]

Who represents radicalism needs reconsideration. It turns out that Mary White Ovington, the author of "The White Brute," is the connecting link between the 1915 suffrage issues of *The Crisis* and *The Masses*. A white new woman, born into privilege and well educated in private schools, Ovington found her life work in African American freedom struggles. An avowed so-cialist, she cofounded the NAACP, along with William English Walling, who is listed in *The Masses* as a contributing literature editor. In 1915, Ovington was working closely with Du Bois on *The Crisis* and she was involved in the daily operations of the NAACP as a fundraiser, lobbyist, branch organizer, and ambassador. According to biographers, Ovington played a mediator role between Du Bois, whom she revered, and the majority white male NAACP board members and funders.[30] In essence, Ovington functioned like a dutiful wife, sister, or daughter, ameliorating conflict and soothing male egos.

Ida B. Wells-Barnett, also a founding member of the NAACP, refused this role. Wells-Barnett was a southern, African American freedom fighter who was an internationally known antilynching activist, investigative jour-nalist, suffragist, and women's rights advocate six years older than Du Bois. In an analysis of why Wells-Barnett has not been given the recognition she deserves, Paula Giddings concludes that she "was marginalized by the civil rights establishment—including those who thought her too militant and yet incorporated her insights into their own strategies without crediting her." Giddings also notes that Du Bois "had few ties with black women activists, save for the wives of his friends" and that he was "closer to many of the white women reformers" like Ovington, whom he may have relied on for "advice on matters concerning women, black and white."[31]

This observation suggests that Wells-Barnett may have been unwelcome in the NAACP not only because of her radical politics, but also because she refused to conform to feminine conventions that required women to play a subservient role. Perhaps Wells-Barnett's story and those of many other African American women who experienced racism in white women's suffrage organizations and sexism in male-dominated racial justice organizations provide a clue about why there are no African American women's writings or drawings in *The Masses* and why it is white women who address black women's oppression in the imaginative literature of both *The Crisis* and *The Masses*. The "Negro woman of the North," Wells-Barnett wrote in 1910, "is given to understand . . . that she is not wanted. The social as well as the in-dustrial edict is: 'Only as a menial—and always that—will you be tolerated.'"[32]

Examining suffrage media rhetoric requires considerations of race in gen-dered radicalism and gender in race radicalism. White women suffragists who were jailed because of their protests in front of the White House, and who subjected themselves to incarceration and forced feeding, were cer-tainly engaging in radical forms of protest. But when some of these women later wrote about how they suffered increased humiliation because they were housed with black women and forced to wear their prison uniforms, are they still so radical? When an African American woman like Nannie Burroughs proclaims in a pro–woman suffrage statement, "The Negro woman is the white woman's as well as the white race's most needed ally in preserving an unmixed race," is this not a radical, black nationalist position?[33] Ultimately, the term "radical" is as contingent as the term "feminist."

Many thanks to Bonnie S. Anderson, Nina Bannett, Nancy Berke, John Drobnicki, Kathy Roberts Forde, Walter Goodman, Carolyn Kitch, Patricia Milanes, Carol Quirke, Michael Rieser, Linda Steiner, and Phyllis E. van Slyck.

Notes

1. David Levering Lewis, *W. E. B. Du Bois: Biography of a Race, 1868–1919* (New York: Henry Holt, 1993), 409. *Masses* 7, no. 1 (November 1915): n.p. *The Crisis* began in 1910 and continues publication to this day. See https://www.thecrisismagazine .com/. *The Masses* began in 1911, ceased publication in 1917, and was subsequently reincarnated as *The Liberator* (1918–24) and then *The New Masses* (1926–48).

2. "Statement of the circulation of *The Crisis*, December 1915." W. E. B. Du Bois Papers (MS 312), Special Collections and University Archives, University of Massachusetts Amherst Libraries, http://credo.library.umass.edu/view/full/mums312-b162 -i421. Elliott M. Rudwick, "W. E. B. Du Bois in the Role of *Crisis* Editor," *Journal of Negro History* 43, no. 3 (July 1958): 214–40. Rudwick notes, "In 1913, there were 30,000 paying readers, and about three-fourths of the copies during this period were sold to Negroes" (214). In *Rebels in Bohemia: The Radicals of The Masses, 1911–1917* (Chapel Hill: University of North Carolina Press, 1982), Leslie Fishbein says that "monthly circulation averaged 14,000, and its readership extended well beyond the bounds of doctrinaire socialists" (18). But no office records or subscription lists exist for *The Masses*. In *Gender and Activism in a Little Magazine: The Modern Figures of The Masses* (Burlington, VT: Ashgate, 2011), Rachel Schreiber says circulation was "40,000 at its peak," and the magazine always relied on outside funding to stay viable (10).

3. Rosalyn Terborg-Penn, *African American Women in the Struggle for the Vote, 1850–1920* (Bloomington: Indiana University Press, 1998), 107–35; Paula Giddings, *When and Where I Enter: The Impact of Black Women on Race and Sex in America* (New York: Bantam Books, 1984), 123–29; Garth F. Pauley, "W. E. B. Du Bois on Woman Suffrage: A Critical Analysis of His *Crisis* Writings," *Journal of Black Studies* 30, no. 3 (January 2000): 390–93.

4. W. E. B. Du Bois, "The Crisis," *Crisis* 1, no. 1 (November 1910): 10.

5. Susan Goodier and Karen Pastorello, *Women Will Vote: Winning Suffrage in New York State* (Ithaca, NY: Three Hills, 2017), 77.

6. Adella Hunt Logan, "Colored Women as Voters," *Crisis* 4, no. 5 (September 1912): 243.

7. *Crisis* 10, no. 4 (August 1915), http://library.brown.edu/pdfs/128895937640750

.pdf; *Masses* 7, no. 1 (October–November 1915), http://dlib.nyu.edu/themasses/books /masseso55. Unless otherwise noted, all subsequent references refer to these issues. There was no October issue of *The Masses*. *The Crisis's* first issue devoted to women's suffrage appeared in 1912: *Crisis* 4, no. 5: "Woman's Suffrage Number." More were to follow. Garth E. Pauley notes that editor Du Bois wrote more than twenty essays on women's suffrage, delivered a speech at an annual National American Woman Suffrage Association convention, which the association subsequently published, and interacted with "several influential suffragists, including Mary Church Terrell, Ida B. Wells, and Jane Addams" (383). See Schreiber for a comprehensive analysis of suffrage illustrations and cartoons in *The Masses*, 125–57.

8. W. E. B. Du Bois, "Forward Backward," *Crisis* 2, no. 6 (October 1911): 244. For a trenchant analysis of white women's racism in the suffrage movement, see Valethia Watkins, "Votes for Women: Race, Gender, and W. E. B. Du Bois's Advocacy of Woman Suffrage," *Phylon* 53, no. 2 (Winter 2016): 3–19.

9. Jeannette Eaton, "To Suffragists," 19. Carrie Chapman Catt founded the Woman Suffrage Party in 1909 and was president of the National American Woman Suffrage Association (NAWSA) in 1900–1904 and 1915–20.

10. After several name changes, Cheyney University is now considered "the oldest Historically Black College/University (HBCU) in the nation" (http://www.cheyney .edu/about-cheyney-university/).

11. Mary White Ovington, "The White Brute," 17–18. Inez Haynes Gillmore, "Stray Thoughts on Chivalry," 22. Gillmore was a cofounder of the College Equal Suffrage League (CESL), an organization that recruited a new generation of young, educated women into the suffrage movement. On Gillmore's labor activism and the founding of the CESL, see Mary K. Trigg, *Feminism as Life's Work: Four Modern American Women through Two World Wars* (New Brunswick, NJ: Rutgers University Press, 2014), 52–53.

12. W. E. B. Du Bois, "Votes for Women," 177.

13. Floyd Dell, "Adventures in Anti-Land," n.p. [5], 6.

14. Max Eastman, "Confessions of a Suffrage Orator," 7, 8, 7, respectively.

15. Faye E. Dudden, *Fighting Chance: The Struggle Over Woman Suffrage and Black Suffrage in Reconstruction America* (New York: Oxford University Press, 2011), 202n16.

16. Mrs. Carrie W. Clifford, "Votes for Children," 185; and Mrs. Mary B. Talbert, "Women and Colored Women," 184, respectively.

17. Reverend Francis J. Grimké, "The Logic of Woman Suffrage," 178.

18. Mrs. Coralie Franklin Cook, "Votes for Mothers," 185.

19. "Doll-Baby" is a term used by *Masses* writers and illustrators to refer to women who valued, and were valued for, their appearance and frivolity. See, for example, Max Eastman, "Confession of a Suffrage Orator," 8; and Maurice Becker's illustration, "Society Cherishes the Doll-Baby Idea" on the same page.

20. See Susan Sontag, *On Photography* (New York: Farrar, Straus and Giroux, 1973), 5. Du Bois, "Votes for Women," 201.

21. "A. Lincoln showing Sojourner Truth the Bible presented by colored people of Baltimore, Executive Mansion, Washington, D.C., Oct. 29, 1864," Library of Congress

Prints and Photographs Division, Washington, DC, http://www.loc.gov/pictures/item/96522312/.

22. In *Sojourner Truth, A Life, A Symbol* (New York: W. W. Norton, 1996), Nell Irvin Painter explores how Truth mythologized her meetings with US presidents, including Lincoln.

23. On references to Lincoln in *The Masses*, see Nina Bull, "In Answer to a Critic," n.p. [4]; and Gillmore,"Stray Thoughts on Chivalry," 22. Christine Stansell, *American Moderns: Bohemian New York and the Creation of a New Century* (New York: Henry Holt, 2000), 68.

24. Ovington, "The White Brute," 17. Subsequent references are included parenthetically in the text.

25. Mary White Ovington, "Letter to the Editor," *Masses* 8, no. 3 (January 1916): 20: "If I did not make the reader feel [Sam's] inevitable helplessness, I shall never write again."

26. Jeannette Eaton, "The Woman's Magazine," 19.

27. Kelsey Percival Kitchel, "The Rains: A Story of Jamaica," 193–97. References are included parenthetically in the text. Census records identify Kitchel as white. She published poems and short stories in newspapers and modernist magazines such as *The Craftsman* and *Smart Set*.

28. Miss N. H. Burroughs, "Black Women and Reform," 187.

29. Goodier and Pastorello, *Women Will Vote*, 141, 74, respectively.

30. Lewis, *W. E. B. Du Bois: Biography of a Race*, 480, 483; Carolyn Wedin, *Inheritors of the Spirit: Mary White Ovington and the Founding of the NAACP* (New York: John Wiley & Sons, 1998), 137–43, 148.

31. Paula Giddings, "Missing in Action: Ida B. Wells, the NAACP, and the Historical Record," *Meridians* 1, no. 2 (Spring 2001): 1, 8. For Du Bois's contradictory attitudes toward women, see Amy Helen Kirschke, "Du Bois and *The Crisis* Magazine: Imaging Women and Family," *Notes in the History of Art* 24, no. 4 (Summer 2005): 35–45.

32. Ida B. Wells-Barnett, "The Northern Negro Woman's Social and Moral Condition," *Original Rights Magazine* 1, no. 2 (April 1910), 83–87; rpt. in *Ida B. Wells: The Light of Truth: Writings of an Anti-Lynching Crusader*, ed. with an introduction and notes by Mia Bay (New York: Penguin Books, 2014), 432–33.

33. On white suffragists' racism, see Trigg, *Feminism as Life's Work*, 64. Burroughs, "Black Women and Reform," 187.

7

A Countermovement on the Verge of Defeat

Antisuffragist Arguments in 1917 Press Coverage

TERI FINNEMAN

Josephine Dodge was brimming with confidence as 1916 came to a close. The sixty-one-year-old president of the National Association Opposed to Woman Suffrage, with its twenty-five state associations and 350,000 members, had presided over her first national convention in Washington, DC, and won reelection to her post.[1] Antisuffrage associations were churning out speakers and literature across the country to further their mission of preventing the expansion of women's suffrage.[2] From 1912 to 1916, twenty-one state suffrage referenda went up for a vote, with only six passing.[3] A story in the *Washington Times* on December 6, the day before the 1916 antisuffrage convention opened, quoted Dodge predicting: "Suffrage is beaten. They will never get another state."[4] Yet within a year, Dodge was replaced at the helm of her national organization; her countermovement inched closer to defeat.

The year 1917 was a turning point in the battle over suffrage; advocates for the women's vote gained ground. Suffragist Jeannette Rankin from Montana became the first woman to serve in Congress. A critical victory at the polls in New York broke a major political barrier by expanding full suffrage to an East Coast state. Further victories in Oklahoma and South Dakota added to the year's momentum as men became increasingly convinced that they should vote in favor of enfranchising women. Suffragists decried the lack of democracy at home as the United States entered World War I. The radical faction of suffrage activists led by Alice Paul made headlines by picketing outside the White House, getting arrested, engaging in hunger strikes, and sitting in jail.[5] Suffrage leader Carrie Chapman Catt took a more moderate approach by launching her "Winning Plan" to unite suffrage advocates and, after decades of focusing on a state-by-state strategy, put the weight of the movement behind securing a federal amendment.[6] With so much momentum from various directions now behind the prosuffrage movement, 1917 became a critical juncture in women's history.

As antisuffragists tried to maintain the legitimacy of their countermovement in the face of repeated setbacks, they made claims—about their own virtues and their opponents' flaws—that were reported in newspapers across America. This chapter uses textual analysis and framing theory in order to more fully understand the antis' rhetorical strategies, at least as they were reported by mainstream journalists. In doing so, I also address criticism that scholars too often dismiss nonfeminist perspectives by simplifying their arguments or downplaying their importance.[7]

Countermovements

Antifeminism has seldom been examined as a countermovement.[8] Indeed, "social movement scholars often ignore the interdependencies" by examining movements without taking into account the actions of the opposition.[9] John McCarthy and Mayer Zald define social movements as "voluntary collectives that people support in order to effect change in society."[10] Their organizations and advocates aim to generate media attention, raise public awareness of a perceived problem, and influence policy.[11] A countermovement is a "conscious, collective, organized attempt to resist or to reverse social change"[12] or "a movement that reacts, usually along conservative or retrograde lines, against a prior movement."[13] This entails amassing human and financial capital to block the proposed change and preserve the status quo.[14] Three conditions are necessary for the emergence of a countermovement: a social movement that shows success, a segment of society that is threatened by the movement, and political allies who step up to support the opposition.[15] In order to discredit the social movement's platform, countermovements engage in counter-framing, that is, attempts "to rebut, undermine, or neutralize a person's or group's myths, versions of reality, or interpretive framework."[16] Through their opposing claims, countermovement organizations and supporters also compete for media and public attention.[17]

Countermovements generally focus on a narrow issue in reactive opposition.[18] In other words, supporters are united in what they are *against* more than what they are *for*; they tend to rely on the social movement to act first before responding. Therefore, they can become "trapped by the negative rhetoric they must employ to counter the movement's claims."[19] Members of the countermovement may use "established myths of the society" to argue against change in order to convince the public of the need to maintain the familiar status quo.[20] One example of an established societal myth is the long-held notion of women's moral authority in the private sphere and their special role in society.[21] Such ideas are useful in status preservation: "declining groups seek to maintain their eroding status by strengthening or creating identifications with groups prestigious in the past."[22] The suffrage movement is especially ripe for this kind of analysis since resistance came from within a demographic group, with a contingent opposed to the expansion of its own rights.[23]

The Antisuffrage Movement

Before examining coverage of the 1917 women's movement, some historical context is important. Although antisuffrage attitudes were common, antisuffragists did not establish formal organizations until the 1880s and 1890s.[24] Antisuffragists in the East initially put little stock in suffrage as a legitimate issue and were dismissive of the West, where suffrage first saw victory and became increasingly widespread. The West was considered too sparsely populated, too radical, and too unsophisticated, therefore making the "experiment" there irrelevant.[25] Antis began to worry, however, when more and more states, particularly eastern states, started considering partial or full enfranchisement.[26] Women opponents thought their way of life and the security of women's distinct roles were "increasingly threatened by the range of progressive movements at the turn of the century."[27] Therefore, like their prosuffrage counterparts, the antis determined they needed more organized, streamlined resistance.[28]

Before state associations officially formed, advocates launched the first antisuffrage newspaper, *The Remonstrance*, in 1890. Its articles claimed that the majority of women did not want to vote and should not be forced into something they didn't want.[29] A common focus was the private sphere. The important role of women in maintaining the home, overseeing the education of children, and upholding morality gave them power that would vanish if women had the right to vote. In a 1904 issue, *The Remonstrance* explained that antis "believe that it is injurious to women and injurious to the state to have women voting on equal terms with men, engaged with them in the turmoil of politics and sharing with them the responsibilities of government."[30] The home should be a refuge from the stresses of business and politics, a "place safe from the necessary evils of a progressive outside world," and both women and men would suffer from the breakdown of separate spheres.[31]

In addition to using periodicals to get their message out, antis also created state associations to organize their opposition. Formed in 1895, the Massachusetts Association Opposed to the Further Extension of Suffrage to Women and the New York State Association Opposed to Woman Suffrage were among the earliest formal organizations of what would eventually become twenty-five state associations with 350,000 members. The New York organization was considered "the most dynamic and influential group of all the organized anti-suffragists in the country."[32] At the 1896 Republican National Convention in St. Louis, Elizabeth Crannell, chairwoman of the New York association, argued that extending suffrage to women would "increase the evils that already threaten to overcome the principles for which our fathers fought."[33] The same year, she also spoke to the Democratic National Convention in Chicago, warning that "womanhood would suffer more than political morality would gain"[34] if suffrage became mainstream. From her perspective, suffrage, and the presumed consequent upheaval of gender roles, was a threat that would unravel civilization.

Religious and biological claims were also commonly deployed in antisuffrage arguments, including the talking point that women couldn't handle the burden of voting.[35] Antis believed that separate spheres were "divinely ordered" and that suffrage was a "selfish, individualistic demand" for women whose role was to put family first.[36] Racial and class tensions also permeated the battle. Antisuffragism became another defensive strategy for maintaining segregation and touting states' rights. Some antis argued that suffrage would destroy white supremacy by allowing women of color to have an equal vote.[37] Fears that immigrants and the poor would be granted equal political status to middle and upper-class women also fueled antisuffrage sentiments in both the North and the South. These women "fought suffrage as a threat to their own positions of privilege"[38] and the access they had to men in positions of power whom they could try to influence.[39] Many antisuffragists were active in community public service and believed women had certain rights in the public sphere.[40] Nevertheless, they thought that men, in their roles as protectors, would do what was best for women, and they cast themselves as representing a silent majority of women who did not want the vote.[41] The antis weren't the only ones, however, using class and race in their arguments. Suffragists also employed racist and classist tactics to advance their cause. They argued that women's votes would counteract "the undesirable part of the electorate," a reference to immigrants and people of color.[42] On both sides of the debate, strategies intended to appeal to middle- and upper-class white men and women left out or discriminated against black, working-class, and immigrant women.[43]

A mix of other issues also influenced antisuffrage attitudes. Maine's association opposed to women's suffrage issued a flyer expressing concern that suffrage would increase the cost to government, spread socialism, increase taxes, and lessen the influence of rural communities since farmers' wives would have a harder time getting to the polls than city women.[44] States also debated the influence of women on prohibition and whether granting women the vote would sway the issue.[45] Many women favored prohibition, regarding easy access to liquor as "the cause of their family problems"—alcoholism, domestic violence, and the spending of the family's money at the saloon.[46] Accordingly, liquor advocates were concerned about enfranchising women.[47]

In the critical final decade before women were enfranchised at the federal level, antisuffragists sought new approaches. After California approved suffrage in 1911, antis formed the National Association Opposed to Woman Suffrage, the first national antisuffrage organization aimed at preventing the spread to additional states.[48] Despite its centralized operation and many well-to-do members, the national organization struggled financially. Tensions flared between state associations and their new central office as they attempted to find adequate resources and time to fight the increasing number of suffrage proposals.[49] Furthermore, they constantly balanced the fact that they were arguing that women should *not* engage in political activity at the same time they themselves were lobbying.[50] The suffragists' increased emphasis on a federal amendment prompted the antis to establish headquarters in Washington, DC, in 1917 to monitor congressional action.[51] In 1917 when the United States entered World War I, antisuffragists faced a new dilemma: they criticized suffragists for campaigning during wartime but also realized they couldn't afford to end their own lobbying.[52] Dodge proposed a wartime truce between the suffragists and antis but her offer was rejected.[53] The war also resulted in an expansion of the antis' scope, since, as is common in wartime, the war evoked concerns about patriotism and loyalty to the United States. Latching onto this sentiment, antis called into question suffragists' allegiance.[54] The anti movement became a conservative defense of the nation against a "radical global social revolution."[55]

In the early 1900s, more women than men were involved in public antisuffrage lobbying; women had come to realize that their silence could be interpreted as agreeing with the suffragists.[56] Yet scholarship has heavily focused on men antisuffragists, if antisuffragists were even mentioned.[57] This study examines news articles from January 1, 1917, to December 31, 1917, archived in Chronicling America, the Library of Congress online database of digitized local and regional newspapers.[58] Small newspapers from across the country were included, since the vast majority of Americans at the time read smaller, more obscure papers, not elite papers.[59] Accessing countermovement rhetoric through these publications, I examined antisuffragists' and suffragists' self-presentations, considering how they framed their own movement and that of their adversaries, that is, how they selected information and made it salient "in such a way as to promote a particular problem definition, causal interpretation, moral evaluation, and/or treatment recommendation."[60] This research examines which arguments used by antisuffragists and which arguments used by suffragists to discredit their opponents gained prominent attention from the press in 1917. In other words, we can see how each side framed the other (and itself) at a turning point, a debate that played out within nationally dispersed newspapers amplifying their final arguments.

The Influence of World War I

Both women and men antisuffragists appealed to emotion and to preservation of the status quo, especially in references to World War I.[61] The war figured predominantly in news articles quoting antisuffrage leaders, with patriotism and the burden of voting being the two major themes. Notably absent was discussion related to more complex perspectives, including race, class, religion, education, conservatism versus progressivism, and local and regional beliefs. Journalists who wrote the news stories analyzed in this sample rarely presented both sides of the issue within a story, and newspapers published antisuffragists' claims without evidence, verification, or context. Furthermore, local and regional newspapers predominantly used commentary from national antisuffrage officials, as opposed to seeking comment from women at the local and state level. In other words, smaller newspapers chose to adopt the national framing of the antisuffrage movement rather than emphasize perspectives at the community level, thereby further limiting contextual information about the debate.

Newspapers around the country ran stories with antisuffragist rhetoric that emphasized the antis' mission to uphold patriotism, an emotional appeal designed to provide contrast with the suffragists. Shortly after the United States entered World War I, for example, the *Tulsa Daily World* ran a story featuring a prepared statement from the antis that declared "there is more need now than ever for a patriotic, conservative body of women, seeking no office or reward, working as nonpartisans for women's welfare and the common good."[62] The national association explained that it would continue its lobbying despite "deploring the necessity for keeping up political work at this time." In other words, the antis knew they needed to defend their continued political activity during wartime while criticizing suffragists for engaging in the same activity. The antis presented themselves as patriots fighting their own battle against an enemy—thereby aligning themselves with a cause of the nation itself, another tactic that became a common countermovement strategy to undermine a progressive social movement—and the newspaper underscored this point with the headline "Anti-Suffragists Decide to Keep Up Strong Fight." Here, the statement and the headline worked together to frame the antis as being self-sacrificing for the good of patriotism and what was right, with the paper selecting "strong fight" as a justifying phrase with its own war connotations.

Antis emphasized that they did not want to lobby during wartime. So, a Connecticut newspaper article quoted antisuffrage leader Alice Wadsworth calling for suffragists to abandon their "agitation" during the war "so that American womanhood can devote all time and energy in strengthening the efficiency of the nation."[63] This again connected strength and patriotism, emotional concepts in wartime that appeal to a broad audience. Wadsworth's use of the phrase "American womanhood," suggesting a level of morality and purity that must be protected, exemplified these (and later) counter-movement activists' strategy of relating their cause to established societal myths—in this case, the role of women as mothers able to heal an ailing nation as they would a child.[64] In the *Omaha Daily Bee*, the Nebraska Association Opposed to Woman Suffrage similarly praised the "loyal, patriotic women" who contributed to the war effort.[65] The argument was that women needed to be selfless and put their country (and the men serving it) first. Indeed, Josephine Dodge made this explicit in urging a renewal of antisuffragists' dedication to the ideal of "America First"—a rallying cry that ran in a Washington, DC, newspaper in 1917.[66] By playing into themes of war and patriotism, these reports targeted readers' emotions.

This strategy was also used in antis' frequent suggestions that suffrage supporters were aligned with pro-German, socialist, and pacifist factions, thereby linking the movement to established myths about these other stigmatized groups. In a Texas newspaper article, antis said a federal suffrage amendment would be a "menace" to the country with "evil effects," such as encouraging the demands of those groups.[67] Under the headline "Call Suffragists Enemies of Nation," a Washington, DC, journalist quoted antis reminding Congress to uphold the Constitution and protect it from "all foreign and domestic enemies."[68] In another story, Wadsworth attributed suffragists' victory in New York to the votes of pro-Germans, socialists, and pacifists, a claim she repeated at the next antisuffrage convention.[69] "We must arouse every real American man and woman to this menace of this triple alliance: socialism, suffragism, pacifism," Wadsworth was quoted as saying.[70]

Several of the antis' word choices are worth noting, particularly menace, evil, enemies, and real. The use of such harsh martial language is striking: it equates a foreign threat to American women wanting enfranchisement. Wadsworth's decision to emphasize "real" Americans—and the reporter's decision to include it—are interesting choices, again tugging at emotion and intending to make people prove they were patriotic by opposing these factions. Suffragists were no longer just a threat to American womanhood but to America itself, an amplification of the antis' prior negative rhetoric. This came after the election defeat in New York and an overall difficult year for the antis' cause. Furthermore, these stories ran in late 1917, more than six months into US involvement in the war. Desperation on the part of the antis and a turbulent wartime climate combined in the press to play into public fears, with newspapers running claims about pro-German and socialist interference without any evidence.

The antis were also quoted as criticizing the suffragists picketing outside the White House, a novel display that unsurprisingly attracted press attention. An Ohio newspaper article featured Wadsworth criticizing the "disloyal and lawless and mischief making company who because of their audacious spirits have more influence upon the electorate than the conservative woman voter would have."[71] In other words, the antis framed suffragists as using underhanded tactics that patriotic conservative women would never employ. A *Richmond Times-Dispatch* story likewise featured antis claiming that suffragists just wanted publicity and were not engaging in honest efforts to win the ballot.[72] Wadsworth hammered this theme throughout July 1917 by calling out the picketers' "seditious and disloyal actions" and "transparent mental dishonesty that is almost inconceivable in persons of 'normal intelligence,'" according to an Indiana newspaper article.[73] Such counter-framing implied that suffragists were unpatriotic and beyond acceptable norms.

Wadsworth tapped into the same patriotic theme to defend her lobbying. She said she was reluctant to accept the leadership of the national antisuffrage organization but felt it was her duty "in the interest of patriotism and national defense."[74] This particular way of justifying the antis' lobbying set them up for accusations of hypocrisy, however, as they were engaging in the same political debates that the antis claimed were too burdensome and unpatriotic for women. Ironically, the argument that political activity was too burdensome for women was the second most prevalent theme in antis' press coverage.

With women increasingly stepping into the public sphere to help the war effort, antis knew their stance was precarious; and their reported responses were primarily negative arguments to preserve the status quo. According to one Oklahoma newspaper, Dodge and fellow anti Alice Chittenden opposed enfranchising women as a reward for serving the country. They argued that women would take the place of men during war but these extra duties in a time of national crisis were enough; women did not need the extra burden of the vote.[75] Prominent anti Marjorie Dorman argued in a Connecticut newspaper that enfranchising women "would be to double the time, the energy, and to largely increase the money used in elections. This would be a needless economic waste."[76] A North Dakota newspaper quoted Dodge arguing that women were already involved in war relief efforts, local organizations, raising children, and housework, and "the ballot is not a reward but a burden."[77] Antis were still using this talking point months later, as evident in an Idaho newspaper citing their arguments that the suffrage amendment needed to be defeated since the extra burden during wartime would be "a grave menace to the country,"[78] an ominous choice of words.

The antis' efforts to arouse emotion appeared repeatedly in news articles, illustrating scholars' later argument that countermovements are "trapped by the negative rhetoric they must employ to counter the movement's claims."[79] As previously noted, journalists in that period did not consistently present both sides of the issue or provide context, thereby allowing claims about economic waste and a national threat to stand without explanation. Nor did local journalists ask local antis to weigh in on the debate. Newspapers merely used national copy and put little other time or resources into the matter, although this was an issue with local and regional impact.

A few other articles are also noteworthy. The *New York Sun* noted that the antis' platform emphasized the constitutional right of each state to settle the question of suffrage for itself.[80] Yet when New York exercised its right—and voted favorably—the antis claimed the vote was illegitimate and alleged pro-German and socialist influence, thereby contradicting their own argument. Furthermore, despite this concern about states' rights, only one article in the sample obliquely mentioned race. One Pennsylvania anti, who also served on the national antisuffrage executive committee, said she agreed with the *New York Times* that the federal amendment would never pass because southern states would not approve women's suffrage.[81] As will be discussed later, press coverage of the suffragists' point of view also rarely mentioned race.

Journalists rarely used men as sources to advocate for the antisuffrage movement in 1917. When they did, they quoted prominent politicians who used harsh rhetoric. For example, a Washington, DC, newspaper quoted Republican Massachusetts representative Joseph Walsh referring to suffrage picketing as "the nagging of iron-jawed angels," while Republican Wisconsin representative William Stafford called the tactic "outlawry."[82] Byron Newtown, a former assistant secretary of the treasury, called suffragists "restless, abnormal women who seem to have a perverted and diseased ambition to do anything and everything except those things which God and nature designed them to do."[83]

Noted Republican politician Elihu Root also criticized the suffragists for taking attention away from war efforts and a "cruel, brutal and arrogant enemy which does not hesitate to murder women and children."[84] Although Root's harsh rhetoric was aimed at war enemies in Europe, the purposeful use of such vehement language was intended to illustrate that suffrage was trivial when the nation had real issues. Like the women antis, men antisuffragists drew upon themes of patriotism, American womanhood, and fear in order to undermine the suffrage movement.

The Suffragists Respond

Meanwhile, press quotes from women and men who favored suffrage provided researched arguments that, at times, pointed out contradictions in their opponents' stances. Interestingly, newspapers were more apt to quote prosuffrage women at the regional and local level, not just national leaders. Coverage also was broader, as suffragists were featured in the press using a variety of tactics to dismiss their opponents, although references to the war were also common.

Newspapers' stories featuring suffragists primarily offered their responses to antis with facts rather than emotion. The same Washington newspaper story quoting opponents who called suffragists "enemies of the nation" also quoted suffrage leaders saying that such a claim was "unfair to America's political leaders, including President Wilson" who had recently supported suffrage.[85] Oddly, antisuffragists provided this statement to the press: they mentioned the argument so they could criticize it. Yet, contrary to their goal, it instead appears as one sentence of rationality in a story full of heated, emotional anti rhetoric. It also was an infrequent instance of journalists including both sides in the same story, seemingly because the antis had already done the work of providing the other side themselves.

The press ran other defenses from suffragists that provided facts. During a speech at the suffragists' annual convention, Mary Hay of New York mentioned the antis' pro-German/socialist accusations and then noted that suffrage received far more votes than the Socialist Party candidate for mayor, disproving the claim that only socialists supported suffrage.[86] In the *Richmond Times-Dispatch*, the president of the Equal Suffrage League of Virginia said antis accused suffragists of being "nothing short of criminal at the present time to waste time, money and energy" when "the world is involved in the greatest war known to history." They furthermore argued that a federal suffrage amendment would "overthrow the whole theory of government" and abolish states' rights, Hay said. She then reminded antisuffragists that states needed to ratify changes to the Constitution and that individual states would get their say.[87] This was an interesting strategy: setting up an emotionally charged argument coming from the antis and then providing a calm, reasoned reply to indirectly make antis seem irrational and uninformed. It is also noteworthy that the newspaper ran the entire anecdote rather than just covering the final punch line. This was a rare instance of the press providing context to readers.

Before leaving for the national suffrage convention, Nebraska suffragist Mrs. W. E. Barkley slyly noted that suffragists and antisuffragists were working so well together on the war effort that this experience would prepare them well for their duties as voters.[88] In a story about the progress that suffrage was making in the Nebraska legislature, another Nebraska suffragist used the same tactic. Mrs. E. M. Fairfield said the antis "have rallied to do patriotic service" and their help with the war effort "demonstrated that woman's place is not in the home."[89] These "compliments" undercut antisuffrage messaging by turning around their patriotic and war rhetoric and showing readers the transition to women in the public sphere had already occurred and was going well.

In a few instances, the press revealed racist tactics used by suffragists to ease the concerns of their opponents. The *Richmond Times-Dispatch* quoted the president of the Equal Suffrage League of Virginia addressing antisuffragist arguments that the South risked "negro domination" if women were enfranchised.[90] "No such danger" existed, she said, as state constitutions already restricted the illiterate vote and "to assume that white women would be less interested than white men in maintaining white supremacy is equally wide of the mark." Similarly, a Delaware newspaper quoted suffragist Florence Hilles as saying that Delaware had far more white women than black women, insinuating that worrying about black women's votes was unnecessary.[91] Otherwise the mainstream press rarely mentioned such attitudes on race.[92] What was also evident was how journalists reinforced suffragists' calculated, calm responses to emotional anti arguments, downplaying rhetoric of "danger," "criminal," and "socialist" fears.

The war also figured prominently in quotes from prosuffrage men. Journalists focused on gathering commentary from prominent men rather than local or regional men. At a public meeting during the New York suffrage convention, Cornell University's president pointed out that European countries already allowed women to vote and asked, "Are we to lag behind while they march forward under the banners of progressive civilization?"[93] He argued that the war "accomplished more for the cause of woman suffrage than centuries of argument and has refuted nearly all the anti-suffrage reasonings," given how women stepped up to support the war. Similarly, Democratic Ohio governor James Cox said it was "unthinkable" that women who sent their sons off to war weren't allowed to participate in government.[94] Former Democratic presidential candidate William Jennings Bryan said women's suffrage was necessary for worldwide peace and prohibition.[95] By referring to antisuffrage arguments as "far-fetched" and "ridiculous," Democratic California representative John Raker was a rare contentious voice. Raker, chairman of the House committee on woman suffrage, said he saw "nothing but absurdity in the claims of anti-suffrage forces that granting the vote to women will encourage pacifism and, for that reason, is backed by pro-Germans."[96] Yet men allies generally were quoted sticking to fact-based arguments rather than using negative or emotional responses, similar to the responses of women suffragists.

Journalists: Neutral, Pro, and Anti

Journalistic bias either for or against the antisuffragists was not glaringly evident across the analysis of the news articles, but it did occasionally occur. Journalistic bias is defined for the sake of this study by word choices that the *reporters* used that illustrated opinion, as opposed to what sources had to say.

A handful of articles included journalistic slant that clearly favored the antisuffrage movement, particularly those in the *Bridgeport Evening Farmer* in Connecticut. One story noted that membership in the state's antisuffrage association was growing "in an extremely satisfactory manner during the last year."[97] The same article praised the speaking skills of prominent anti Marjorie Dorman, who made "strong points" and was able to "refute certain claims made by the suffragists concerning the 'demand' for the vote." A few weeks later, the newspaper again touted the organization's membership gains and its educational approaches that reached "indifferent" women whose "eyes opened" after hearing their arguments.[98] In Montana, the state that had just elected the first woman to Congress, the *Daily Missoulian* covered a local high school government vote that denied women access to membership. The reporter wrote: "Skirts will never rustle the floor of the House, for the vote was strongly anti-suffrage. . . . What would the House do with girls in its membership to confound the presiding officer with embarrassment and to refute the logic of representatives with feminine inconsistency?"[99] Yet this kind of support for the antisuffragists was rare in journalistic word choices.

Journalists used varying strategies when suggesting suffrage support. Some were factual and, therefore, less obvious, such as when stories reported the lack of antisuffrage speakers at events, thereby implying a lack of local popularity for their views.[100] The *Columbus Commercial* ran a story about a former president of an Iowa antisuffrage association who converted after visiting her children in Wyoming and California, which were among the early states to grant women the right to vote.[101] With the headline "Former Anti Makes Suffrage Speech," one could interpret this article as suggesting that antisuffragists could be changed with more education. Other articles were much more blatant in their dismissal of the antis. The *Evening Star* in Washington, DC, predicted that an antisuffrage organization "will soon go out of existence,[102] while the *Hickory Daily Record* in North Carolina said "equal suffrage is one of the surest things in the world."[103] New York antisuffragists who gave up and instead turned their attention to helping the war effort were called "wise girls" in the *Wheeling Intelligencer*.[104] One journalist called the activists "foolish little antis," adding "though the dodo bird and dinosaurs are gone, the anti has not made up her mind exactly how she will adapt herself to the new condition, should it arise."[105] These instances of bias did not occur often in the sample analyzed, yet the sharper language used by prosuffrage journalists is notable compared to the suffragists themselves.

Conclusion

Antisuffrage leader Alice Wadsworth once said war was temporary, but suffrage would "affect the life and government of our nation until the very end of existence."[106] Perhaps ironically, it was war that gave suffrage the boost it needed. News coverage of the antisuffragists in 1917 offers a historical precedent for what researchers studying social movements would later find: countermovements tend to be trapped in negative rhetoric and are more focused on what they are against than what they are for, while also trying to grasp onto established societal myths to reinforce their claims. Negative, emotional rhetoric that played into public fears defined the antis' countermovement frame in 1917 press coverage, while the press portrayed suffragists as providing reasoned progressive arguments that contradicted and undermined the antis. After all, how could women entering the public sphere to help with wartime shortages be unpatriotic and unable to handle an additional burden? Furthermore, antis were caught in a Catch 22: they were lobbying in the public sphere during wartime, thereby undercutting the very societal myths about women's role that they were trying to promote.

Even in local and regional newspapers, news reports predominantly quoted national figures to speak for the views of antisuffrage women, antisuffrage men, and prosuffrage men. This suggests that newspapers predominantly ran whatever national copy was given to them, rather than trying to localize the issue. Interestingly, there was more of a mix of national and local women used as prosuffrage sources, which arguably enhanced the credibility of their argument, making support seem more widespread and mainstream. The full extent of journalists' choices in antisuffrage news stories is unclear; determining the full scope of content available for publication and how much of it journalists chose to publish is impossible. Still, this coverage demonstrates what the press did select as relevant to include and what readers could have learned about this countermovement through their local newspapers. This analysis illustrates how the press amplified the political framing strategies of two political groups trying to defeat one another in a national battle.

Arguably, the suffrage debate was nearly seventy years old by the late 1910s and the public of the era should have been well versed in it. Yet news reporting at this critical time lacked context and complexity, and coverage of the countermovement emphasized its fear tactics. That coverage left gaps for readers who lacked understanding of the various reasons for and against the movement and what was factual versus what was fear-mongering. As 1917 drew to a close, antisuffrage rhetoric that women could not handle the public sphere and that society would break down if women voted simply did not align with the reality of what people at the time saw for themselves—that women were indeed making valuable contributions during wartime and already voting by the millions in individual states across the country. A message tied to the past was no match for the present, setting up the defeat of this countermovement.

Special thanks to South Dakota State University's scholarly excellence funds for supporting this research.

Notes

1. Anne Myra Benjamin, *Women against Equality: The Anti-Suffrage Movement in the United States from 1895 to 1920*, 2nd ed. (Morrisville, N.C.: Lulu Publishing Services, 2014); Anastasia Sims, "Beyond the Ballot: The Radical Vision of the Antisuffragists," in *Votes for Women! The Woman Suffrage Movement in Tennessee, the South, and the Nation*, ed. M. S. Wheeler (Knoxville: University of Tennessee Press, 1995), 105–28.

2. Elizabeth V. Burt, "The Ideology, Rhetoric, and Organizational Structure of a Countermovement Publication: *The Remonstrance*, 1890–1920," *Journalism & Mass Communication Quarterly* 75, no. 1 (1998): 69–83.

3. Susan E. Marshall, "Ladies against Women: Mobilization Dilemmas of Anti-feminist Movements," *Social Problems* 32, no. 4 (1985): 348–62.

4. "Say Women Did Not Re-elect Wilson," *Washington Times*, December 6, 1916, 12.

5. Katherine Adams and Michael Keene, *Alice Paul and the American Suffrage Campaign* (Urbana: University of Illinois Press, 2008).

6. Jacqueline Van Voris, *Carrie Chapman Catt: A Public Life* (New York: Feminist Press, 1987).

7. Karen Celis and Sarah Childs, "The Substantive Representation of Women: What to Do with Conservative Claims?" *Political Studies* 60, no. 1 (2012): 213–25; Jane Jerome Camhi, *Women against Women: American Anti-Suffragism, 1880–1920* (Brooklyn, NY: Carlson Publishing, 1994); Manuela Thurner, "'Better Citizens without the Ballot': American Antisuffrage Women and Their Rationale during the Progressive Era," *Journal of Women's History* 5, no. 1 (1993): 33–60.

8. Melissa Blais and Francis Dupuis-Déri, "Masculinism and the Antifeminist Countermovement," *Social Movement Studies* 11, no. 1 (2012): 21–39, doi: 10.1080/14742837.2012.640532; Kristy Maddux, "When Patriots Protest: The Anti-Suffrage Discursive Transformation of 1917," *Rhetoric & Public Affairs* 7, no. 3 (2004): 283–310; David S. Meyer and Suzanne Staggenborg, "Movements, Countermovements, and the Structure of Political Opportunity," *American Journal of Sociology* 101, no. 6 (1996): 1628–60; Erin Steuter, "Women against Feminism: An Examination of Feminist Social Movements and Anti-Feminist Countermovements," *Canadian Review of Sociology* 29, no. 3 (1992): 288–306.

9. Lee Ann Banaszak and Heather L. Ondercin, "Explaining the Dynamics between the Women's Movement and the Conservative Movement in the United States," *Social Forces* 95, no. 1 (2016): 404–5, doi: 10.1093/sf/sow051.

10. John McCarthy and Mayer Zald, *The Trend of Social Movements in America: Professionalization and Resource Mobilization* (Morristown, NJ: General Learning Press, 1973), 2.

11. Meyer and Staggenborg, "Movements, Countermovements."

12. Tahi L. Mottl, "The Analysis of Countermovements," *Social Problems* 27, no. 5 (1980): 620.

13. Blais and Dupuis-Déri, "Masculinism," 28.

14. Mottl, "The Analysis of Countermovements."

15. Meyer and Staggenborg, "Movements, Countermovements"; see also Janet Saltzman Chafetz and Anthony Gary Dworkin, "In the Face of Threat: Organized Antifeminism in Comparative Perspective," *Gender and Society* 1, no. 1 (1987): 33–60.

16. Robert D. Benford and David A. Snow, "Framing Processes and Social Movements: An Overview and Assessment," *Annual Review of Sociology* 26, no. 1 (2000): 626; Robert Benford, *Framing Activity, Meaning, and Social-Movement Participation: The Nuclear Disarmament Movement* (Austin: University of Texas Press, 1987).

17. Meyer and Staggenborg, "Movements, Countermovements."

18. Blais and Dupuis-Déri, "Masculinism"; Burt, "Ideology"; Mottl, "The Analysis

of Countermovements"; Ralph H. Turner and Lewis M. Killian, *Collective Behavior* (Englewood Cliffs, NJ: Prentice-Hall, 1972).

19. Elizabeth V. Burt, "Journalism of the Suffrage Movement: 25 Years of Recent Scholarship," *American Journalism* 17, no. 1 (2000): 77.

20. Mottl, "The Analysis of Countermovements," 628; Turner and Killian, *Collective Behavior*; Burt, "Ideology."

21. See Paula Baker, "The Domestication of Politics: Women and American Political Society, 1780–1920," *American Historical Review* 89 (June 1984): 620–47.

22. Clarence Lo, "Countermovements and Conservative Movements in the Contemporary U.S.," *Annual Review of Sociology* 8, no. 1 (1982): 109; Seymour Martin Lipset and Earl Raab, *The Politics of Unreason: Right Wing Extremism in America, 1790–1977*, 2nd ed. (Chicago: University of Chicago Press, 1978).

23. Marshall, "Ladies against Women."

24. Massachusetts Historical Society, "Massachusetts Association Opposed to the Further Extension of Suffrage to Women Records," http://www.masshist.org /collection-guides/view/fa0121; Benjamin, *Women against Equality*; Thurner, "Better Citizens."

25. Billie Barnes Jensen, "In the Weird and Wooly West: Anti-Suffrage Women," *Gender Issues* 32, no. 3 (1993): 41–51.

26. Lee Ann Banaszak, *Why Movements Succeed or Fail: Opportunity, Culture, and the Struggle for Woman Suffrage* (Princeton, NJ: Princeton University Press, 1996); Camhi, *Women against Women*; Jensen, "In the Weird and Wooly West"; Steuter, "Women against Feminism."

27. Steuter, "Women against Feminism," 292.

28. Camhi, *Women against Women*.

29. Library of Congress, "Woman's Suffrage in the Progressive Era," http://www.loc .gov/teachers/classroommaterials/presentationsandactivities/presentations/timeline /progress/suffrage/remonst.html; Burt, "Ideology."

30. "A Duty to Keep Still?" *Remonstrance*, 1904, 2, cited in Burt, "Ideology."

31. Susan Goodier, *No Votes for Women: The New York State Anti-Suffrage Movement* (Champaign: University of Illinois Press, 2013), 5.

32. Goodier, *No Votes for Women*, 9.

33. "Address of Mrs. W. Winslow Crannell," July 8, 1896, Historic Cherry Hill Collections, Albany, NY.

34. "Address of Mrs. W. Winslow Crannell," July 16, 1896, Historic Cherry Hill Collections, Albany, NY.

35. Maddux, "When Patriots Protest."

36. Goodier, *No Votes for Women*, 38.

37. Susan Marshall, *Splintered Sisterhood: Gender and Class in the Campaign against Woman Suffrage* (Madison: University of Wisconsin Press, 1997).

38. Marshall, "Ladies against Women," 5; Camhi, *Women against Women*.

39. Goodier, *No Votes for Women*; Marshall, *Splintered Sisterhood*.

40. Thurner, "Better Citizens."

41. Thurner, "Better Citizens."

42. Goodier, *No Votes for Women*, 41.

43. Belinda Southard, *Militant Citizenship: Rhetorical Strategies of the National Woman's Party, 1913–1920* (College Station: Texas A&M University Press, 2011).

44. National American Woman Suffrage Association Records, Anti-suffrage literature, box 39, Manuscript Division, Library of Congress, Washington, DC.

45. Camhi, *Women against Women*.

46. Jo Freeman, *A Room at a Time: How Women Entered Party Politics* (Lanham, MD: Rowman and Littlefield, 2000), 29.

47. Freeman, *A Room at a Time*, 29.

48. Benjamin, *Women against Equality*.

49. Marshall, *Splintered Sisterhood*.

50. Marshall, *Splintered Sisterhood*.

51. Camhi, *Women against Women*.

52. Benjamin, *Women against Equality*.

53. Benjamin, *Women against Equality*.

54. Benjamin, *Women against Equality*; Maddux, "When Patriots Protest."

55. Maddux, "When Patriots Protest," 285.

56. Goodier, *No Votes for Women*.

57. Maddux, "When Patriots Protest"; Marshall, *Splintered Sisterhood*.

58. Four searches were conducted using the terms antis, anti-suffrage, National Association Opposed to Woman Suffrage, and "antis and suffrage" within ten words of each other. Results were sorted by relevance, with a sample of 397 articles from thirty-six states and Washington, DC, analyzed.

59. Frank Luther Mott, *American Journalism: A History, 1690–1960*, 3rd ed. (New York: Macmillan, 1962), 548.

60. Robert Entman, Jörg Matthes, and Lynn Pellicano, "Nature, Sources, and Effects of News Framing," in *The Handbook of Journalism Studies*, ed. Karin Wahl-Jorgensen and Thomas Hanitzsch (New York: Routledge, 2009), 177.

61. Burt, "Journalism of the Suffrage Movement."

62. "Anti-Suffragists Decide to Keep Up Strong Fight," *Tulsa Daily World*, April 27, 1917, 8.

63. "Drop Suffrage Parlay in War," *Bridgeport Evening Farmer*, May 3, 1917, 12.

64. This ties into a broader study about the role of mothers in World War I and how the press aided the Wilson administration in creating the concept of the "Patriotic Mother of the Great War." See Ana C. Garner and Karen Slattery, "Mobilizing Mother: From Good Mother to Patriotic Mother in World War I," *Journalism & Communication Monographs* 14, no. 1 (2012): 5–77.

65. "Suffragists at War Over Referendum," *Omaha Daily Bee*, June 11, 1917, 5.

66. "350,000 Women Offer Services to President," [Washington, DC] *Evening Star*, February 18, 1917, 2. This still resonates with audiences 100 years later.

67. "Says Suffrage Amendment Would Be Menace to U.S.," *El Paso Herald*, November 23, 1917, 5.

68. "Call Suffragists Enemies of Nation," [Washington, DC] *Evening Star*, November 23, 1917, 15.

69. "Anti-Suffragists Open Convention," [Washington, DC] *Evening Star*, December 11, 1917, 20.

70. "Victory of Suffragists in New York," *Bridgeport Evening Farmer*, December 13, 1917, 11.

71. "Heads the Antis," *Democratic Banner*, July 27, 1917, 2.

72. "Antis Step into Arena," *Richmond Times-Dispatch*, July 3, 1917, 1.

73. "Big Slam at Pickets Is Letter," [Hammond, IN] *Lake County Times*, July 30, 1917, 6.

74. "Heads the Antis," *Broad Ax*, July 28, 1917, 3.

75. "Women Want Some Peace in Time of War," [Ardmore, OK] *Daily Ardmoreite*, April 18, 1917, 3.

76. "Liquor Interests and Anti-Suffragists Are Forced into Alliance," *Bridgeport Evening Farmer*, February 28, 1917, 5.

77. "Don't Want Ballot as Price for Patriotism," *Bismarck Tribune*, May 15, 1917, 8.

78. "Suffragists to Demand the Ballot," *Boise Evening Capital News*, December 9, 1917, 15.

79. Burt, "Journalism of the Suffrage Movement," 77.

80. "Antis Say Suffs Won on Pacifism," *New York Sun*, November 23, 1917, 7.

81. "Vote Thrust upon Them, Antis Fear," *Philadelphia Evening Public Ledger*, November 8, 1917, 3.

82. "House Votes to Create Suffrage Committee," [Washington, DC] *Evening Star*, September 25, 1917, 9.

83. "Appointment Pleases Anti-Suffrage Forces," [Washington, DC] *Evening Star*, October 7, 1917, 16.

84. "Root Opposes Suffrage," [Pendleton] *East Oregonian*, September 27, 1917, 8.

85. "Call Suffragists Enemies of Nation," [Washington, DC] *Evening Star*, November 23, 1917, 15.

86. "Women Mean to Have Amendment," *Albuquerque Morning Journal*, December 14, 1917, 2.

87. "Dwells on Human Side of Municipal Survey," *Richmond Times-Dispatch*, November 23, 1917, 5.

88. "Vote Yes on Both Amendments," *Omaha Daily Bee*, December 5, 1917, 10.

89. "Omaha Women Rejoice at Progress," *Omaha Daily Bee*, April 21, 1917, 2.

90. "Dwells on Human Side of Municipal Survey," *Richmond Times-Dispatch*, November 23, 1917, 5.

91. "Suffrage Discussed before the General Assembly," *Newark Post*, February 21, 1917, 6.

92. Because of the nature of the source material analyzed from the Chronicling America database, this study doesn't include coverage in the black press.

93. "War Has Helped Woman Suffrage," *Barre [VT] Daily Times*, August 31, 1917, 3.

94. "Mrs. Catt Raps U.S. Democracy," *South Bend News-Times*, May 14, 1917, 8.

95. "Bryan in Nashville," [Huntington, TN] *Carroll County Democrat*, February 2, 1917, 1.

96. "Antis' Pacifism Argument Ridiculous, Raker Declares," [Washington, DC] *Evening Star*, December 27, 1917, 15.

97. "Antis Not Surprised at Suffragist Action," *Bridgeport Evening Farmer*, January 19, 1917, 7.

98. "Anti-Suffrage Organization Adds to Its Membership," *Bridgeport Evening Farmer*, February 2, 1917, 13.

99. "'House' Denies Entry to Women in Membership," *Daily Missoulian*, October 17, 1917, 4.

100. "Suffrage Loses at Farmers' Meeting," [Brattleboro] *Vermont Phoenix*, January 5, 1917, 9; "Suffrage Bill Passed by Big Majority," *Washburn [ND] Leader*, January 19, 1917, 5.

101. "Former Anti Makes Suffrage Speech," *Columbus Commercial*, March 15, 1917, 3.

102. "School for Woman Voters," [Washington, DC] *Evening Star*, November 17, 1917, 2.

103. "Boosting the Cause," *Hickory [NC] Daily Record*, October 26, 1917, 2.

104. No headline, *Wheeling Intelligencer*, November 21, 1917, 4.

105. "Vote Thrust upon Them, Antis Fear," *Philadelphia Evening Public Ledger*, November 8, 1917, 3.

106. "Woman Suffrage," *Chariton [MO] Courier*, August 17, 1917, 4.

8

Discourses of Race and Masculinity in the Nashville Press

"A White Man's Country and a White Man's Government"?

JANE MARCELLUS

As the debate over whether or not Tennessee would become the final state to ratify the Nineteenth Amendment heated up in Nashville during the summer of 1920, competing newspapers in the state capital took opposing views. The more liberal *Nashville Tennessean,* published by former US Senator Luke Lea, supported ratification, while former railroad executive Edward Bushrod Stahlman's *Nashville Banner* remained opposed. As I argued in a previous study, the *Tennessean's* stance that summer was roughly aligned with progressive "New South" views, while the *Banner's* was decidedly "Old South."[1]

Explicit in the *Banner's* coverage were notions about white masculinity. "Can Anybody Terrorize Tennessee Manhood?" asked a broadside, originally produced by suffrage antis but reprinted in the newspaper.[2] Although *Banner* coverage of the 1920 special legislative session was generally factual, particularly during an era when "objectivity" was not yet an established norm,[3] it adopted a vehement anti position when the amendment passed. "Go to Mass-Meeting, Ryman Auditorium, Tonight. Will Make Protest Against Ratification," a multideck headline urged *Banner* readers.[4] According to the *Banner,* as the band played "Dixie," House Speaker Seth Walker praised House members who voted against suffrage, proclaiming: "Forty-seven names have been signed in the blood of the South to keep this a white man's country and a white man's government." Leading the antisuffrage rally himself, *Banner* publisher Stahlman declared there was "real manhood in Tennessee."[5]

The *Tennessean*, meanwhile, focused much of its coverage that summer on the upcoming presidential election, which pitted Democrat James M. Cox against Republican Warren G. Harding. Anticipating ratification, the paper's repeated focus on Cox primed women to vote for the Democratic candidate in November. One story distinguished among "three kinds of men"—those that men like and women dislike, those that women like and men don't, and those liked by both sexes. Cox was the rare third kind, wrote New York "woman correspondent" Zoë Beckley, adding, "I believe women will vote for him."[6] However speculative, Beckley's emphasis on "kinds of men" suggests that masculinity was a contested, rather than an inherent, trait.

Beyond the papers' respective positions on the amendment itself, a close reading of suffrage coverage suggests that what was at stake for both newspapers was, at least in part, competing views of southern white masculinity. Most blatant in the *Banner*, with its rhetoric about the "blood of the South" echoing Civil War sentiments, it appeared more subtly in the *Tennessean*, whose publisher, Lea, was an ardent suffrage supporter. To explore that, I build on my 2010 study, using discourse theory to interrogate how masculinity was constructed in Nashville newspapers in the years leading up to 1920. I ask, specifically, how and when competing discourses emerged and how those views intersected with race at the height of the Jim Crow era.[7]

Tennessee remains important not only because it provided the thirty-sixth of forty-eight states needed for ratification but also because it has been a rich site of contested views on social progress in the South, including racial equality. In 1820, Elihu Embree, slaveholder turned abolitionist, started one of the first newspapers in the United States devoted solely to manumission.[8] During the Civil War, many residents of East Tennessee sided with the Union and sought to create a separate state, similar to West Virginia's secession from Virginia.[9] Since the height of the Jim Crow era coincided with the culmination of women's seventy-year effort to gain the vote nationally, and since racial equality and women's suffrage both presented distinct but not unrelated challenges to white male hegemony, focusing on white masculinity in southern newspapers provides an understudied context for the suffrage struggle.

Discourse Theory, Masculinity, and Southern "Suffragents"

Discourse concerns "the production of knowledge through language," said Stuart Hall, referencing Michel Foucault. More than a linguistic concept, discourse "defines and produces the objects of our knowledge," constructing topics and governing the way they can be talked about.[10] Foucault contended

that discontinuities in discourse, rather than cause-and-effect relations between events, should be at the heart of historical analysis.[11] Traditional history
"enables us to isolate the new against a background of permanence," yet the
resulting discourse is "no more than the repressive presence of what it does
not say"—a "not-said" with its own power.[12]

Sean Nixon argued that gender identities, including masculinity, are not
"unitary and fixed" but "subject to social and historical variation." He stressed
the importance of understanding "the specific discursive codes and conventions through which masculinity is signified."[13] While work on women's suffrage has long problematized male dominance, the idea of competing versions
of masculinity has been a "not-said," implicit yet rarely acknowledged. This
is particularly true of hegemonic and recuperative masculinity, relatively
recent terms that are nonetheless critical in looking at the historical "dis-
continuity" presented by women's suffrage. Noting that the term "hegemonic
masculinity" emerged in the 1980s via feminist studies of patriarchy, R. W.
Connell and James Messerschmidt define it as "the pattern of practice . . .
that allowed men's dominance over women to continue." Not necessarily
"normal" but "certainly normative," hegemonic masculinity embodies "the
currently most honored way of being a man," requiring "all other men to
position themselves in relation to it." Rarely violent, though supported by
force if necessary, hegemonic masculinity is characterized by "ascendency
achieved through culture, institutions, and persuasion."[14]

The post–World War I years were critical for contested gender roles not
only because of the suffrage movement, but also because more women sought
education, careers, and financial independence in that era. But even as masculinity reasserted itself in articles and advertisements mocking suffrage and
women's equality, some men took leadership roles in promoting the vote.
As Brooke Kroeger shows, the "suffragent" movement began in the North,
but southern male support emerged, too.[15] In 1888, *Memphis Daily Appeal*
editor J. M. Keating wrote: "The right of women to suffrage is no longer a
subject of mockery, jibe, or jest. Intelligent people realize the injustice of
withholding the ballot from women."[16] One Tennessee "honor roll" listed
117 prosuffrage "gallant heroes." Notably, the listed included Lea, a member
of both the Tennessee Men's Ratification Committee and the Men's League
for Woman Suffrage.[17]

Nashville Suffrage Coverage Begins

The first suffrage article published in the *Nashville American*, the newspaper that became the *Tennessean*, ran in 1895, when Mrs. John Ruhm edited

a lengthy piece headlined "Equal Rights Department." A compendium of prosuffrage arguments by several authors, it refuted the claim that women's exclusion from military service should exclude them from voting, since risking death in childbirth was a feminine type of patriotism. Although Ruhm, wife of a Union Army officer,[18] presented an arguably "northern" perspective, she included "A Southern Woman's View" by Mrs. Virginia D. Young: "Whatever is for the good of woman is equally for the happiness of man. The sexes are hemispheres whose equality makes the perfect whole, the oneness of two."[19] Overall, the article underscored traditional gender roles but saw them as complementary, different but supposedly equal—arguably consistent (if wrongheaded) with the Jim Crow stance on race.

Lea, aged twenty-eight, started the *Tennessean* in 1907, hoping to compete with both the *American* and the *Banner*, which Stahlman had owned since 1893.[20] The *Tennessean* absorbed the *American* in 1910, creating a two-newspaper town.[21] The papers reflected their owners' backgrounds and widely opposing political views. Lea, a wealthy descendent of pro-Union Nashville mayor John Lea,[22] graduated from the prestigious University of the South and Columbia University Law School. A prohibitionist, he was often at odds with Stahlman, a self-made pre–Civil War German immigrant and former railroad executive thirty-six years Lea's senior.

Suffrage coverage in both papers was sporadic after the turn of the century, sometimes running in the "Society" section. The first glimpse of the competing papers' mixed discourses about race, masculinity, and suffrage appeared in stories on the fifth annual convention of the Tennessee Equal Suffrage Association in January 1912 at Nashville's Hermitage Hotel. The *Tennessean's* lengthy page-one write-up referenced the "Notable Assemblage of Tennessee Womanhood," its gallant tone reminiscent of southern courtliness toward white women. Overtly prosuffrage, the story declared that "splendid reports" signaled the meeting would be "one of the most important held in the history of the state's organization," though Governor Ben Hooper told suffragists he was "wobbling" on the cause.[23] In contrast, *Banner* coverage appeared inside, downplaying the issue's importance, a strategy it would repeat until 1920. A dry rundown of committee agendas appeared on page 13 on opening day, with a story on page 3 at convention's end.[24] The second story consisted primarily of quotes from Mrs. John Turney's closing statement referencing the Fifteenth Amendment: "We are American citizens and the Constitution of the United States says, 'The citizens' right to vote shall not be denied or abridged on account of race, color, or previous condition of servitude.'"[25] Though Turney did not mention race overtly, the inference was that if black men could vote, women should, too—the stance of the National

Woman Suffrage Association before it merged with the American Woman Suffrage Association to form NAWSA in 1890.[26]

Despite emerging patterns, inconsistencies appeared, particularly involving race. Later in January 1912, the *Tennessean* ran an exoticized view of suffrage and female power in a full-page feature headlined, "Where the Women Rule the Men," about the Tuaregs, a nomadic people of the Sahara.[27] The lengthy subhead—"How Female Suffrage Works Out among the Tuaregs, Where Men Go Veiled, Everything Belongs to the Wife, a Husband Can't Stay Out at Night, and Every Man Has to Do Just as Some Woman Tells Him"— emphasized the wrongheadedness of female power, as did the illustrations. A drawing of an unveiled woman was captioned, "Note the Uncovered Face and Self-Reliant Expression," while captions beneath small drawings suggested problems with Tuareg social equality: "When He Snares Her, He Has to Give Her All His Goods," followed by "All She Lets Him Have is a Stick and a Box to Put His Clothes In" and "He Has to Mind the Baby and Cook the Food." A copyright notice indicated the story's British origins, though the lead contrasted America and Africa in light-versus-dark terms: "Woman suffrage is only just beginning to make real headway in enlightened America. In darkest Africa, however, it is an old story." Factually accurate in that the Tuareg are a nomadic, matriarchal, and matrilineal people,[28] the story nevertheless spun it as a cautionary tale. In the Jim Crow South, it could be read as a warning against black female power specifically. Certainly, its inclusion suggests that the *Tennessean* waffled when race was part of the story.

The following year, the *Tennessean* took a prosuffrage stance in a promotional piece about the planned Washington suffrage parade preceding Woodrow Wilson's presidential inauguration. The wire story noted that a dinner at New York's Hotel Astor for women suffragists and the Men's League for Woman Suffrage would be "a mutual affair, which is significant of what suffrage really means—cooperation."[29] This was a first prominent mention of male suffragists. When the parade occurred, both papers seemed neutral, running stories at the top of page one. The evening of the parade, the *Banner* ran an Associated Press story headlined "Kaleidoscopic Picture of Ever Shifting Color" with a deckhead noting the "Great Army of Suffragists" marching to "Cheers of Thousands" and another deck emphasizing women's "Unanimity" in demanding the ballot. No doubt filed before the events of the day unfolded, the story began with unusual (for the *Banner*) prosuffrage optimism: "This was woman's day of political crowning glory, short of actually possessing the universal right to vote." Noting that "men and women alike joined in the demonstration," the story described the costumes, line of march, and "business-like" planning.[30] The next morning, the *Tennessean*'s banner headline announced the "First Democratic Inaugural in Twenty Years," with equal headlines over its two main stories, Wilson's inauguration on the left and the suffrage parade on the right. "Suffrage Pageant a Near Riot," read the headline atop an AP story emphasizing the "taunts and jeers" hurled at marchers, who responded by "marching stoutly along." Inez Milholland "distinguished herself" by "riding down a mob" while an unnamed woman "struck a hoodlum a stinging blow across the face" when he insulted her. "The mounted police rode hither and yon, but seemed powerless to stem the tide of humanity."[31]

In their parade coverage, both papers' prominently placed wire stories, with headlines reflecting the copy, suggested neutrality, but other articles published around that time were more discursively complicated in two stories regarding male support. In February 1913, Lea's paper emphasized men's role in "Will Men Help Woman Suffrage in Tennessee?" Covering a local speech by a Kentucky suffragist, the story stressed the speaker's argument that Tennessee men should "take a place in the front rank" of enfranchising the state's women.[32] Yet in May, a front-page *Tennessean* story, datelined Washington, reported on the upcoming Senate race in Alabama. Headlined "Danger to Laws of South" with five decks including "Means Big Negro Vote" and "Would Overturn Laws of Alabama and Every Other State," it focused on the contest between incumbent Joseph F. Johnston and suffrage supporter Richmond Pearson Hobson, stressing "the sagacious old senator" and his intent to make suffrage a central issue, since most Alabamians opposed voting "for the fair sex."[33] Even in the prosuffrage *Tennessean*, the discursive approach was again complicated when it came to race, with Jim Crow attitudes about "danger" of the "Negro vote" (which effectively meant black women) affirmed in story placement and headlines.

After the parade, the *Banner* rarely covered suffrage prominently, though briefs occasionally appeared in the weekly "What Women Are Doing Worth Hearing About." Covering an entire page in the news section on Saturday evenings, this "women's page" consisted of short items ranging from club news to dances to domestic news. It usually occupied page three or four, opposite a regular feature titled "Tennessee Confederate Regiments," consisting of updates on aging soldiers half a century after the Civil War. The juxtaposition of these two regular items illustrates the world created for *Banner* readers—one in which women's news is brief and segregated and the "lost cause" of the South is still relevant. The world created by the *Tennessean* favored suffrage but remained cautious when race was involved.

Suffrage Coverage Expands

World War I began in Europe in 1914, dominating the front pages of both papers until the Armistice was signed in 1918. But 1914 also brought more suffrage coverage, with the *Tennessean* becoming consistently more prosuffrage and the *Banner* somewhat more anti.

For example, the *Tennessean* began to run columns penned by suffragists. In March, Turney wrote "Suffragists Will Show Their Strength," a lengthy piece about Alice Paul's plan for a "national demonstration" in Washington that May. "There have been pageants, and there have been processions, and there have been demonstrations . . . the object being to visualize to the reluctant and the imaginative public the greatly increasing strength of the suffrage movement. None of these demonstrations approach in size or importance the mighty demonstration the Congressional Union announces for May 2 and 9, 1914," she wrote.[34] Published at a time when ads were not always clearly marked and the lines between news and the emerging field of public relations sometimes blurred, the piece demonstrates how the *Tennessean* allowed suffragists to disseminate their views directly, as the *Banner* would do by 1920 for the antis. When May 2 came, the *Tennessean* ran a front-page story about suffrage "Rally Day" to coincide with the Washington event, headlined, "Nashville Is Dressed in Best Bib and Tucker in Honor of Occasion." Yellow suffrage colors were to be "seen everywhere" and the mayor proclaimed a half-holiday for the event, which began downtown and ended at Centennial Park two miles away.[35] Although this particular story did not focus on either masculinity or race, the fact that suffragists negotiated their own space in the male-owned *Tennessean* illustrates one way that Tennessee women, to use Kroeger's title phrase, "used men to get the vote."

If news stories about suffrage ran on the *Banner*'s news pages, it was often negative, as several July papers illustrate. "Women Suffer Another Reverse," announced a July 1 headline, though the brief was simply about the US House Rules Committee postponing a vote on the amendment and what was meant by "another" is not clear. That same month, a story from London about Emmeline Pankhurst's arrest appeared prominently on page one, and "Dr. Shaw Regrets Women's Action" emphasized the split between suffragists over picketing the White House. A particularly disturbing story, "Woman's Figure Swings by Neck," ran in a visually prominent position inside. This AP story, datelined Washington, told of "the figure of a woman with a rope around her neck" swinging from the House wing of the US Capitol. Although the figure was a plaster model for a marble statue representing (ironically) peace, sightseers asked a sculptor working nearby about it. "A suffragette barred out of the Capitol," he quipped—his joke being the point of the story.[36] Although the story originated with the AP in Washington, the *Banner*'s decision to run a joke about lynching suffragists clearly suggests racial overtones—a subtle warning that suffragists deserved the same demeaning violence often reported in stories about the lynching of "Negroes."

Special Suffrage Section

In August, the *Tennessean* published a thirty-two-page special suffrage magazine insert. Compiled by society editor Madge Hall, it included "no less than 20 suffragists from all parts of the country" who were "among the great army of women" trying to advance suffrage, said an advance. Referencing men, the advance claimed that where women voted, conditions improved and "the prejudice which has long stood in the way of women voting has gradually disappeared until it is now hard to find a thoughtful and observant man" opposed. Masculinity, as constructed here, was seemingly genteel— "thoughtful and observant" manhood as embodied, arguably, by Lea, the opposite of the rancorous Stahlman.[37]

Only the cover for the thirty-two-page special section has survived in archives,[38] but its image is revelatory. Patterned after a Pears Soap ad from around 1890 in which an older woman scrubbed a little boy,[39] the suffrage cover showed a middle-aged woman roughly scouring the head of a man upon whom the word "Politics" was emblazoned. Though bald and mustachioed, the man was child-size, so the woman towered over him, immobilizing him with her hand on his head, like the child in the original. The caption on both was "You Dirty Boy!" but rather than "Pears Soap," the steaming pot beside the knockoff was labeled "Woman Suffrage." Clearly equating the vote with women's sacred maternal role, the drawing suggested that suffrage would expand women's power to clean up dirty (male) politics the way a mother scrubs an errant son into submission.

The suffrage version of this image was not original to the *Tennessean*, instead originating in Britain.[40] What is intriguing, though, is not only the way the drawing incorporated ideas about race and the British Empire that began to appear in Pears ads once the Boer War broke out in 1899, but also the way the repurposed image (like the Tuareg story) found still new meaning in the Jim Crow South. The Boer War–era Pears ads depicted the soap as literally scrubbing black skin white. As Anne McClintock noted, one 1899 *McClure's Magazine* ad announced that "the virtues of cleanliness" made the soap "a potent factor in brightening the dark corners" for the "cultured of all nations."[41] Hall pointed out the class implications, since Pears apparently had the power "of washing off the soot, grime and dirt of the industrial slums and their inhabitants—the unwashed poor."[42] In the suffrage version, the man and woman were both white, as in the pre–Boer War ad on which it was modeled, but here the child had become the adult male embodiment of "Politics," his arms blackened, one by "Graft" and the other "Crooked Methods," effectively equating dirty politics with blackened (if not naturally black) skin. Empowered by the vote, the white woman here will scrub this blackness from the white man's skin, purifying "Politics" and theoretically transforming this "dirty boy" into a "not-said"—a "cultured" man whose politics (and skin) are clean and white.

NAWSA Comes to Nashville

NAWSA held its national convention in Nashville November 12–17, 1914, on the heels of the Southern States Suffrage Conference in Chattanooga. The *Tennessean* covered the Chattanooga conference on page one, amplifying Mrs. O.H.P. Belmont's prediction of victory.[43] Both papers welcomed NAWSA to Nashville, the *Banner* with two stories on November 7, one in "What Women Are Doing Worth Hearing About" announcing "women of notable achievements" who would "give great impetus to the cause of equal suffrage in this section." A second story again noted the prominent women, including Shaw, Jane Addams, and Carrie Chapman Catt. A front-page story, "Suffragists Throng City," on November 11 also welcomed the women.[44] On November 12, the *Tennessean* ran an opinion piece by Alice Stone Blackwell, "Why Women Should Vote" followed by "Our Guests, The Suffragists" on November 15. The second story said Nashville was "proud of its guests" who were "women of intelligence and attainments" representing "a great and vital principle of equal rights . . . between man and woman."[45] It seemed as if Stahlman and Lea were vying to outdo each other in their welcome—a marked contrast with the reception NAWSA received in Louisville in 1911, when *Louisville Courier Journal* editor Henry Watterson vilified them as "a dangerous influence for evil."[46]

Both papers covered the convention on the front page. *Banner* coverage emphasized NAWSA's declaration of nonpartisanship, noting, "This meeting in Nashville promises to be, perhaps, the most notable in the history of the movement that has made rapid strides toward the goal set in the nearly a half century since its existence." Yet the *Banner* didn't hesitate to focus on women's appearance, quipping, "Much interest was also added to the occasion by the group of attractive young girls drawn from the social circles of the younger element who were serving as ushers."[47] In contrast, the next morning's coverage in the *Tennessean* applauded the movement's increasingly aggressive policies. "That a complete revolution in the policy of the woman's suffrage movement in the quest of the women for the ballot is about to change the passive endurance of a denial of franchise into a vigorous demand for the vote was manifested Thursday afternoon," read the somewhat cumbersome lede. The lengthy jump on page two detailed Lea's support as US senator and that of Governor Hooper (no longer "wobbling" as in 1912) alongside increasingly "progressive" views in Tennessee and the South.[48] In contrast, the *Banner* stressed divisiveness among suffragists, with the phrases "Clash," "Ranks Divided," "Mooted Question," and "Contention" all used in the several deckheads above a story about policy discussions.[49] Intriguingly, the page layout left it unclear whether the banner headline, "Progress of Battle Is a Puzzle," applied to the suffrage story or adjacent war news. Employing war discourse to shape its suffrage coverage, *Banner* editors were able to suggest inevitable defeat.

Lea addressed the convention, with the *Tennessean* running the text of his speech and the *Banner*, unsurprisingly, avoiding it. His opening remarks reveal a gallant demeanor:

> I am embarrassed by not knowing how to address this distinguished audi-ence. Should I address this assemblage, representing the intelligence and wisdom of American womanhood, as "fellow citizens," I would not only violate the state, but the federal, constitution, for neither of these sacred instruments recognizes a woman as a "citizen." Nor can I meet the situation by referring to you as "people," because in the eyes of the law, women are not "people." Much as I regret it, I must address you "my disenfranchised friends," who, in spite of your learning, your cultivation and your intel-ligence, are neither citizens nor people.

Lea's emphasis on "cultivation" suggests a courtly manner implicitly directed toward white women of the privileged class, though he did not use those words. In the lengthy speech referencing Julius Caesar, original sin, and the argument over whether women have souls, Lea refuted the logic of antis' arguments. A staunch prohibitionist, he noted that where legal, "women's suffrage has opened more schools and closed more saloons than all other political movements combined." Reinforcing gender roles, he said voting would not lower "one iota the standard of motherhood, of wifehood and of womanhood, a standard of which every woman is proud and which every man reverences and worships." Echoing Mrs. John Ruhm's 1895 argument, he told the group, "It is as brave to give life as to inflict death."[50] While race was not mentioned in convention coverage, it was emphasized as a point of pride in local culture. The *Tennessean* ran a story on the Fisk Jubilee Singers' performance on November 11, noting that it might be repeated for the suffragists (whether this occurred is not clear). "Real music," the lead declared, meant "Southern negro folk songs."[51] Blacks were not important as political entities, but were valued as entertainers whose music supposedly exemplified southern culture—a "must-see" for white convention-goers.

Besides Lea, several men addressed the NAWSA convention, including Chicagoan Charles Hallinan, vice president of the National Men's League for Woman Suffrage. It may be for that reason that men's involvement became the focus of two brief stories in the *Tennessean*, one headlined "Nashville Men Stand on Street in Rain to Hear Suffrage Talks" (noting one suffragist's comment that Nashville was the only city in the country where men had stood outside in a drizzle downtown to hear their arguments), the other reporting the formation of a Tennessee men's league. "Probably the most advanced step in the woman's suffrage movement in Tennessee was made Monday afternoon when the Tennessee Men's League was launched in the loggia of the Hermitage Hotel," it began. Between thirty and forty men had joined, with hope that it would grow to one hundred.[52]

Finally, both papers ran ads for a "Thrilling, Sensational, Death-Defying Event" featuring a race between Katherine Stinson, flying a biplane, and her sister, Marjorie, in an Overland racing car on the last day. Sponsored by the Nashville Equal Suffrage League, the event was to take place at the fairgrounds, with suffrage speeches. The *Tennessean* called Katherine "a licensed girl aeroplane pilot," and the ad said Orville Wright taught her to fly. She would drop a large dummy "illustrating how spies may be dropped behind enemies' lines at night," followed by a "rain of roses" attached to small parachutes.[53] These items suggested a mix of symbols—the bravery of a woman piloting over (imaginary) enemy territory and the reassuring femininity of red roses. In this Monday afternoon spectacle in Nashville, as the Battle of Ypres raged in France, the discourse of women's bravery had gone beyond the traditional prosuffrage views of Mrs. Ruhm and Lea, brought to town by northerners during a national convention.

Anticipating Suffrage

Governor Ben Hooper told the NAWSA conventioneers that women's suffrage was "coming," but the issue rarely made bold headlines again in Nashville until 1920. Nevertheless, coverage was frequent in the *Tennessean*, which began a Sunday column, "Suffrage News and Notes," in 1915. Edited by Mrs. W. J. Morrison, "press correspondent" for the Nashville Equal Suffrage

League, the column ran briefs promoting suffrage. "The management takes this occasion . . . to say that it is contributing this space with pleasure, having always been in hearty sympathy and given loyal support to the cause of woman's suffrage," *Tennessean* editors announced.[54] It often shared a page with "society" news, sometimes alongside "Poultry Dep't," a column about raising turkeys, often a wife's job on the farm. But sometimes it ran with news about men's fraternal organizations.[55] Much of the content was reprinted, such as a Dorothea Dix piece on women jurors.[56] It often began with a short poem or suffrage song—new words to an old tune. One with a southern twist was "Happy Day" to be sung to the tune of "Dixie," repurposing a nineteenth-century classic about the Old South as a "land of cotton" (picked by slaves) to give the song new meaning in which women are empowered:

> We want to vote for a bright tomorrow
> Dawn of hope and end of sorrow
> Happy day, happy day
> Happy day for the world!

Later lines included

> We want to vote as wives and mothers,
> With our husbands, fathers, brothers,
> Happy day, happy day
> Happy day for the world

and

> We are not fools and we're not crazy
> We're not bad, corrupt nor lazy
> Happy day, happy day
> Happy day for the world[57]

Insights into the relationship between suffragists, the press, and men were revealed in *Tennessean* coverage about an internal conflict among suffragists. In a heated suffragist meeting about a local court case, disparaging remarks were made against the *Tennessean*, according to its page-one story, which mixed reporting and opinion. "Apparently forgetting that *The Tennessean* was the pioneer newspaper in the state to take up the fight for woman's suffrage, Mrs. [Leslie] Warner, . . . according to those present, unmercifully 'rapped' the paper." The story ran under several deckheads, including "Men Are to Assist in Battle for Act," apparently referencing a call for "mere men" reporters to leave. The sole male reporter (presumably the story's author) retreated to the balcony, but was "eyed suspiciously" and asked to wait downstairs.

This same story reported on the suffragists' discussion about "negro women anxious to take advantage of their franchise rights" and whether they would vote as their "white sisters" directed. A suffragist who had met with the Negro women noted that "Southern [white] women would tell them the best thing to do," hoping to ward off "unscrupulous politicians of their own race."[58] The story is indicative of the role identity politics, particularly race, sometimes played, even in coverage by the prosuffrage newspaper. Although the reporter and editors set aside neutrality to comment on male involvement, they did nothing to check the white suffragists' attitude of noblesse oblige toward black women.

When the state suffrage association met in Chattanooga in June, the *Banner* story ran on an inside cover headlined "News about Women and Personal Mention." Despite visual prominence, little of the copy concerns suffrage, instead featuring an elegant portrait of Warner, as outgoing president, opposite a larger, unrelated portrait of young Miss Lucy Cloud, a local family's "charming house guest." Small portraits of suffragists ran below. The page constructed suffrage as "society" discourse, focusing on delegates' elegant appearance, though a brief news item ran inside.[59] Unsurprisingly, the *Tennessean* covered the meeting above the fold on page one with a story on Abby Crawford Milton's election as president, noting, "It was brought to the attention of the body that Mrs. Milton's husband is editor of the *Chattanooga News* and that he had always stood by woman suffrage and had defended it through his paper"—an apparent follow-up on the earlier row over Warner.[60] (George Fort Milton was a Men's League member and Lea's friend.)

The state meeting happened to coincide with news out of Washington: the US Senate's upcoming decision on the amendment. The *Tennessean* had been following the amendment through Congress. The *Tennessean* ran several stories, notably "Senate Passes Bill to Grant Women Votes" and a localizer, "Women Cheer News of Victory of Suffragists," both on page one. The local story announced "wild jubilation."[61] The *Banner* ran news of US Senate passage on page thirteen, the AP story headlined simply, "Long Fight Won by Suffragists."[62]

Conclusion

An inconsistent story emerges from the convergent discourses of masculinity, race, and women's suffrage as seen in Nashville newspapers in the years preceding ratification. The *Tennessean* championed suffrage enthusiastically. It might even be argued that Lea, with his relentless front-page predictions of victory, gave the women of America the vote as surely as did Harry T. Burn, the twenty-four-year-old state legislator whose last-minute reversal at his mother's behest ushered in ratification.[63] Lea took women seriously. As he told NAWSA members in 1914, he saw them as wise, intelligent, cultivated citizens. For the most part, suffrage was serious news in the *Tennessean*, usually not blended discursively with "society" as in the *Banner*, at least after 1914. Yet when race was integral to a suffrage article, warning signs, arguably against black women's power, appeared. Examples include the Tuareg story, the Pears soap image, and white suffragists' assumptions about black women needing their counsel. All reinforced Jim Crow assumptions about race even while supporting suffrage itself. Moreover, as evidenced in his 1914 speech to NAWSA, Lea's own tone was gallant, implicitly constructing suffragists as white and middle-class. They were "ladies," whether he used the word or not. In this way, both in his speech and through his newspaper, Lea took on at least some of the role of the courtly southern gentleman, perhaps with a modern New South twist. Intriguingly, as the vote on ratification neared, he turned the spotlight from suffragists themselves to Cox's bid for the presidency, focusing on a man who favored suffrage but, as evidenced in his own autobiography, was no "suffragent."[64]

The *Banner*, meanwhile, downplayed suffrage, running coverage inside or constructing it in a society-page context, a strategy that reinforced traditional gender roles and thus hegemonic masculinity. At times, women's physical appearance was highlighted. As much as the *Tennessean* predicted victory, Stahlman's *Banner* predicted defeat. The eruption of verbal violence in its "blood of the South" discourse following ratification thus seems to have come out of nowhere. Beyond hegemonic masculinity, the bold headlines urging antis to "rally at the Ryman" exemplify recuperative masculinity[65]—the notion that male dominance must be shored up when threatened. Perhaps such attitudes had lay dormant, emerging only occasionally in decisions to run, for example, the wire story quipping about a statue as a lynched suffragist. That Stahlman took on the "blood of the South" discourse is as curious as Lea's adoption of the gallant southern gentleman, considering that Stahlman was a pre–Civil War German immigrant and Lea's family roots lay in the Union. Both illustrate the continued male-centered focus in newspapers and more broadly in society, despite ratification.

The author thanks librarians at the James E. Walker Library at Middle Tennessee State University and at the Tennessee State Library and Archives in Nashville.

Notes

1. Jane Marcellus, "Southern Myths and the Nineteenth Amendment: The Participation of Nashville Newspaper Publishers in the Final State's Ratification," *Journalism & Mass Communication Quarterly* 87, no. 20 (Summer 2010): 241–62.

2. "Can Anybody Terrorize Tennessee Manhood?" *Nashville Banner*, August 12, 1920, 20. The broadside was produced by the Southern Women's League for the Rejection of the Susan B. Anthony Amendment. Josephine A. Pearson Papers, Tennessee State Library and Archives, http://teva.contentdm.oclc.org/cdm/ref/collection/p15138coll27/id/55.

3. Early journalism educator Willard Grosvenor Bleyer pointed out that most daily newspapers shaped the news according to the views of their publishers, who acted as community opinion leaders. Willard Grosvenor Bleyer, "Introduction," in *The Profession of Journalism: A Collection of Articles on Newspaper Editing and Publishing, Taken from the Atlantic Monthly*, ed. Willard Grosvenor Bleyer (Boston: Atlantic Monthly Press, 1918), xvii–xviii.

4. "Go to Mass Meeting, Ryman Auditorium, Tonight; Will Make Protest against Ratification," *Nashville Banner*, August 19, 1920, 1.

5. "People Protest Suffrage Action," *Nashville Banner*, August 20, 1920, 1–2.

6. Zoë Beckley, "Cox a Man the Women Voters of America Will Believe In," *Nashville Tennessean*, July 25, 1920, 8.

7. The Jim Crow era occurred between post–Civil War Reconstruction and the civil rights movement. It was characterized by "Black Codes" mandating segregation in schools, railroads, workplaces, and public facilities, along with poll taxes and other efforts to limit blacks' voting rights. Repressive codes and lynching increased during the 1900s and 1910s. J. E. Hansan, "Jim Crow Laws and Racial Segregation." *Social Welfare History Project, 2011*, http://socialwelfare.library.vcu.edu/eras/civil-war-reconstruction/jim-crow-laws-and-racial-segregation/; and Douglas O. Linder, "Lynchings: By Year and Race," http://www.famous-trials.com/sheriffshipp/1084-lynchingsyear.

8. Durwood Dunn, "Elihu Embree," *Tennessee Encyclopedia*, Tennessee Historical Society, October 8, 2017, http://tennesseeencyclopedia.net/entries/elihu-embree/.

9. Eric Lacy, *Vanquished Volunteers: East Tennessee Sectionalism from Statehood to Secession* (Johnson City: East Tennessee State University Press, 1965), 122–26.

10. Stuart Hall, "The Work of Representation," in *Representation*, 2nd ed., ed. Stuart Hall, Jessica Evans, and Sean Nixon (Los Angeles: Sage, 2013), 29.

11. Michel Foucault, *The Archaeology of Knowledge and the Discourse on Language*, trans. A. M. Sheridan Smith (New York: Pantheon, 1971), 3–15.

12. Foucault, *Archaeology of Knowledge*, 2, 25.

13. Sean Nixon, "Exhibiting Masculinity," in *Representation*, ed. Hall, Evans, and Nixon, 294 and 296.

14. R. W. Connell and James W. Messerschmidt, "Hegemonic Masculinity: Rethinking the Concept," *Gender and Society*, 19, no. 6 (December 2005): 832.

15. For a discussion of the term "suffragent," see Brooke Kroeger, *The Suffragents: How Women Used Men to Get the Vote* (Albany: SUNY Press, 2017).

16. Carol Lynn Yellin and Janann Sherman, *The Perfect 36: Tennessee Delivers Woman Suffrage* (Oak Ridge, TN: Iris Press, 1998), 130.

17. Yellin and Sherman, *Perfect 36*, 127–34.

18. John Ruhm was US District Attorney in Nashville. Ruhm, who was white, had served in the Union Army as quartermaster for the 15th Regiment, US Colored Infantry. After the war, he advocated education and other reforms for the poor. See "Finding Aid for the John Ruhm Letter," MS 2228, University of Tennessee Libraries, Special Collections, http://dlc.lib.utk.edu/spc/view?docId =ead/0012_000687_000000_0000/0012_000687_000000_0000.xml.

19. "Equal Rights Department," ed. Mrs. John Ruhm Sr., *Nashville American*, May 9, 1895, 10.

20. David E. Sumner, "*Nashville Banner*," *Tennessee Encyclopedia*, March 1, 2018, https://tennesseeencyclopedia.net/entries/nashville-banner/.

21. Mary Louise Lea Tidwell, *Luke Lea of Tennessee* (Bowling Green, OH: Bowling Green State University Popular Press, 1993), 21–22, 32; David E. Sumner, "*Nashville Tennessean*," *Tennessee Encyclopedia*, March 1, 2018, https://tennesseeencyclopedia .net/entries/nashville-tennessean/.

22. Tidwell, *Luke Lea of Tennessee*, 7.

23. "Suffragists from All Over State Convene; Address by Governor," *Nashville Tennessean*, January 11, 1912, 1, 5.

24. "Suffragettes of Tennessee," *Nashville Banner*, January 10, 1912, 13.

25. "Tennessee for Equal Suffrage," *Nashville Banner*, January 12, 1912, 3.

26. A lawyer who wrote the constitution for the Nashville Equal Suffrage League, Turney in 1913 became chair of the Tennessee branch of the Congressional Union, which evolved into the National Woman's Party. Yellin and Sherman, *Perfect 36*, 149; "Detailed Chronology, National Woman's Party History," 2, https://www.loc.gov /collections/static/women-of-protest/images/detchron.pdf.

27. "Where the Women Rule the Men," *Nashville Tennessean*, January 21, 1912, SM8. The copyright notice says, "American-Examiner, Great Britain Rights Reserved."

28. "Who Are the Tuareg?" Smithsonian Institution, https://africa.si.edu/exhibits /tuareg/who.html.

29. "Suffragettes Preparing for Big Washington Pageant," *Nashville Tennessean*, February 2, 1913, 4C.

30. "Kaleidoscopic Picture of Ever Shifting Color," *Nashville Banner*, March 3, 1913, 1.

31. "Suffrage Pageant a Near Riot," *Nashville Tennessean*, March 4, 1913, 1 and 2.

32. "Will Men Help Woman Suffrage in Tennessee?" *Nashville Tennessean*, February 12, 1913, 5.

33. Ralph Smith, "Danger to Laws of South," *Nashville Tennessean*, May 22, 1913, 1A.

34. Mrs. John E. Turney, "Suffragists Will Show Their Strength," *Nashville Tennessean*, March 2, 1914, 5.

35. "Rally Day for Equal Suffrage," *Nashville Tennessean*, May 2, 1914, 1 and 7.

36. "Women Suffer Another Reverse," *Nashville Banner*, July 1, 1914, 13; "Mrs. Pankhurst Is in Jail Again," *Nashville Banner*, July 8, 1914, 1; "Dr. Shaw Regrets Women's Action," *Nashville Banner*, July 4, 1914, 2; "Woman's Figure Swings by Neck," *Nashville Banner*, July 15, 1914, 7.

37. "Progress of Woman Suffrage," *Nashville Tennessean*, August 30, 1914, 6A.

38. It is missing from both the Tennessee State Library and Archives and the *Tennessean*'s own collection.

39. "Pears Soap Poster," 1890, Pictorial Press, Ltd./Alamy Stock Photo, https://www .alamy.com/stock-photo-pears-soap-poster-about-1890-131516373.html.

40. It was apparently the work of Frederick William Pethick-Lawrence, a British baron married to suffragist Emmeline Pethick and himself publisher of left-wing, prosuffrage newspapers. See Miranda Garrett and Zoë Thomas, *Suffrage and the Arts: Visual Culture, Politics, and Enterprise* (London: Bloomsbury, 2018), 271n44. See also Frederick Pethick-Lawrence, *Fate Has Been Kind* (London: Hutchinson & Co., 1943), 83.

41. Anne McClintock, "Soap and the Commodity Spectacle," in *Representation*, ed. Hall, Evans, and Nixon, 272.

42. Stuart Hall, "The Spectacle of the 'Other,'" in *Representation*, ed. Hall, Evans, and Nixon, 231.

43. "Mrs. Belmont Predicts Victory," *Nashville Tennessean*, November 11, 1914, 1.

44. "Suffrage Leader's Opinion of Two Organizations for Tennessee," *Nashville Banner*, November 7, 1914, 2; "Suffragists to Come Next Week," *Nashville Banner*, November 7, 1914, 4; "Suffragists Throng City," *Nashville Banner*, November 11, 1914, 1, 14.

45. Alice Stone Blackwell, "Why Women Should Vote," *Nashville Tennessean*, November 12, 1914, 2B; "Our Guests, the Suffragists," *Nashville Tennessean*, November 15, 1914, A6.

46. Kroeger, *The Suffragents*, 82–83.

47. "Suffrage Advocates of Nation Meet Here," *Nashville Banner*, November 12, 1914, 1, 14.

48. "Suffragists in Lively Debates," *Nashville Tennessean*, November 13, 1914, 1, 2.

49. "Clash in Suffrage Session Continues," *Nashville Banner*, November 13, 1914, 1.

50. "Suffragists Addressed by Lea," *Nashville Tennessean*, November 14, 1914, 4.

51. "Big Crowd Hears Negro Melodies," *Nashville Tennessean*, November 11, 1914, 5.

52. "Nashville Men Stand on Street in Rain to Hear Suffragists," *Nashville Tennessean*, November 15, 1914, 1A; "Suffrage League Formed by Men," *Nashville Tennessean*, November 17, 1914, 7.

53. Advertisement, *Nashville Banner*, November 16, 1914, 14; "Girl Aviator to Fly at State Fairgrounds This Afternoon," *Nashville Tennessean*, November 17, 1914, 2.

54. "Suffrage News and Notes," ed. Mrs. W. J. Morrison, *Nashville Tennessean*, November 7, 1915, SM2.

55. "Suffrage News and Notes," ed. Mrs. W. J. Morrison, *Nashville Tennessean*, December 26, 1915, SM4.

56. Dorothy Dix, "Women on Mirandy on Jurors," in "Suffrage News and Notes," ed. Mrs. W. J. Morrison, *Nashville Tennessean*, December 19, 1915, 5.

57. "Suffrage News and Notes," ed. Mrs. W. J. Morrison, *Nashville Tennessean*, January 30, 1916, SM3. "Suffrage News and Notes" disappeared in 1918.

58. "Women Refuse to Leave Fight to Mrs. Warner," *Nashville Tennessean*, May 18, 1919, 1, 11.

59. "News about Women and Personal Mention," *Nashville Banner*, June 1, 1919, n.p.; "Prominent Women Delegates to State Suffrage Association," *Nashville Banner*, June 1, 1919, 3.

60. "Mrs. G. F. Milton Heads Woman Suffrage Body," *Nashville Tennessean*, June 6, 1919, 1.

61. "Senate Passes Bill to Grant Women Votes," *Nashville Tennessean*, June 5, 1919, 1; "Women Cheer News of Victory of Suffragists," *Nashville Tennessean*, June 5, 1919, 1.

62. "Long Fight Won by Suffragists," *Nashville Banner*, June 5, 1919, 13.

63. For information on Harry T. Burn, see Anastatia Sims, "Woman Suffrage Movement," *Tennessee Encyclopedia,* https://tennesseeencyclopedia.net/entries/woman-suffrage-movement/.

64. Cox does not mention suffrage in his autobiography, even when discussing the 1920 election. James M. Cox, *Journey through My Years* (New York: Simon & Schuster, 1946).

65. Coined in 1999, the phrase refers to a backlash against equality sought by feminists. As such, it leads to policies favoring patriarchy. Bob Lingard, Martin Mills, and Marcus B. Weaver-Hightower, "Interrogating Recuperative Masculinity Politics in Schooling," *International Journal of Inclusive Education* 16, no. 4 (April 2012): 407–21; Martin Mills, Wayne Martino, and Bob Lingard, "Getting Boys' Education 'Right': The Australian Government's Parliamentary Inquiry Report as an Exemplary Instance of Recuperative Masculinity Politics," *British Journal of Sociology of Education* 28, no. 1 (2007): 5–21.

9

The Facilitators

Elites in the Victory of the Women's Suffrage Movement

BROOKE KROEGER

In the 1910s, among the many supporters who lifted the women's suffrage movement out of its nineteenth-century "doldrums"[1] and onto victory footing were civic, religious, academic, business, and social luminaries who formed or became active in new suffrage organizations. Throughout the decade, top movement leaders such as Anna Howard Shaw, Carrie Chapman Catt, Harriot Stanton Blatch, and Alice Paul cultivated and embraced elite new recruits and the much-needed resources they brought: fresh arguments, political and financial assets for the state-by-state and national campaigns; fluid access to useful contacts in their social and professional spheres; and an outsized ability to present the suffrage movement in the popular press in a flattering, more broadly engaging new light.

Because of the position the elites of suffrage occupied in their social and professional worlds—men of affairs and socialites with VIP aura—they brought heightened value to the suffrage associations and committees that organized around their prominence or expertise. Businessmen populated the finance committees. Attorneys helped with legislative and policy efforts. Those with political clout worked the legislatures. Society women organized and underwrote events and strategic initiatives. Orators traveled the speaker circuits and from the pulpits, preachers preached. Long before their involvement with suffrage, newspapers and magazines tracked their comings and goings, which upped the news value of their speeches, staged events, big donations, and myriad other interventions on the movement's behalf. Note also that the editors, publishers, and well-known writers in their midst were men with significant influence or outright editorial control over the popular mainstream newspapers and magazines they ran, wrote for, or owned. This, too, worked to the movement's advantage.

As Congress passed the federal suffrage amendment in 1919, Catt, then president of the National American Woman Suffrage Association (NAWSA), credited the thousands of "evoluters" over seven decades whose work and sacrifice had made it possible for the women of every state in the union to vote. "A long array of such noble souls rises in memory as one looks backward over the years," she wrote in a page-long essay for the *New York Times*; "women who had the vision of the righteousness of the equality of rights between the sexes, men who dare to espouse a despised cause."[2]

The social and professional elites who organized for suffrage in the 1910s figure prominently in Catt's "noble" array, both the fashionable high-society women and the broad base of influential progressive men of all political parties who were often, but not always, the husbands, brothers, sons, or lovers of ardent women activists. Both served the movement as resource mobilizers, as framers of effective arguments, as funders of movement initiatives, and as political and media influencers. All these functions are key to any social movement's success.

Several recent books on women's suffrage examine the roles of elites as individuals and as members of organized forces both within and outside of groups they joined, advised, or led.[3] Unlike celebrity endorsers, who are most often in-but-not-of a movement, these men and women were in it and of it. "Auxiliaries"[4] was the term used by James Lees Laidlaw, the national president of the Men's League for Woman Suffrage, to describe the members of his organization. There are no precise numbers, but in 1913, a lengthy essay in the *Trend* by Robert Cameron Beadle, the Men's League's second secretary-treasurer, put membership at "several thousand" in chapters in twenty-five states and across the world.[5] In those four years, the league sent representatives to the annual international suffrage conventions in Stockholm, London, and Budapest; held a national convention of its own; and marched in all but one of the major New York and in Washington, DC, parades. Their actions always attracted press attention, either in the main coverage or in curtain-raisers and sidebars. Men in a women's movement have never stopped being unexpected, thus giving their commitment to suffrage a gendered dimension, too. This was true in the media long after men on the parade line became so commonplace the crowds stopped their brickbats and catcalls.

Repeated mentions in newspapers and magazines document the regular notice both men and women elites invariably attracted at assemblies, dinners, and mass and smaller planning meetings; during major and minor legislative and fundraising drives; at conventions; in parlors, pageants, and parades; on hikes or state-traversing and national automobile recruitment trips; at fundraisers; and at teas and fairs on their vacation estates. The major suffrage movement archives preserve evidence of their efforts as organizers, underwriters, and de facto or deliberate publicists.[6] Glamour, charisma, upbringing, access, and position made this possible, along with the overt and subtle privileges their social and professional class accorded, including available leisure time; economic wherewithal; real estate; influential social, business and political circles; and, as noted, smooth media access. Elite impact also threads through the news-generating direct, indirect, and in-kind financial support these men and women provided either to NAWSA or to its more radical rival, Alice Paul's National Woman's Party (NWP), first called the Congressional Union.

This chapter examines the critical support that social and professional elites provided from about 1909 to 1919 to help take the suffrage movement over the finish line in state and federal campaigns. It emphasizes their roles as media influencers and the attention they generated for the acts they performed; for the celebrity-like appeal they bestowed on their organizations; and as media industry giants themselves—the writers, editors, and publishers of some of the most widely read publications of the day. I briefly review applicable concepts from social movement research and provide examples to showcase how social and professional elites mattered as framers, funders, facilitators, and media influencers in both the state and national suffrage battles.

The Value of Elites in Social Movements

Scholars ascribe special importance to elite engagement and effective media strategy as aspects of success, both in the suffrage campaign saga and in the success formulation of social movements more generally.[7] Roger Karapin counts the support of elites as one of three key factors that led to the suffrage "opportunity spiral" of the 1910s; in other words, a successive swirl of gains that "increased the movement's power and success chances," which in turn brought support from politicians "who now had to face female voters or at least began to see women's suffrage as likely to be adopted in their states."[8] I would add that the news-generating actions of social and professional elites, as elites, was as significant as the other resources their involvement brought, and that elites in the 1910s figure as an intrinsic aspect of the other two factors he names: interaction among the state suffrage campaigns and in the momentum-producing suffrage victories of the decade after a fourteen-year drought. For example, in 1912, Frederick Nathan and his wife, Maud, head of the New York Consumers' League, campaigned by car in Ohio, Wisconsin, and Texas as those legislatures debated the suffrage question, and in 1914, the Men's League's Laidlaw and his wife, Harriet Burton Laidlaw, a major figure in the New York State campaign, drove west to recruit in Montana on what the *New York Evening Post* called a "Whirlwind Tour." The two-column headline in the *Billings Gazette* billed the couple as "Eastern Society Suffragists."[9]

Elite movement presence throughout the decade spurred the mobilization of additional moral, cultural, organizational, informational, and human resources. The sociologists Bob Edwards and John McCarthy explain how moral resources enhance a movement's legitimacy, inviting solidarity, sympathy, and backing. Cultural resources include conceptual tools and specialized knowledge. Organizational resources facilitate recruitment and the dissemination of information. Human resources are labor, leadership, and "value-added components"[10] such as skills, savvy, and unique expertise. For the suffrage campaign in its last lap, the elites threw significant weight into all five of these arenas and through these efforts, into the refashioning of the movement's mass media profile.

Mass media, writes the social movement theorist William Gamson, is the "master arena," one that buffets the efforts of social movements and over whose coverage activists and movement leaders have little or no reliable influence or control. He offers three reasons: the needs of "the gallery," that is, the "players in every other arena," who rely on mass media to disseminate news of the public acts they perform; the assumption of all the players in the policy process that mass media influence is pervasive; and the way mass media both spreads word of changes in language use and political consciousness and signals broader cultural changes in civil society. Journalists, he adds, play the dual role of deciding what to quote and who to take seriously as important players.[11] Applying these concepts to the suffrage movement's ending years illuminates the benefit the campaign received from the active organized presence of social and professional elites in its midst: both as men and women whom reporters reflexively wrote about, and as industry giants who influenced or controlled what came off the presses. In practice, it meant that the journalistic acts of shaping and framing, and the ambient media whims and biases of more than a few of the major newspapers and magazines of the period, worked reliably in the movement's favor.

Francesca M. Cancian and Bonnie L. Ross, studying suffrage movement coverage in the *New York Times* and magazines listed in the *Reader's Guide to Periodic Literature*, concluded that the publicity generated by new tactics in the movement's revival period after 1907—easy-to-report stunts and events, such as parades, pageants, and open-air meetings—had a "multiplier effect" that accelerated movement expansion.[12] They note two approaches to understanding the relationship between social movements and the media: one, that coverage will reflect the interests or perspectives of the power elite and that once government, big business, labor leaders, and other members of the political establishment accept a movement's goals, considerable coverage will follow; and two, that the internal culture of media organizations is key, suggesting that if it is difficult for reporters, writers, and editors to get information about a movement or if they find its concepts too abstract to explain to readers, little or no coverage will follow. The authors conclude that sound analysis requires both approaches. Their study, however, does not consider the specific impact of elite engagement in the movement's last years in and of itself, which likely accounts for an appreciable measure of the improved quantity and quality of coverage. I would submit that in that climactic decade, the visible involvement of the movement's newfound elites with the compound benefits of their easy-to-cover movement participation and their baked-in press access, multiplied the multiplier. Their very presence as suffrage supporters brought welcome headlines, even in publications as editorially hostile to the movement as the *New York Times*.

Thus, social and professional elites represented a novel constituency in the suffrage panoply. Before the 1910s, few men of position or high-society women were suffrage movement figures, so the arrival of so many elites was newsworthy. But so were the assets they brought—note again the added gendered value, too—as men of position willing to use their privileged influence in the movement's favor, and as women widely admired for style, grace, and social status, who engaged in the cause with their gloves off.[13] Both even worked the streets when duty called.

As Media Influencers

True, during this ten-year push, many campaign strategies that crossed all class lines generated surges of welcome publicity, among them, the grand parades, rallies, and pageants, organized for everyone from NAWSA and NWP headquarters, and publicity-generating stunts like the "Be a Suffrage Fan" fans distributed at a New York Giants–Chicago Cubs game in May 1915, or an 18,000-foot-long petition signed by four million women and driven cross-country from Oregon to the White House that December, impressive enough to bring an admiring greeting from President Woodrow Wilson.

The elites cast media lures of a different sort. Their contributions as publicity assets had several overt and subliminal dimensions, because of the attention they automatically attracted as society figures, because their suffrage activism made them exemplars of a new gender model for men and women of their social stratum, and because so many of them owned, edited or wrote for major publications, an overwhelmingly men's province at the time. The suffrage work of elites simply provided yet another reason to write about figures already in the public consciousness from other contexts. Moreover, when a newspaper or magazine story mentioned a name from its upper-class readership, even antisuffrage newspapers like the *New York Times* restrained the impulse to mockery so evident in its editorials, and notwithstanding a playful headline, "The Deeper Notes to Join the Soprano Chorus" over its front-page scoop about the Men's League in formation. Because of who they were, society denizens such as Katherine Duer Mackay and her media magnate husband Clarence Mackay, the Laidlaws, and Alva Smith Vanderbilt Belmont could rely on respectful treatment in the press, the inevitable references to women's dress notwithstanding.[14] For all these reasons, the presence of elites transformed the movement's public caricature. "The Type Has Changed" reads the caption under Boardman Robinson's 1911 sketch in the *New York Tribune* of two suffragists, one dowdy, one dazzling. Two years later, at the 1913 suffrage convention in Washington, DC, a *Tribune* writer even went so far as to admire the matronly Anna Howard Shaw in her "shimmering gray silk."

Suffragists among the elites elicited news coverage in other ways. Rosalie Gardiner Jones and Louisine Elder Havemeyer engineered major spectacles— long suffrage recruiting hikes from New York City to the capital in Albany in 1912, and from New York City to Washington, DC, for the 1913 parade. Havemeyer took charge of a six-week-long torch relay rally by motorcar from the easternmost tip of Long Island to Buffalo in the summer of 1915. Major publications published the poems and columns of Alice Duer Miller, notably the prosuffrage *New York Tribune* under Helen Rogers Reid and her prosuffrage husband, the publisher Ogden Mills Reid.[15] Vira Boarman Whitehouse and Norman de Rapelye Whitehouse, a stockbroker, brought society gloss, as did Narcissa Cox Vanderlip and Frank Vanderlip, the president of what is now Citibank. Both couples were top figures in the New York campaign. Late in 1917, right after passage of the New York suffrage referendum, the *New York Times* gave front-page coverage to the wartime offer to Vira Whitehouse from George Creel, the head of the White House's Committee on Public Information (CPI), to be a special agent in Switzerland who would promote the US interests through speeches, the distribution of literature, and other "informative activities."

THE TYPE HAS CHANGED.

FIGURE 9.1. "The Type Has Changed," cartoon by Boardman Robinson for the *New York Tribune*, February 24, 1911, 7.

Creel's offer was not incidental. Up until April of 1917, when the United States entered World War I and Wilson appointed him to head the CPI, Creel, a widely published writer and editor, was the Men's League's astute publicity chairman. He knew firsthand the work Whitehouse had done over several years to help the state referendum pass. As the league's publicity chairman, Creel ran that office like a military operation. The left-hand column of his committee's stationery lists his team's dozens of name-brand writers and editors, from William Allen White to Walter Lippmann. It is readily apparent how editors and publishers involved in the suffrage campaign helped guide prosuffrage coverage. For instance, the all-male editorial advisory board for the special February 1915 all-suffrage issue of *Puck* included Ogden Reid of the *Tribune*; Oswald Garrison Villard of *The Nation* and *New York Evening*

Post; William Dean Howells of the *Atlantic*; Arthur Brisbane of the *New York Journal*; John O'Hara Cosgrave of the *New York World*; Norman Hapgood, of *Harper's Weekly* at the time; S. S. McClure of *McClure's*; Frank Munsey of *Munsey's*; Erman J. Ridgway of *Everybody's*; and Hamilton Holt of *The Independent*.

Throughout the period, news reports reflected the way elite involvement helped transform the movement's frumpy humorless image into one that portrayed a much broader coalition with its own elegant coterie of attention-getting socialites and their prosuffrage men. The attention they attracted expanded the movement's ability to disseminate news across the social classes and to spread ideas, publicity, and propaganda to audiences well beyond the movement's standing, albeit growing base.

As Elites in Organizations

Some scholars give special attention to the precocity of western states in granting women the vote in the late 1800s. On the East Coast, only New York prevailed and not until 1917.[16] The sociologists Holly McCammon and Karen Campbell attribute much of the western advantage to two factors: suffragists in those states who framed arguments to dovetail with common beliefs, and regional political and gendered opportunities that worked in the movement's favor. Help came from the region's state and territorial procedures for changing voting rights and from the support of elected governmental officials who then became advocates. In addition, western suffragists were quicker to capitalize on changing societal beliefs about the roles of women in the broader culture—beyond home and children—as women pursued higher education, entered the professions in ever greater numbers, and became outspoken supporters of political and social causes.[17]

New York experienced a similar phenomenon, but not until the 1910s, when so many of its socially, professionally, and politically connected new recruits formed or joined new suffrage organizations. According to Mc-Cammon and Campbell, the number of suffrage organizations was not a key success factor in the West, since some states that granted the franchise had many such associations and others had few. In New York, however, organized support in diverse configurations initially *did* matter. As the 1910s dawned, new suffrage organizations solidified support from various constituencies and built their membership rosters. Adept at priming the publicity pump, Alva Belmont formed her Political Equality Association to link white women of wealth with African American women and others. The welcome she gave to African Americans made the national press, as she sought to address that

glaring deficit.[18] "Mrs. Belmont Invites Negro Women to Join the 'Cause,'"
read one headline in the *Detroit Free Press*.[19] To increase visibility, in Manhattan, the Bronx, Brooklyn, and Long Island,[20] she opened eleven "street-front
suffrage settlement clubs" that offered space for meetings, classes, reading
rooms, and entertainment. Harriot Stanton Blatch's organization for wage-
earning women is another example,[21] as was the Collegiate League, which
had chapters on most of the prestigious men's and women's college campuses,
notably Columbia, Harvard, and Vassar.

Exclusivity was part of the strategy in the creation of several organizations.
Back in September 1908, one of the most visible of these upstart groups,
Katherine Mackay's Equal Franchise Society, sent letters of invitation to high-
profile white socialites and influential men. The Men's League did likewise,
to prominent men in New York State or women in good position to recruit
them. Only later, as the Men's League went national, did it broaden its call to
include prosuffrage men of all social classes. When Mackay, with the help of
Blatch, started her organization, the *New York Times* emphasized its society
roots. A *New York Times Sunday Magazine* splash featured the influential
men on the new society's roster and why they had thrown their support to
the women's cause. Headlined "Well-Known Men Advocate It," the piece
quoted George Harvey; the philosopher and Columbia University professor John Dewey; another Columbia professor, Charles Sprague Smith, also
director of the People's Institute; and Rollo Ogden, a *New York Evening Post*
editorialist, who, in 1919, became editor of the *New York Times*.

Thus, NAWSA's leadership cleverly anointed elite figures with leadership
roles in semi-autonomous groups. The strategy deepened individual commitment to the cause and encouraged those who signed on to involve others
in their social and professional circles, even if only for ad hoc support. Like
attracted influential like, thus broadening the movement's reach within these
useful societal and professional ranks. The elite groups that formed in the
1910s also listed row upon row of honorific vice presidents and executive and
advisory committee members. More to the point, upper and professional
class involvement with the suffrage cause was newsworthy. The resulting
publicity helped increase support for suffrage among those in the strongest
position to help with the movement's most urgent financial, political, and
governmental aims, needs, and goals. That publicity also helped convince
reluctant legislators and legions of workaday men—voters—to cast their
ballots for suffrage.

In 1907–8, the well-publicized back-to-back US speaking tours of two
privileged British suffragettes (as they were called in the UK), Anne Cobden-
Sanderson and Viscountess Ethel Snowden, coincided with the emergence

of New York's exclusive Colony Club as a primary base for the recruitment of prosuffrage white society women.[22] With Blatch's assistance, Mackay convened her Equal Franchise Society in 1908 with the aim, the *New York Times* said, of taking suffrage's "organized work more into the ranks of society than it has yet been." At about the same time, Oswald Garrison Villard proposed the Men's League to Anna Shaw, who was NAWSA's president at the time. She found his idea compelling, coming as it did from the son of movement activist Fanny Garrison Villard and grandson of the abolitionist and suffragist William Garrison, not to mention Villard himself, the editor and publisher of *The Nation* and the *New York Post*. In proposing the league, Villard was mindful of Cobden-Sanderson's public rebuke of the "idle luxurious lives" of rich American women and the indifference to the cause of American men. The press repeatedly reported her insulting remarks and the *Post* editorialized about it. In giving Villard NAWSA's blessing to form the Men's League, Shaw pointed out the failure of previous efforts to involve men of his stature—the ones the movement needed. Although she did not mention it, not even the early individual public support for the cause from figures as august as Garrison, Frederick Douglass, and William Dean Howells, editor of the *Atlantic*, had changed the movement's fortunes in the nineteenth century.

Both Dewey and Rabbi Stephen S. Wise joined Villard as Men's League cofounders. They invited the young writer and editor Max Eastman to be the league's first secretary-treasurer. At the time, Eastman, Dewey's protégé at Columbia, already had been published in the *Atlantic Monthly*, the *North American Review*, and the *International Journal of Ethics*. Even with the aid of his mother, the Reverend Annis Ford Eastman, it took him nearly a year, until November 1909, to recruit a 150-man roster impressive enough to announce publicly. At least 100 attention-commanding names were Villard's ideas.

The financier and philanthropist George Foster Peabody, a bachelor at the time, became nominal head of the New York State league. Its effective leader was James Lees Laidlaw, the league's national president, a financier who could trace his heritage back to colonial days through fifty different lines. The league's first organized event in December 1910 attracted some 600 often namedrop-worthy banquet attendees who garnered excellent press attention, as did the guest of honor, the Vicountess Snowden. In May 1911, the Men's League fielded somewhere between 80 and 100 marchers for the second annual New York Suffrage Day Parade. The verbal abuse they endured along Fifth Avenue galvanized even greater involvement among this vanguard of men, whom the press and public pejoratively demeaned as "suffragents," "mere men," "husbandettes," or "suffrage husbands." Not only did they march in ever growing numbers in all the subsequent major parades, including a 1912 New York torchlight extravaganza. They also oversaw a historically themed Men's League pageant in 1914. Twice, when police protection failed the marchers, in New York, and then again in DC, the men used their clout in vehement press-generating protest.

Mission overlap was rife among the New York suffrage organizations that formed in the 1910s, so evident in the involved organizations listed on the cover of that February 1915 all-suffrage issue of *Puck*: the Empire State Campaign Committee, the New York State Woman Suffrage Association, the Woman Suffrage Party, the Equal Franchise Society, the Collegiate League, the Men's League for Woman Suffrage, and the Women's Political Union.[23] Only that November, after the failure of New York's first suffrage referendum vote, did these seven groups consolidate. Gertrude Brown, New York's state suffrage president (whose husband, Raymond Brown, was a former newspaperman and illustrator),[24] told the *New York Times* how proud each group had been of its separate identity. "But we are convinced that maintaining these lines of demarcation is foolish and wasteful and each organization is now anxious to see the combination and centralization of forces made permanent."

As Framers of Arguments

If the brief characterizations that appear in newspaper and magazine articles of 1879 and 1894 are accurate, the East was well behind the West in updating the way its most prominent figures framed arguments.[25] In the late nineteenth century, McCammon and Campbell explain, western suffragists discovered the greater effectiveness of "expediency" arguments, which avoided arousing opposition, over "justice" arguments that were more threatening to the status quo, such as the wrongness of denying a citizen a right as basic as the franchise. "Bridge-framing"—arguments that worked well for both movement insiders and outsiders—also proved effective.[26] By the spring of 1909, Max Eastman was commanding substantial press attention as he crisscrossed New York State making speeches for the movement. The suffrage speeches of Rabbi Wise, a major figure in Reform Judaism, attracted coverage, as did Wise's contretemps with another high-profile but antisuffrage Reform rabbi, Joseph Silverman. They argued over a prosuffrage resolution that Wise managed to push through a regional rabbinical council over the objections of Silverman, who was presiding. The *New York Times* devoted the better part of a column to the clash of the rabbis, under a cascading headline.[27]

Eastman distinguished himself on the platform and generated press attention by casting aside "stale old arguments" to offer a shift in emphasis more in line with what he called "popular thought." His stock speech disposed of two of the most common efforts to persuade: that giving women the vote would be just and that it would purify politics. Instead, he argued that what the country needed was not "beautiful cloistered saints" but human beings out in the world, acting on their convictions. He added contemporaneous tropes: during the 1909 New York shirtwaist workers strike, for example, he emphasized the degrading treatment of women strikers who had so little recourse. As a suffrage speaker in demand, Eastman often gave the keynote, but also appeared on tour with Belmont and, for other bookings, with Shaw. For her part, Katherine Mackay was adept at packing the houses with key civic and political leaders from among her social peers, but also made headlines with her plea that a vote for mothers was a vote for children. She promoted this at the major public events that she organized and underwrote until her divorce from Mackay curtailed her involvement.[28]

John Dewey and his wife, Alice, like Belmont, made newsworthy efforts to counter the movement's exclusion of African Americans. In February 1911, the *New York Times* reported that on the strength of a report in another unidentified newspaper, the leasing company of the Deweys' Harlem apartment building had filed an injunction to stop the couple from inviting "Negroes" to a suffrage meeting in their home. The Deweys declined to confirm or deny the report, so with only an unconfirmed newspaper item as evidence, the legal action failed. Nonetheless, the *Anti-Suffragist Newsletter* quoted the *Baltimore Star* as saying, "If the woman suffragists wish to gain converts for their cause in the States lying south of the Mason and Dixon line, they have gone about it in a queer way." W. E. B. Du Bois, as editor of the NAACP's *Crisis*, was not a Men's League member, but put forth strong prosuffrage arguments in a series of editorials and published several special suffrage issues of the magazine. He repeatedly encouraged his African American readers to support women's suffrage, despite the hostility or indifference they had good reason to feel from past and ongoing mistreatment. "We must remember," he wrote, "that we are facing a great question of right in which personal hatreds have no place."[29]

Laidlaw's 1912 mission statement for the Men's League (which surfaced in a Canadian newspaper in a syndicated column by Fola LaFollette's husband, the playwright George Middleton) makes the organization's raison d'être clear: to bring into the fold those men who needed to see masses of other men on board before they could acknowledge their personal support, and to structure a way to persuade voters not yet persuaded. The statement acknowledged the "long and burdensome" nature of a quest by nonvoters to convince legislators to support their plea when legislators were responsible only to voters. "If a well-organized minority of men voters demand equal suffrage," Laidlaw argued, "they will get it."

CHIVALRY VERSUS JUSTICE

Why the Women of the Nation Demand the Right to Vote

By GEORGE CREEL

Decorations by Edward A. Wilson

THERE is no good quarrel with honest opposition to equal suffrage. Not only is the right to disagree guaranteed by the Constitution, but it is highly essential that every important political change should encounter antagonism in order to guard against hasty and ill-considered action.

The woman who has no need of the vote herself, and resists it as an added and unwelcome responsibility, may be selfish but she is frank. The man who holds that the opposite sex is not sufficiently intelligent to use the ballot wisely may be prejudiced but he is courageous. Men and women alike who feel that equal suffrage does not contain any effective remedy for admitted injustices and evils, may lack faith but they are sincere. Such as these are straightforward fighters who do not fear the open, and they are entitled to all the amenities of well-tempered debate.

There is neither frankness, courage nor sincerity, however, in those controversialists who deny that the American woman is touched at any point by wrong, oppression or wretchedness, and whose implacable enmity to her enfranchisement is masked by glowing hyperboles that paint her as a peach-cheeked, rose-lipped queen buried to the dimpled chin in love and homage.

In America to-day there are about nine million women who work, many of them engaged in the pleasant professions and wholesome industries, to be sure, but the large majority engulfed in dismal and degrading drudgeries. In the face of this economic revolution that has leveled so many protective walls, how is it possible to grant good faith to the continued insistence that "woman's place is the home?"

The platitude, in effect, contends that these weary millions are not working from any real necessity, but possess homes in which they could remain did they but have the proper spirit and desire. According to its reasoning, the sea of frenzied backs is caused by nothing more vital than discontents and unrests.

Look where one will, women may be seen creeping across the icy floors of office buildings, aight in, night out, scrubbing up the dirt of a man's day; toiling in mills and factories ten and twelve hours a day; plying swift needles in fire-traps; breathing the stifling air in steam laundries; making gewgaws in darksome tenements at an average wage of two cents an hour, or tearing fingers in the damp shucking sheds of the Gulf Coast States.

Does any one honestly believe that these driven souls are doing these things because they like it? Or that their presence in such employments is adequately explained by the assumption of "marital unrest," or "dissatisfaction with the humdrum of domestic life," or the "desire to obtain pin-money for vanities?"

AN equal measure of just resentment is aroused by the twin declaration that suffrage will entail "the disintegration of the American home." Here again there is the bland theory of vine-clad cottages and dense walls of fragrant honeysuckle behind which every right-thinking woman sits in security surrounded by her babes.

What of the squalid holes in the thirteen thousand licensed tenements of New York City alone, where whole families and boarders often sleep, eat and work in a single room, toiling long, weary hours for incredible pittances? What of the old doghouses, dilapidated carriage sheds and noisome barracks in which padrones herd the cannery workers of Delaware, Maryland, Louisiana and Mississippi? Or the ragged tents of miners on the bleak hillsides of the coal mining states? Or the sickening hovels of the coal and steel districts in Pennsylvania? Or the paper-walled shacks of the cotton mill towns where sleep waits on terrible exhaustion?

What greater "disintegration" can come to these "homes" where families rot in despair, and boys and girls grow to maturity stunted in mind and body?

There is no intent to cry down chivalry or desire to repress a single poetic impulse. It is well indeed that men should hold the mother sex in

tender, reverent regard, and it is to be hoped that love will never lose its romance and idealism. It is asserted, however, that true chivalry must have justice as its firm foundation. The kind that ignores crying evils and patent wrongs in favor of high-sounding periods is nothing more than veneered hypocrisy.

There can be no denial of the imperative nature of the equal suffrage issue. Eleven states and one territory have granted woman the ballot, and in all others it is the principal agitation and demand. Why, then, is it not a high duty to free the discussion of all falsities, smugnesses and obvious claptrap so that honest, sincere argument may have a clear field.

What is more fair, for instance, than the demand that men who grow maudlin in praise of the "American queen" must be prepared to show that, in their particular city and state, the women are treated fairly and decently? Or that those who insist that the "fair sex" does not need the vote be called upon to prove that the women in their sections are without grievance?

In plain words, let chivalry be arraigned and made to justify itself. Is it the thing of perfect honor and protective tenderness, deep-rooted in adequate laws, or only buncombe designed to cloak prejudice, sordid motives and evil privileges? There are many cases, the citation of which will not only make the point clear, but may also lead to a better understanding of the bitternesses and ugly resentments that are clouding and confusing the entire equal suffrage question.

SENATOR TILLMAN, of South Carolina, for instance, bases his opposition upon the belief that the ballot will "mar the beauty and dim the luster of the glorious womanhood with which we have been familiar," and prefaces all of his attacks by the insistence that his "known reverence for good women" will prevent him from being understood.

The slightest inquiry into this beauty and luster, however, develops almost unspeakable conditions. The statute-books of South Carolina do not contain one single law for the protection of the working woman, thousands of whom are in the cotton mills. The father is the sole and despotic owner of the children, being able to deed them away from the mother if he wishes, and there are no laws that permit a wife to control her own property or her own earnings.

No matter how drunken, worthless or brutal a husband may become, divorce is practically impossible, and if the woman flees the roof that such conditions have made unbearable, the state regards her almost as a fugitive slave who may not be fed or sheltered.

South Carolina is one of the few commonwealths that still permit children of twelve to be worked eleven hours a day, and as if this did not give sufficient opportunity to the robbers of cradles, birth certificates are not required, and the entire appropriation for factory inspection is but three thousand five hundred dollars a year.

It also stands almost alone in refusing to declare prostitution an outlaw industry, nor is the loathsome business of procuring frowned upon by an act of any kind. The one protection against lust is the Unwritten Law, which, says the state's foremost citizen, "is the best law to protect woman's virtue that I ever heard of."

Why bother about prevention when the guilty men may be "shot down like dogs?" There are, to be sure, many women without the necessary father or brother, but it is assumed that such as these would merely mention their needs to any chivalrous gentleman that happened to be passing. A simple matter, a trifling courtesy, since it has been loudly declared that the slayers would be acquitted "without the jury leaving the box."

Nor is this all that is done for the American queen in the "glorious state that smiles under the moral rays of God's blessed sunshine. Education is not permitted to unsettle her placid contemplation of the beauties of her special brand of chivalry, for all the efforts of the women have not been able to secure the passage of a compulsory

(Continued on Page 24)

FIGURE 9.2. First page of "Chivalry versus Justice," article in the March 1915 *Pictorial Review*, with decorations by Edward A. Wilson.

A California banker, John Hyde Braly, considered his finest life accomplishment the work of his California Political Equality League and its goal of awakening men to the importance of women's suffrage. In 1914, the attorney Gilbert E. Roe, in an eye-opening speech that became a popular pamphlet, dissected all the ways New York law discriminated against women. Eminent men of science filled an entire page of the February 15, 1914 *New York Times*, giving the lie to assertions of women's biological and intellectual inferiority.

A 1911 article in the *Century* by Judge Ben B. Lindsey of Colorado and George Creel provided evidence of how well women's suffrage was working in the West. Their piece functioned as a counter to the journalist Richard Barry's antisuffrage reportage in *Pearson's* and *Ladies' Home Journal*. In the years before Creel's 1917 White House appointment, he wrote numerous cause-supporting articles for popular mass circulation magazines, like one in *Pictorial Review* titled, "Chivalry versus Justice: Why the Women of the Nation Demand the Right to Vote." NAWSA republished it as a pamphlet, as it did a number of Max Eastman's speeches and essays and those by other influential men. Throughout the decade, eminent suffragists like Dewey and Wise argued the prosuffrage case in published symposia, or collections of short essays or opinion statements on a given subject. They would present fresh arguments, or at least rely on their personal appeal as presenters of well-worn ones. And Creel, a real movement firebrand, engineered provocative months-long letter-to-the-editor skirmishes with the antis in the *New York Times*. That changed once Creel accepted Wilson's appointment at CPI. Given his then daily contact with President Wilson, NWP and NAWSA suffrage leaders would still seek him out, but his new position left him unable to advocate for suffrage publicly, or perhaps even privately, since the president had not yet decided to support the federal initiative.[30]

As Funders

As the Nineteenth Amendment passed in 1919, Carrie Chapman Catt, writing for the *New York Times*, expressed gratitude to those men, who, "like the women, lived in strictest economy so that there should be more to give to the woman's cause." For many of the elites who signed on in those last years, "strictest economy" is not the operative term.[31] Like other wealthy women who supported the movement with transformative gifts,[32] generosity does not appear to have impinged on their lavish lifestyles. Their contributions attracted notice in the press. Clarence Mackay's fortune was the reason Katherine Mackay could split costs with Alva Belmont to promote and stage an important Albany mass meeting that cost them what today would be $70,000.

Both women told a *New York Sun's* reporter they were "glad of it." Although Mackay's largesse ended with her divorce, Belmont had no such issue. Long before she became active for suffrage, she had divorced a Vanderbilt and inherited a fortune from Belmont at his death. No gift, however, matched the largess or the headlines of the bequest of a woman who was not even a movement activist, Miriam Folline Leslie, the widow of the eponymous publisher of *Frank Leslie's Illustrated*, her third husband. To NAWSA, she left the entirety of her nearly two-million-dollar estate, much of which she earned with her "editorial eye and business acumen," having merged some titles and added new ones. She turned the failing company she inherited from Leslie into a moneymaker.[33]

The suffrage movement had other wealthy funders and fundraisers, powerhouses such as Vira Boarman Whitehouse and the *Tribune's* Helen Rogers Reid.[34] Both of their husbands were Men's Leaguers, active on the campaign finance, legislative, or publicity committees. George Foster Peabody was the Men's League's "financial mainstay" from the start, and Belmont's underwriting enabled NAWSA to establish impressive New York City headquarters alongside those of her Political Equality Association until she switched allegiance and became a benefactor of Alice Paul. The brick mansion that was NWP headquarters in Washington, DC, which Belmont also financed, is now the Belmont-Paul Women's Equality National Monument.[35]

In-kind contributions took many forms. In 1914, the men-only policies of two exclusive New York City clubs, the Lotos and the Manhattan, thwarted women reporters from crossing their thresholds to cover the first meeting of a men's campaign committee for the federal initiative. Laidlaw immediately offered the ground floor and cafeteria of his family's banking offices as an alternative venue. "Manhattan Club Doors Closed to Fair Reporters and Equal Rights Champions Distressed by Rule That Causes Woe," was the headline in the *Tribune*. The Laidlaws organized suffrage teas at Hazeldean, their Long Island summer estate, which became the subject of a photo-filled 1915 feature in the *Atlanta Constitution*. "Health, Beauty and Happiness Are Matters of Diet," the headline read; "Food and the Ballot Interdependent, Says Mrs. Laidlaw."[36]

The Laidlaws also set the pace in on-the-spot contributions. At the 1913 state convention, the *Tribune* reported their pledge of a hundred dollars a month for twenty-five straight months—more than $60,000 today—to support the upcoming 1915 suffrage referendum campaign, the one that failed. In short, elites brought keen social, organizational, and fundraising skills from their professions as attorneys, clergy, journalists, and financiers, or from their social and charitable endeavors. Both their presence and their finesse as recruiters attracted other new supporters in just as good a position to meet urgent movement needs, even if only on an ad hoc basis. In 1912, Catt acknowledged in an interview with the *New York Morning Telegraph* how in two short years, the movement's men, "the thinking men of our country—the brains of our colleges, of commerce and literature," had become "a blessing to us."[37]

As Enablers of Political Opportunity

Political opportunities, broadly defined, include signals of increased receptivity to a movement's goals from elected and governmental officials.[38] For the suffrage campaign, the apparent prototype for mobilizing a broad swath of East Coast elites in the 1910s was the playbook Catt developed more than a decade earlier for the Colorado campaign, her call for "centralized control of affiliate organizations, systematic precinct canvassing, endorsements from all political parties," "elite leadership," and a "society plan" designed, in her words, to "enhance movement respectability."[39] Historians explain that with politicized elite women as the target, momentum in Colorado began with six Denver clubwomen who founded the Colorado Equal Suffrage Association. The western movement won the support of political office-holders, who had the potential to become suffrage allies.[40]

The proximity to political power of many of the men of suffrage provided another boon. Along with Creel, the attorney Dudley Field Malone held two successive top patronage posts in the Wilson administration, rewards for his California campaigning for candidate Wilson in 1911. Malone courted California's newly minted women voters by promising the presidential hopeful's eventual support for the federal suffrage amendment. Malone's life before, during, and after suffrage (political campaigns, controversial causes, celebrity divorce lawyer in Paris, bon vivant, attorney in the Scopes trial, business manager for Channel-swimmer Gertrude Ederle and boxer Gene Tunney) never seemed to leave the nation's front pages.

Deployment of elites had more radical uses, too. By tactical intention, women with pedigree were among the sixteen picketers from Alice Paul's NWP that Washington, DC, police arrested in 1917: Eunice Dana Brannan, the wife of the president of Bellevue Hospital and the daughter of the late *New York Sun* editor, Charles A. Dana; Florence Bayard, a daughter of a former secretary of state and ambassador to Britain; Elizabeth Selden Rogers, a sister-in-law of a former secretary of war, Henry L. Stimson, and a descendant of Roger Sherman, one of the signers of the Declaration of Independence; Alison Hopkins, the wife of J.A.H. Hopkins, who chaired New Jersey's Progressive State Committee during Wilson's 1916 presidential campaign; and Matilda

Gardner, wife of the syndicated columnist Gilson Gardner. The protesters' husbands had access to the president and protested to Wilson immediately and in person. The *New York Times* and *Washington Post* gave the arrests front-page coverage, with the *Times* drawing attention to the women's social station.

In time, the flame turned hotter under top political figures who played both sides of the suffrage question, not only the mayors, city council members, state representatives and governors, but also congressmen and presidential contenders from Theodore Roosevelt to Wilson. Dudley Malone, who at the time was the clandestine lover of Alice Paul's lieutenant, Doris Stevens, went the furthest in pushing the cause. To protest Wilson's recalcitrance, he abruptly resigned his coveted presidential patronage post as collector of the Port of New York, generating front-page coverage across the country and worshipful appreciation from both NAWSA and the NWP leaders. Alice Duer Miller wrote a poem in his honor, published in the *Tribune*. Several Men's Leaguers enjoyed close ties to Wilson, including George Foster Peabody and even Rabbi Wise, who until the Democrat Wilson's run for the presidency was a Republican.

As it turned out, the Great War itself, in many ways, created suffrage's greatest political opportunity. Although it was likely not the only reason, Wilson credited the sacrificial engagement of women suffragists in the war effort for his sharp turn toward support for the constitutional amendment campaign, but only in the year before Congress passed it.

Men's Leaguers extended their value with pro bono legal, financial, political, and business acumen, their standing as academics and clergy, or their access to usefully influential peers in local, state, and national government. Because their support was organized, expertise of this nature and variety was easy to summon[41] and all their good works were news fodder. Their useful connections and admired popular standing provided what NAWSA described in its official history as "invaluable help" as they transformed the hen-pecked pejorative "suffrage husbands" into a title of distinction.

Conclusion

Peabody's actions on behalf of women's suffrage exemplify all the key reasons why the organized engagement of elites as framers, funders, facilitators, and influencers mattered so greatly in the movement's success. By the time that he became president and chief benefactor of the New York Men's League, his business and philanthropic activities had long been well chronicled in the press. As a former treasurer of the Democratic Party and a prominent, active Wilson supporter, he had a warm relationship with the president throughout both of his terms in office, even after declining Wilson's offer to join his first cabinet as secretary of the treasury.[42] In 1911, just as NAWSA was gathering in Kentucky for its annual convention, Peabody, a University of Georgia alumni, wrote to the editor of the *Athens Banner* to defend the suffrage movement, prompted by a *Louisville Courier-Journal* editorial against it. The *Atlanta Constitution* reprinted Peabody's letter to the *Banner*, after describing the respected Georgia-born financier as one of the men of suffrage "impelled by the duty they feel of a just cause." Peabody repeatedly spoke out publicly on behalf of the movement and persuaded those in his circle, including his late-life wife, Katrina Trask, the wealthy widow of his partner, Spencer Trask, who announced her influential support just days before the New York State vote. Framer, funder, facilitator, media influencer: the same story outline could easily apply to any number of men and women in this subset of suffrage movement actors and their versatile roles in the movement's ultimate success.

In New York at least, the positive impact of the involvement of the suffrage elites lingered long after the vote was won. With the hindsight of 1933, the New York State League of Women Voters, a NAWSA successor organization, emblazoned the names of eighty-three all-time, all-state suffrage greats on a bronze plaque that still hangs in the State House in Albany. Mackay and Belmont are likely pointed omissions, given that Mackay's involvement ended with her divorce and that Belmont threw her support to Alice Paul. Still, the names of nearly a fifth of those honored on the plaque also appear in the New York Social Register of 1917, that is, women plus Laidlaw.[43] Given that the New York campaign was nearly sixty years old before society men and women began joining in appreciable numbers, and that those earlier decades probably included many others who may have been equally deserving of such recognition, it is notable that this honor would go to so many elites from the movement's last decade. Their long-forgotten names appear in the company of the suffrage movement's earliest and most enduring state and national movement paragons: Susan B. Anthony, Elizabeth Cady Stanton, Shaw, and Catt, still alive until 1947, who had earlier paid poignant homage to suffrage's "long noble array."

Again, just as valuable was the celebrity-style media attention that the wider public's interest in the elites attracted casually, often simply because they occupied boxes at a Carnegie Hall suffrage event or seats at a banquet, or because they were respected writers, editors, or publishers of popular mainstream publications who doubled as canny undeclared campaign publicists. In the aggregate, the activism and media celebrity status of this organized high-prestige group pressed and held down almost every strategic campaign button. They brought momentum. They brought panache. The value of the multichannel media conduit they opened is hard to overestimate. They made the effort "easier and happier work," in James Lees Laidlaw's mission statement phrase, because they joined in it.

Notes

1. Eleanor Flexner, *Century of Struggle: The Woman's Rights Movement in the United States* (Cambridge, MA: Belknap Press of Harvard University Press, 1975), 256. Also, for a good statistical and narrative summary of the dramatic growth of the movement in the 1910s, see Roger Karapin, "Opportunity/Threat Spirals in the U.S. Suffrage Movement and German Anti-Immigration Movements," *Mobilization* 16, no. 1 (February 2011): esp. 70–71.

2. Carrie Chapman Catt, "Why Suffrage Fight Took 50 Years," *New York Times*, June 15, 1919, 82.

3. Brooke Kroeger, *The Suffragents: How Women Used Men to Get the Vote* (Albany: SUNY Press, 2017). (Please note unless otherwise indicated, this book, with its extensive endnotes, is the source of cited material in this essay, retrievable digitally via name or word search or by consulting its index.) Also published in 2017: Susan Goodier and Karen Pastorello, *Women Will Vote: Winning Suffrage in New York State* (Ithaca, NY: Cornell University Press, 2017); Joan Marie Johnson, *Funding Feminism: Monied Women, Philanthropy, and the Women's Movement, 1870–1967* (Chapel Hill: University of North Carolina, 2017); Johanna Neuman, *Gilded Suffragists: The New York Socialites Who Fought for Women's Right to Vote* (New York: NYU Press, 2017).

4. "Women Citizens Pledge Votes to Nation's Welfare," *New York Times*, November 8, 1917, 1.

5. R. C. Beadle, "The Men's League for Woman Suffrage of the State of New York," *Trend*, 6, no. 2 (November 1913): 266–75. The states he named were New York, Illinois, Iowa, Kansas, Kentucky, Maine, Minnesota, Missouri, Montana, New Hampshire, Ohio, Pennsylvania, Tennessee, Texas, Virginia, Connecticut, Maryland, New Jersey, Massachusetts, California, Colorado, Oregon, Washington, Georgia, and Delaware.

6. See especially the Women's Suffrage Collection at the Schlesinger Library, Harvard University; the Woman Suffrage and Women's Rights Collection in the Archives & Special Collections Library at Vassar College; the Suffrage Collection 1850–2009, Five College Archives & Manuscript Collection, Sophia Smith Collection, Smith College; and the Library of Congress.

7. See the numerous references listed in Deana A. Rohlinger and Catherine Corrigall-Brown, "Social Movements and Mass Media in a Global Context," in *The Wiley Blackwell Companion to Social Movements*, 2nd ed., ed. David A. Snow, Sarah A. Soule, Hanspeter Kreisi, and Holly J. McCammon (New York: John Wiley & Sons, 2019), 131–46, esp. 142–47.

8. Roger Karapin, "Opportunity/Threat Spirals in the US Women's Suffrage and

German Anti-Immigration Movements," *Mobilization* 16, no. 1 (January 2011): 72. Before the Washington State victory of 1910, no state campaign had succeeded since Utah's in 1896. "Those gains increased the movement's power and success chances," Karapin writes in describing the spiral, "which in turn helped it gain the support of politicians who now had to face female voters or at least began to see women's suffrage as likely to be adopted in their states."

9. "Eastern Society Suffragists Make Plea for Equal Ballot," *Billings Gazette*, February 7, 1914, 8.

10. Bob Edwards, John D. McCarthy, and Dane R. Mataic, "The Resource Context of Social Movements," in *The Wiley Blackwell Companion to Social Movements*, ed. Snow, Soule, Kriesi, and McCammon, 79–97; and in previous editions: Bob Edwards and John D. McCarthy, "Resources and Social Movement Mobilization," in *The Blackwell Companion to Social Movements*, ed. David A. Snow, Sara A. Soule, and Hanspeter Kriesi (Malden, MA: Blackwell Publishing, 2004, 2007), 125–28.

11. William A. Gamson, "Bystanders, Public Opinion and the Media," in *The Blackwell Companion to Social Movements*, ed. Snow, Soule, and Kreisi, 242–61, esp. 243.

12. Francesca M. Cancian and Bonnie L. Ross, "Mass Media and the Women's Movement, 1900–1977," *Journal of Applied Behavioral Science* 17, no. 1 (January 1981): 13–15.

13. Heather McKee Hurwitz and Alison Dahl Crossley, "Gender and Social Movements," in *The Wiley Blackwell Companion to Social Movements*, ed. Snow, Soule, Kreisi, and McCammon, 537–52, describe gender-related opportunities and constraints as "central to the emergence, nature and outcomes of social movements." For descriptions of how gendered opportunity structures (e.g., the changing or accepted role of women at a given point in history) shape the dynamics, organizations, and outcomes of social movements, see Holly J. McCammon and Karen E. Campbell, "Winning the Vote in the West: The Political Successes of the Women's Suffrage Movement, 1866–1919," *Gender and Society* 15, no. 1 (February 2001): 55–82. See also Sidney Tarrow, *Power in Movement: Social Movements, Collective Action, and Politics* (Cambridge: Cambridge University Press, 1996), 88, 98, 170–86.

14. See myriad entries in archival repositories (e.g., Proquest Historical, news papers.com, fultonhistory.com) for 1909 to 1920 for the search terms "Mrs. Frank Vanderlip" and "suffrage" or for "Mrs. Norman deR. Whitehouse" and "suffrage."

15. See generally, Neuman, *Gilded Suffragists*; Kroeger, *Suffragents*; Johnson, *Funding Feminism*, all well indexed.

16. Fabio Rojas and Brayden G. King, "How Social Movements Interact with Organizations and Fields: Protest, Institutions, and Beyond," in *The Wiley Blackwell Companion to Social Movements*, ed. Snow, Soule, Kriesi, and McCammon, 203–19.

17. McCammon and Campbell, "Winning the Vote in the West," 55–82.

18. On Belmont, see Johnson, *Funding Feminism*, 23, 42–43; Neuman, *Gilded Suffragists*, 55–56, 112, 146; Goodier and Pastorello, *Women Will Vote*, 71–73.

19. "Mrs. Belmont Invites Negro Women to Join the 'Cause,'" *Detroit Free Press*, February 7, 1910, 10.

20. See Sylvia D. Hoffert, *Alva Vanderbilt Belmont: Unlikely Champion of Women's Rights* (Bloomington: Indiana University Press, 2011.)

21. In 1907, Blatch founded the Equality League of Self-Supporting Women, later renamed the Women's Political Union.

22. See Neuman, *Gilded Suffragists*, 5–22.

23. "Woman Suffrage Number," *Puck* 77, February 13, 1915, cover, 1.

24. "Former Hawley Company Official Started Career as Reporter and Artist," *New York Herald-Tribune*, May 1, 1944, 12. Ray Brown was a newspaperman and illustrator, who worked for the *Chicago Times*, later the *Chicago Times-Herald*, and in New York was a vice president of the Hawley Advertising Company. Gertrude Brown was also a concert pianist.

25. See, for example, "The Minority Report on Equal Suffrage," *Harper's Weekly*, April 26, 1879, and fifteen years later, "Women's Voices Heard," *Boston Globe*, January 19, 1894, 4.

26. McCammon and Campbell, "Winning the Vote in the West," 55–82.

27. Brooke Kroeger, "Wise vs. Silverman, or New York's Historic Rabbinical Women's Suffrage Smack-Down," *Tablet*, April 27, 2017, https://www.tabletmag.com/jewish-arts-and-culture/books/230486/wise-vs-silverman-womens-suffrage.

28. "Mrs. Mackay Pleads for Equal Suffrage," *New York Times*, January 16, 1909, 18; and "Mrs. Clarence H. Mackay Shows Devotion to Cause," *Boston Globe*, July 27, 1909, 7.

29. W. E. B. Du Bois, "Woman Suffrage," *The Crisis* 9, no. 5 (April 1915): 283.

30. See Kroeger, *The Suffragents*, for indexed references to Creel, Barry, Lindsay, Dewey, and Wise.

31. Neuman, *Gilded Suffragists*, 51–56.

32. See generally, Johnson, *Funding Feminism*.

33. Johnson, *Funding Feminism*, 39–40.

34. Neuman, *Gilded Suffragists*; Johnson, *Funding Feminism*.

35. The Belmont-Paul Women's Equality National Monument website: https://www.nps.gov/bepa/index.htm.

36. Antonia Petrash, *Long Island and the Woman Suffrage Movement* (Charleston, SC: History Press, 2013), 87–97. "Health, Beauty and Happiness Are Matters of Diet," *Atlanta Constitution*, July 25, 1915, B16.

37. Theodora Bean, "The Greatest Woman in Suffrage and the Greatest Story Ever Written About Her," *New York Morning Telegraph*, December 29, 1912.

38. Marco Giugni, "Political Opportunities: From Tilly to Tilly," *Swiss Political Science Review* 15, no. 2 (February 2009): 361–68.

39. Rebecca J. Mead, *How the Vote Was Won: Woman Suffrage in the Western United States, 1868–1914* (New York: NYU Press, 2004), 64.

40. See both McCammon and Campbell, "Winning the Vote in the West," 65; and Mead, *How the Vote Was Won*, 64.

41. For a concise version of how editors opened the gates to featured suffrage coverage, see Brooke Kroeger, "When the Media Elite Threw Their Fedoras into the

Ring for Women's Rights," November 16, 2017, https://www.gothamcenter.org/blog /when-the-media-elite-threw-their-fedoras-into-the-ring-for-womens-rights.

42. Letter, Peabody to Wilson, March 20, 1913, as cited in Louise Ware, *George Foster Peabody: Banker, Philanthropist, Publicist* (Athens: University of Georgia Press, 1951), 167.

43. Brooke Kroeger, "A New Book Pays Tribute to the Society Women Who Paved the Way for Suffrage," *Town & Country*, September 5, 2017, https://townandcountrymag .com/society/tradition/g12158824/suffragents-brooke-kroeger. Sixteen names on the plaque are in the 1917 *Social Register*.

10

After Suffrage

An Uncharted Path

MAURINE BEASLEY

Four years after the Nineteenth Amendment was added to the US Constitution, a determined Eleanor Roosevelt and a group of like-minded women interested in social welfare legislation sat all night long outside a room at the Democratic National Convention. They had been appointed to a committee ostensibly to prepare planks for a party platform of special interest to women voters. With Roosevelt as chair, the group had worked for three months to compile recommendations that encompassed the objectives of leading women's organizations. These included equal pay for women workers, an end to child labor, and measures to secure safe and healthy working conditions. Unfortunately, they waited in vain. As the sun rose, the all-male Resolutions Committee voted to refuse to allow the women to present their proposals. Committee members obviously wanted to keep power solely in their own hands.[1]

Roosevelt, having begun her own political career as a helpmate to her husband, Franklin D. Roosevelt, but also a voice in her own right, found the 1924 convention a bitter learning experience. In fact, women's suffrage turned out to be far less meaningful than both men and women had expected. As Gail Collins, the first woman editorial page editor of the *New York Times*, concluded eight decades later, "The shock for suffragists was that it hardly seemed to have any consequences at all." Collins's survey of history noted that women generally voted the way their husbands and male relatives did, "because they shared the same loyalties to class, ethnic group, and region."[2] Political bosses, saloonkeepers, and employers of child labor, who had feared that women would try to vote to reform society, could breathe a sigh of relief. Women did not vote as a bloc or disrupt a white male power structure.

Men in charge would not need to pay much attention to women voters. As Roosevelt learned, women who sought to propose legislation soon found that men politicians refused to consider them equal political partners.

In retrospect, US women were never likely to constitute a solid voting bloc. On the one hand, while reliable data on women's voting habits after suffrage is sparse, the number of votes cast in the 1920 election represented only a 30 percent increase over the total four years earlier. That is, the percentage of eligible voters who cast ballots in 1920 went down.[3] Scholars have not agreed as to why more women did not vote. Obviously, women did not see suffrage as a reason for ending voluntary associations such as women's clubs in favor of activities within political parties.[4] But some women were not allowed to cast ballots at all. Suffrage leadership, seeking support from white southern women, had decided years earlier not to protest a growing movement to institute segregation and voter suppression in states of the former Confederacy.[5] Segregated states managed to keep African American women, as well as African American men, from the polls. The middle-class and upper-class white women, with some working-class allies, who dominated the suffrage campaign had overlooked questions of race, while claiming that women voters would bring a moral force to politics by pushing social welfare reforms that men had been loath to institute. They soon learned that the ballot did not necessarily advance the idea that women were morally superior.

In the first volume of her autobiography, Roosevelt expressed her disappointment at discovering during the 1924 Democratic National Convention that women were "of very little importance," commenting that they waited "outside the door of all important meetings."[6] Committed to advocacy for the less fortunate, such as immigrant women toiling in sweatshops, Roosevelt did not abandon her objective of seeking change within the Democratic Party. Having followed her husband's lead, and busy with her five children and the social duties expected of the wife of a rising political figure, Roosevelt did not work for suffrage; she converted to suffrage only after he came out for it in 1911 while a state senator in New York.[7] Once suffrage was gained, however, and Roosevelt began to take part in Democratic party politics herself, she recognized the significance of voting. In the early 1920s she was politically active not only as the surrogate for her husband while he was recuperating from infantile paralysis, but also to develop her own intellectual and organizational abilities that previously had been submerged in the lifestyle of an upper-class wife and mother. Her dual endeavors gave her an unusual opportunity to analyze the situation of women in politics after suffrage. In what she wrote about herself and in what was written about her, she pointed out that women needed patience, diligence, and experience to make use of the vote. Most of all they needed role models who were not men.

Eleanor Roosevelt Calls for Women "Bosses"

Writing in 1928 in *Red Book*, a popular women's magazine, Roosevelt lamented that women "have no actual influence or say at all in the consequential councils of their parties."[8] Although major political parties reorganized after suffrage to provide roles for women on their local, state, and national committees, "there is a widespread male hostility—age-old, perhaps—against sharing with them any actual control," she continued.[9] The only way to get men to accept women in all party affairs would be "to elect, accept and back women political bosses."[10] Recognizing the negative connotation of the term "boss," she described "bosses" as political leaders who exercised authority in a particular area. "Against the men bosses there must be women bosses who can talk as equals, with the backing of a coherent organization of women voters behind them," Roosevelt emphasized. Without the ability to choose leaders, she saw women voters as helpless, trapped in "incoherent anarchy."[11]

Did Roosevelt see herself as a "boss"? Possibly. The same year that the *Red Book* article appeared, she was named director of women's activities for the Democratic Party. She also headed a woman's advisory committee backing the unsuccessful presidential campaign of Al Smith. In the same election Franklin Roosevelt won the governorship of New York. Probably due to the visibility of both Roosevelts, the *Red Book* article gained considerable attention. A *New York Times Magazine* interview with Roosevelt was headlined "A Woman Speaks Her Political Mind."[12] The interviewer praised her political knowledge, yet carefully pictured her as a wife and mother of five children whose "upbringing has been her first consideration. She believes that a woman fitted to serve her community or her country can show that fitness best in the management of her own home."[13] As Blanche Cook, Eleanor Roosevelt's biographer, pointed out, the interview illustrated the double bind for women in politics. To be accepted they had to be seen more as homemakers unselfishly interested in serving others and less as energetic players in the world of politics.

This chapter uses various periodicals to illustrate the challenges, rebuffs, and controversies that swirled around the former suffragists after the Nineteenth Amendment took effect in 1920. It offers an overview that shows how postsuffragists fought among themselves, with some emphasizing the right of women to work outside the home on the same basis as men. Others were less interested in equality than in measures to improve conditions for mothers and children within domestic settings, and laws protecting women workers at the lower end of the economic scale. The chapter concludes by considering whether periodicals framed suffrage in a way that made exercising the ballot seem more of a burden on women than a cause for jubilation.

The Roosevelt article and interview are typical of women's political presence in the periodicals of the day. These involved cultural conflicts over both the image and reality of women's interests as well as the way women did or did not make use of the vote. Having been so focused on one objective—winning the vote—after 1920, suffragist activists were left adrift, veering off in different directions and philosophically unable to unite on a single path forward that resonated with the nation's twenty-six million newly enfranchised women voters. Warring factions among women soon agreed on one point: gaining the vote did not mean that women had acquired political power.

Indeed, after World War I ended in 1918, suffrage, with its de facto exclusion of black women in the South and limited use by poor white women, as well as opposition from middle-class and upper-class matrons content with traditional roles, composed a relatively small dimension of women's experience. Taking advantage of increased economic and social freedom that stemmed from participating in the war effort, during what became known as the Roaring Twenties, women expressed themselves in matters of dress and conduct apart from the ballot box. In the popular imagination, suffragists seemed dull and old-fashioned compared with the "flapper," a young woman who wore short skirts, bobbed her hair, smoked cigarettes, and was far more willing than her mother to experiment with sex.

At the same time antisuffragists upheld a conservative role for women in the face of change; they opposed women competing with men at the polls. Even on the eve of passage of the suffrage amendment, the National Association Opposed to Woman Suffrage plausibly claimed in 1918 to have 450,000 women members. Suffrage was opposed by a host of regional, business, and religious interests: southerners did not want to enfranchise more black voters; wealthy brewers worked behind the scenes with saloonkeepers to defeat suffrage; eastern city political machines covertly backed by the Catholic Church fought suffrage, as did big business, which feared women's suffrage would disturb profits. Members of antisuffrage organizations believed the emerging feminist philosophy threatened their privileged way of life, which they based on the idea of separate spheres for men and women.

The *Woman Patriot*, the virulent publication of the National Association Opposed to Woman Suffrage, called feminism "a disease."[14] This journal first appeared in Washington, DC, in 1918, and represented a merger of three antisuffrage newspapers, *The Remonstrance* (which dated back to 1890), *Anti-Suffrage Notes*, and the *Women's Protest*. Dedicated to waging war on what it called "the two great enemies of our civilization, feminism and socialism," the *Woman Patriot* claimed urban immigrant women were attracted to socialism and that these women would flock to the polls, while women on farms and in small towns would largely stay at home once enfranchised.[15] The weekly continued until 1932, picturing communists as plotting to take over the United States and opposing efforts to outlaw child labor on grounds poor children should not be deprived of the right to work. It attacked federal legislation designed to aid women and children, contending government should not interfere with childrearing. Other periodicals in the 1920s manifested different degrees of interest in the act of women voting. Advertisements in mass circulation women's magazines featured attractive "flappers" and happy housewives rather than earnest individuals studying political issues. Advertisers apparently sensed that many women had tired of the long battle over suffrage.

The National Woman's Party Sees Limitations of Suffrage

Headed by the single-minded activist Alice Paul, the National Woman's Party (NWP), which had represented the militant wing of the suffrage movement, quickly recognized that the vote itself did not change women's status. NWP's magazine *Equal Rights*, founded in 1923, was the chief publication of the day that dared to use the word "feminist" to describe itself. In a declaration of principles published in the first issue of *Equal Rights*, the NWP argued, "women today, although enfranchised, are still in every way subordinate to men before the law, in government, in educational opportunities, in the professions, in the church, in industry and in the home."[16] It issued twenty-nine separate demands for equity, including an end to discrimination in professions and erasing the double standard of sexual conduct so that women would receive the same treatment as men for venereal diseases and the same punishment for sex offenses. The declaration insisted that women should have the same inheritance rights as men, as well as the right to sit on juries, obtain divorces on the same grounds as men, keep their own names after marriage, control their own earnings and property, and act as equal partners in marriages.

In 1924, the year that the Democratic Party's Resolutions Committee shut out Roosevelt and her committee, *Equal Rights* warned that women had little place in men's third-party movements. If parties had separate women's divisions, women were excluded from general participation in decision-making, and "their autonomy was curtailed by dependence on men for financing," the magazine pointed out; if there were no separate division, women were still "out of the main current of the movement."[17] As Roosevelt had learned, the same could be said for the position of women in major political parties.

The NWP focused solely on constitutional equality. It drew up and campaigned for an amendment to the US Constitution that stated: "Men and women shall have equal rights throughout the United States and in every place subject to its jurisdiction." Introduced in Congress for the first of several times in 1923, it was originally named for Lucretia Mott, the early suffragist heroine. In later decades the language of the proposed amendment was changed only slightly. In 1972 Congress passed the now-named Equal Rights Amendment in this form: "Equality of rights under the law shall not be denied or abridged by the United States or any state on account of sex." Although the ERA still is pending before state legislatures, so far it has not been ratified by the necessary thirty-eight states so has not become law.

Women's Organizations Fight Proposed Equal Rights Amendment

Almost all women's organizations that had backed suffrage strongly opposed this equal rights amendment. Roosevelt stood with those who feared that it would wipe out protective legislation for working women. This opposition, reported in the news media of the day, tore apart what was left of the suffrage movement, although the primary suffrage organization, the National American Woman Suffrage Association (NAWSA), already had transitioned itself into the nonpartisan League of Women Voters (LWV).[18] Reformers, many of whom were teachers and social workers, had been mainstays of the NAWSA, which represented a far larger constituency than the NWP and had a much longer history of fighting for suffrage. NAWSA had contended women voters would be "social housekeepers" who were morally superior to men, although it also used the somewhat contradictory argument that women deserved the ballot because they were human beings equal to men. The LWV was committed to careful study of issues before taking positions on proposed legislation regardless of political affiliations. It opposed this new amendment in common with leading women's associations including the National Consumer League, which fought against sweatshops; the American Association of University Women; the Women's Trade Union League (which enlisted upper-class women as well as workers to improve working conditions for women); the General Federation of Women's Clubs; the Young Women's

Christian Association; and the National Council of Jewish Women. While these organizations had argued that women deserved the ballot, each was considerably more moderate than the NWP and had an agenda that was broader than voting and political activity.

The weakness of this coalition was readily apparent in what happened to NAWSA after passage of the Nineteenth Amendment. Before suffrage NAWSA had counted several million members. When NAWSA transformed itself into the LWV, barely more than 100,000 joined the new organization.[19] The LWV urged members, who were organized in state and local units, to improve the political process by educating themselves on legislation, to seek out the best possible legislation and candidates regardless of sex. For example, the LWV and other women's organizations supported legislation to combat infant mortality and deaths of mothers in childbirth. Congress passed this act in 1921, fearing that women would use the ballot to retaliate against politicians who did not support women's issues. As it turned out, it need not have been concerned. The first legislation to provide federal funds for medical care, the act provided matching funds to states to set up prenatal clinics and public health centers. Faced with resistance from the American Medical Association (AMA), not all states moved to implement the legislation. The AMA argued that it took health care away from individuals and delivered it into the impersonal hand of government.[20] The NWP also opposed the act as an example of the kind of special interest legislation for women that it wanted to eliminate. In 1929 Congress, no longer afraid of outrage from newly enfranchised women, voted to discontinue the program. By then, the political world realized that women voters "need not be granted any special concessions."[21]

The LWV drew in women willing to give money, time, and talent to political issues and provided an outlet for reform-minded voters. Roosevelt gained some of her initial political skills in the LWV. As historian Susan Ware commented, "Its brand of intensive study, training for citizenship and sophisticated political action show one direction that women took in public life after they won the vote in 1920."[22] But many women had no time or inclination to master the intricacies of policies and politics.

Both the Democratic and Republican parties set up clubs for women voters, but many women still viewed voting as a masculine activity. Party newsletters pleaded with women to register and vote and stressed that voting did not endanger women's femininity. Club activities often ran the risk of not being taken seriously. Emily Newell Blair, vice-chair of the Democratic National Committee, raised the question "Are Women a Failure in Politics?" in *Harper's* in 1925, answering that their progress was slow.[23] In 1926, for example, *The Bulletin*, a slick-paper magazine published under Blair's direction by the Woman's National Democratic Club in Washington, DC, reprinted an item from the *New York Sun* to show what others were saying about the club. Making light of the club's mission, the *Sun* delivered a slap at the well-dressed upper-class women pictured in *The Bulletin*: "Those who feared that politics would make women mannish may calm their fears. The Woman's National Democratic Club has reversed the role and put politics into ruffles. . . . The new clubhouse on New Hampshire Avenue right in the heart of Washington's most exclusive residential section and itself one of the finest old homes on the street, is the last word in putting 'ritz' into politics."[24]

The LWV promoted its activities in the *Woman Citizen*, formerly the NAWSA organ. Before women voted in their first presidential election in 1920, it pictured a blind woman on its cover and asked readers, "Are You Blind Politically?" referring to women's need to educate themselves before casting ballots.[25] In 1921 the publication declared itself an independent women's journal, although it continued to devote four pages in each issue to LWV activities. The *Citizen* dealt with a wider array of topics than *Equal Rights* and stayed away from the feminist label. With a circulation of 20,000 in the 1920s compared to little more than 2,000 for *Equal Rights*, it aimed expansively at acting as "the mirror of the life of the up-to-date intelligent woman."[26] As such, the issue of voting was mingled with other causes. The magazine's support of the peace movement led to charges from the Daughters of the American Revolution, then engaged in an "anti-Red" campaign, that the LWV was radical and unpatriotic, charges that the LWV determinedly refuted.[27] Reflecting a middle-class reformer's interests, the *Woman Citizen* condemned lynching, which was murder by mobs, mainly in the South, to control African Americans. And in line with most women's organizations of the day, it strongly backed prohibition and pressed for an amendment to outlaw child labor, a goal that was never achieved.[28]

Its efforts to serve a relatively diverse readership continued through the 1920s, but the magazine encountered financial problems despite its respectable circulation. As a result, it curiously decided that its name, the *Woman Citizen*, was too militant for prospective subscribers. According to its advertising department, the name had become "a handicap, both in attracting new readers and in appealing to advertisers for their business. Too many people read in the name a magazine devoted to women in politics and *nothing else*."[29] With this backdrop, suspect in the minds of some, in 1928 the publication reappeared as the *Woman's Journal*, taking the name of a publication that went back to the early years of the suffrage campaign. The editor announced the new name did not imply a "limited political field for the magazine."[30] Nevertheless, it folded in 1931.

Equal Rights, which managed to struggle on until 1954, had a far more defined scope. It focused on the Mott Amendment, arguing it was needed because suffrage itself did not eliminate legal inequalities in citizenship, economic opportunity, or social status. It downplayed objections from women's organizations and reformers like Roosevelt who contended that wiping out legal inequality would invalidate protections for women workers such as maximum-hour laws and bans on employment at night or in jobs presumed to be dangerous. In its quest for passage of the Mott Amendment and laws for equality on the state level, *Equal Rights* rarely diverted its attention to other issues. The main exceptions were articles on suffragists' tactics under Paul's leadership, such as picketing the White House and undertaking hunger strikes after being arrested that had brought drama and increased visibility to the suffrage campaign.[31] The magazine also covered international aspects of the equal rights movement and applauded the achievements of NWP members, generally well-educated individuals from elite backgrounds. Attacking discrimination against women, *Equal Rights* portrayed professional women, some of whom were unmarried or involved in same-sex relationships, as dedicated professionals, intent on proving they could succeed as well as men if given equal opportunities.

Journalist Ruby Black Defends against Attacks on Feminists

For instance, Ruby A. Black, the associate editor of *Equal Rights*, wrote a three-page article in 1924 on the discrimination facing qualified women journalists. An exception to many NWP members in that she grew up in relative poverty, Black wrote from firsthand experience. The eighth of nine children born to a pioneer farming family in East Texas, Black had worked her way through the University of Texas, graduating Phi Beta Kappa, by teaching in rural schools and mastering tasks on a country newspaper. The first woman editor of the *Daily Texan*, the university's student newspaper, she had taught journalism at the University of Wisconsin, where she had been a graduate student in economics. She later served as labor editor at a St. Louis daily newspaper. Still, she was unable to find work on a newspaper in the nation's capital, the headquarters of the NWP, since she refused to work, like most women journalists, on women's and society newspaper sections.

Black had joined the NWP at the University of Texas. When she married Herbert Little, a reporter for the United Press in Madison, Wisconsin, in 1922, both agreed she should become a "Lucy Stoner." This term honored women like Lucy Stone, a nineteenth-century suffrage leader, who kept their birth names instead of taking their husbands'. Black's desire to use her own name led to a test case brought by the NWP, on the legality of requiring women to be identified as "wife of" on passports.[32] Ironically, Black herself did not benefit when passports finally were issued to married women in their own names. She had sought a passport because she expected Little to be transferred from Madison to Europe. Instead, United Press sent him to Washington, DC, where he quickly moved ahead in journalism, while Black floundered. Initially she was unable to pay her share of the couple's expenses, a blow to her feminist commitment to economic independence, an NWP tenet. Eventually she established her own news bureau to dispatch political news to newspapers outside Washington, but she never caught up with Little in pay.

Black also submitted freelance articles to magazines, especially on topics that did not fit easily within the pages of *Equal Rights*. In 1925 she sold an article on "Jobs for Women" to *The Nation*, arguing that the increase of 500,000 working women in various fields from 1910 to 1920 alarmed men who wanted to keep more lucrative jobs for themselves.[33] She built this article on statistical information, but she also strove to write about the growth of an unfavorable perception of feminism, particularly by young women. Having given up her graduate study to follow her husband, Black resented the fact that feminists were pictured in the public eye as single women uninterested in the opposite sex and obsessed with causes that purported to elevate women at the expense of men. "'Feminism' has become a term of opprobrium," declared Dorothy Dunbar Bromley, a writer in *Harper's* in 1927. To Bromley, the word conjured up visions of charmless spinsters in flat heels or "the current species who antagonize men with their constant clamor."[34]

Black's attempts to publish articles defending feminists against such attacks had little success. In one unpublished manuscript she wrote: "In the *Atlantic Monthly, Good Housekeeping* and *Vanity Fair*, magazines hardly similar, within the last half-year I have read accounts of the feminist who regards marriage as trivial and the necessity of bearing children as troublesome . . . and thinks she can live without marriage and children."[35] While Black admitted the difficulty of caring for children while managing a successful career, she insisted the feminist "is willing to experiment in ways to improve that machinery."[36] Eventually Black did just that—having a baby girl in 1932 while determinedly continuing her news bureau and tackling the "machinery" problem by importing a widowed relative from Texas to live with the family and bring up her daughter.

Black was pleased when her face appeared on the cover of *Equal Rights* in 1928. In contrast to the numerous pictures of staid, middle-aged women usually seen in the publication, the illustration showed the slightly built Black as a boyish-looking young woman with bobbed hair and bangs.[37] An accompanying story announced that she covered Congress and other Washington news for forty-one newspapers, thereby gaining "another great victory over that great Army whose motto seems to be 'No, we don't want a woman.'"[38] It urged readers who visited the Capitol press galleries to ask, "Who is that little boy?" and predicted they would be told with a smile, "That's no little boy, ma'am, that's Ruby A. Black, from Texas." To *Equal Rights* and the NWP, women deserved the opportunity to shed old roles and compete with men even to the extent of personal appearance. It apparently did not recognize, as did Black in her unpublished manuscripts, that many women wanted a traditional home and family.

New organizations arose like the National Federation of Business and Professional Women (BPW), which was ambivalent, if not entirely negative, on an equal rights amendment in the 1920s but still sought to promote more opportunities for women, including equal pay. Founded in 1919, the BPW appealed to women who held white-collar office jobs as well as women who owned their own businesses or were professionals. In later years these women pushed against protective legislation, which they saw as a barrier to moving ahead, in the federation's monthly magazine, the *Independent Woman*. Started in 1920, the publication served to unify previously isolated organizations of business and professional women in forty-three states that had federated the previous year, inspired by the success of the suffrage movement. Less elite than the American Association of University Women (AAUW), which was open only to college graduates, BPW had no educational requirements for membership. Many members held low-paid clerical positions but aspired to move up in the business world.

Independent Woman's first issue, in January 1920, set the tone for the decade ahead. The cover featured a silhouette of Judge Jean Norris in what the magazine called "her most judicial attitude," captioned, "The First and Only Woman Judge of a New York Court."[39] Accompanying comments said the cover illustration suggested "the high honors to which women may now aspire, and also, in its dignity and feminine grace, we think it typifies the best that woman has to contribute to public life."[40] An editorial scoffed at a bulletin from the Department of Labor that presented a model personal budget for women employed by the US government, who typically were paid less than men. The editorial questioned statisticians who allowed single women almost nothing for recreation because they assumed "some of these expenses would be met by young men."[41]

Independent Woman carried little content on voting in its early issues, instead generally highlighting activities of individual clubs and upbeat stories about federation members who loved their jobs. The magazine avoided partisan political content, although many BPW members were Republicans who favored limits on government. Social reformers were more likely to be Democrats. The July 1921 issue, whose cover featured a silhouette of a mother presenting a birthday cake to her small daughter, was typical: articles offered career advice by promoting new fields for women, such as dental hygiene and playground supervision. Occasionally *Independent Woman* hit directly at men. An editorial headlined "Everybody Satisfied" aimed to humorously reassure women who did not expect to marry. It said, "Sometimes it is far easier to mourn for the husband we have never had than to live with the one we have married, something of a consolation to the unmarried business woman when some man tells her that woman's place is in the home."[42] White faces filled its pages. Like the LWV and the AAUW, the BPW was unwilling to challenge racial segregation nationally.[43] While women's organizations had some local units comprised of African Americans, the central governing bodies refused to integrate for decades.

Periodicals Question the Success of Suffrage

As the 1920s went by, the question of whether suffrage had failed or succeeded attracted considerable journalistic attention.[44] A related debate emerged over whether the "flapper" style of short skirts, backseat petting, and illicit drinking had led to a decline in morality among young women. In 1921 the *Literary Digest* asked college editors, along with editors of religious publications and newspaper journalists, to weigh in on this question. No consensus emerged on morality. Somewhat similarly, the *Literary Digest* surveyed newspaper editors on "Why More Women Don't Vote," and came up with the weak conclusion that women needed "a little more education."[45] Everyone acknowledged, however, that women's roles were changing. As one commentator said, "It was not merely that now women could vote, or that they dared to bare their knees, although both facts were important. . . . Some writers suggested that an assault was being mounted against the very principle of masculine supremacy."[46] Since women now were gaining independence economically by working outside the home, they "no longer were willing to personify the morality which men had never lived up to."[47] But, the assault was against a double standard of morality in private life, not against male supremacy in politics.

Women were not the only ones who appeared lukewarm about use of the ballot in the 1920s. The distinguished political theorist Walter Lippmann found an alarming lack of interest in politics among all voters. Writing in the

Atlantic Monthly, he faulted national leadership in both the Republican and Democratic parties for failing to recognize questions of the day that truly engaged the public, such as the resurgence of the Ku Klux Klan and arguments over evolution.[48] Lippmann agreed with others that the public had tired of public affairs after the disillusionment of World War I, but he saw multiple causes for uninterest in political activity: "Politics carried on for justice, for liberty, for prestige, is never more than the affair of a minority. . . . For the great majority of men political ideals are almost always based upon and inspired by some kind of economic necessity and ambition."[49] He contended the prosperity of most of the country during the 1920s led the public to close its eyes to civic responsibility: "Nothing a man could hope to gain by voting for politicians, and by agitating for laws, was likely to be half so profitable as what he could make by participating in the boom."[50] Presumably Lippmann intended his analysis to include women voters, since his argument was based on economic grounds. By 1920 over one-fifth of women held jobs outside the home, although many worked for low pay. During the 1920s the number of women in the labor force grew 26 percent. Over 500,000 of the new workers held clerical jobs and another 450,000 were classed as professionals. [51]

Conclusion

To suffragists, the vote loomed large as a means of acquiring rights. By the time women finally won their right to vote, they already had secured some rights important to the middle class, such as the right to enter professions and graduate schools (albeit not without facing discrimination), and to maintain guardianship of their children.[52] Therefore, many of the suffragists who voted in 1920 saw enfranchisement as the culmination of their struggle, a desirable end in itself. If women who went to the polls in the 1920s voted mainly to uphold the status quo, it may have been because they too were profiting from general economic affluence and an easing of societal barriers. If they did not vote, perhaps they saw little reason to do so. During the 1920s traditional marriage and homemaking, which remained the occupations pictured in mass circulation women's magazines, continued to be the norm for most women. The NWP lost membership and barely survived. If women did not have all the rights the NWP stood for, possibly women thought they already had what they needed.

A dismal view of women's use of the ballot marked a 1927 *Woman Citizen* article, "Women's Faults in Politics," by Frank R. Kent, a well-known political analyst.[53] He concluded that suffrage had failed because women had not voted as a bloc or as important elements within established parties, but merely reflected the views of men. In his eyes, women had promised to do far more with the ballot than they had delivered. An earlier series in the *Woman Citizen*, however, "Women Who Won" followed by "More Women Who Won," heralded the electoral victories of woman candidates and was far more affirmative about women's voting.[54]

In general, periodicals of the day, as these examples have shown, portrayed women as outsiders trying to break into political circles where they were not wanted because they had little to offer in the way of votes. No female "bosses," as Eleanor Roosevelt advocated, had appeared. Some articles blamed women for not doing more with the ballot so they would gain more respect. Others urged women to further educate themselves politically, or, in the case of *Equal Rights*, to insist on a specific objective. Although some articles praised women for their political efforts, more took issue with women's performance and pictured voting as a task that women had not learned to do well.

What was missing from the coverage was analysis of the subject that had fractured the woman's movement and kept women from operating as a bloc either outside or inside established political parties. That was the issue of protective legislation for working women. If the postsuffragists could have compromised on the need for limited regulation of working conditions instead of demanding either complete equality or separate standards for women workers, perhaps women might have voted in more of a bloc. According to historian William Chafe, suffragists never clearly explained their goals for the vote.[55] After they gained it, hundreds of discriminatory state laws remained, although many women may not have realized this. To Chafe the leaders of the suffrage movement should have recognized the need for additional women's rights as well as for workplace regulation.[56] Periodicals of the day offered little content to help them move in this direction. Publications seemed more interested in voting itself than in the complexities surrounding it.

In 1995 the LWV commissioned a book, *A Voice of Our Own: Leading American Women Celebrate the Right to Vote*, to commemorate the seventy-fifth anniversary of woman suffrage. In a chapter on "Lessons from the Woman Suffrage Movement," Lucinda Desha Robb of the National Archives wrote, "As odd as it may sound, one of the most important lessons of the woman suffrage movement may be the relative unimportance of suffrage all by itself. . . . The vote alone should never be the goal; the goal is what you can do with the vote."[57] It is a lesson the American public still is learning.

Notes

1. Blanche Wiesen Cook, *Eleanor Roosevelt*, Vol. 1, *The Early Years, 1884–1933* (New York: Viking, 1992), 350.

2. Gail Collins, *America's Women: 400 Years of Dolls, Drudges, Helpmates, and Heroines* (New York: William Morrow, 2003), 338.

3. Kristi Andersen, *After Suffrage: Women in Partisan and Electoral Politics before the New Deal* (Chicago: University of Chicago Press, 1996), 51.

4. Susan Ware, *Modern American Women: A Documentary History* (New York: McGraw-Hill, 1997), 143.

5. Sheila Rowbotham, *A Century of Women: A History of Women in Britain and the United States* (New York: Viking, 1997), 41–42.

6. Eleanor Roosevelt, *This Is My Story* (New York: Garden City Publishing Co., 1937), 354–55.

7. Cook, *Eleanor Roosevelt*, 195.

8. "Women Must Learn to Play the Game as Men Do," *Red Book*, April 1928, as reprinted in *What I Hope to Leave Behind: The Essential Essays of Eleanor Roosevelt*, ed. Allida M. Black (New York: Carlson Publishing, 1995), 195.

9. Roosevelt, "Women Must Learn to Play the Game as Men Do," 197.

10. Roosevelt, "Women Must Learn to Play the Game as Men Do," 198.

11. Roosevelt, "Women Must Learn to Play the Game as Men Do," 198.

12. S. J. Woolf, "A Woman Speaks Her Political Mind," *New York Times Magazine*, April 8, 1928.

13. As cited in Cook, *Eleanor Roosevelt*, 1: 370.

14. David R. Spencer, "The *Woman Patriot*," in *Women's Periodicals in the United States*, ed. Kathleen L. Endres and Therese L. Lueck (Westport, CT: Greenwood Press, 1996), 437–46.

15. As quoted in Spencer, "*Woman Patriot*," 440.

16. *Equal Rights*, February 17, 1923, 5.

17. "The Women of the Progressive Movement," *Equal Rights*, December 6, 1924, 338.

18. NAWSA had been led for years by Carrie Chapman Catt, a widely admired former school superintendent who, as a young wife, had been one of the first woman newspaper reporters in San Francisco and was known for her international work as a pacifist as well as for her involvement in the international woman suffrage alliance. After Congress passed the Nineteenth Amendment in 1919, Catt shepherded the hard-fought fourteen months' battle for ratification by individual states. Already at the 1919 NAWSA convention Catt had called for the organization to shift itself into a league of women voters to provide voter education.

19. Susan Ware, introduction to LWV Papers, 1918–1974, v., Manuscript Division, Library of Congress, Washington, DC.

20. Christine Lunardini, *What Every American Should Know About Women's History* (Holbrook, MA: Bob Adams, 1994), 201–3.

21. Allan J. Lichtman, *Prejudice and the Old Politics* (Lanham, MD: Lexington, 2000), 163.

22. Ware, introduction to LWV Papers, v.

23. Emily Newell Blair, "Are Women a Failure in Politics?," *Harper's*, October 1925, 513–22.

24. "What People Say About the Club," *Bulletin*, June 1928, 18.

25. *Woman Citizen*, September 4, 1920, cover.

26. Kathleen L. Endres, "The *Woman Citizen*," in *Women's Periodicals in the United States*, ed. Endres and Lueck, 429–34.

27. Endres, "*Woman Citizen*," 433.

28. Endres, "*Woman Citizen*," 433.

29. As quoted in Endres, "*Woman Citizen*," 433.

30. Endress, "*Woman Citizen*," 433.

31. Linda Lumsden, "*Equal Rights*," in *Women's Periodicals in the United States*, ed. Endres and Lueck, 73–77.

32. Susan Henry, *Anonymous in Their Own Names: Doris E. Fleischman, Ruth Hale, and Jane Grant* (Nashville, TN: Vanderbilt University Press, 2012), 110–11.

33. Ruby A. Black, "Jobs for Women," *Nation*, December 9, 1925, 648.

34. Qtd. in Collins, *America's Women*, 328.

35. Black, "Spontaneity and Spinsterhood," box 4, Ruby A. Black Papers, Manuscript Division, Library of Congress, Washington, DC.

36. Black, "Spontaneity and Spinsterhood."

37. Cover, *Equal Rights*, April 7, 1928.

38. Dorsey Cole, "Ruby A. Black," *Equal Rights*, April 7, 1928, 68.

39. Therese L. Lueck, "*National Business Woman*," in *Women's Periodicals in the United States*, ed. Endres and Lueck, 207–8.

40. Lueck, "*National Business Woman*," 207.

41. Lueck, "*National Business Woman*," 208.

42. "Everybody Satisfied," Editorial, *Independent Woman*, July 21, 1921, 7.

43. Sara M. Evans, *Born for Liberty* (New York: Free Press, 1989), 234.

44. Sara Alpern and Dale Baum, "Female Ballots: The Impact of the Nineteenth Amendment," in *History of Women in the United States*, Vol. 18, pt. 2, *Women and Politics*, ed. Nancy F. Cott (Munich: K. G. Saur, 1994), 535.

45. Alpern and Baum, "Female Ballots," 535.

46. Beatrice M. Hinkle, "Against the Double Standard," in *The Culture of the Twenties*, ed. Loren Baritz (Indianapolis: Bobbs-Merrill, 1970), 280.

47. Baritz, ed., *The Culture of the Twenties*, 280.

48. Walter Lippmann, "The Causes of Political Indifference To-Day," *Atlantic Monthly*, February 1927, as reprinted in *The Culture of the Twenties*, ed. Baritz, 145–58.

49. Lippmann, "The Causes of Political Indifference," 152.

50. Lippmann, "The Causes of Political Indifference," 150.

51. William H. Chafe, *The American Woman: Her Changing Social, Economic, and Political Roles, 1920–1970* (New York: Oxford University Press, 1972), 50.

52. Aileen S. Kraditor, *The Ideas of the Woman Suffrage Movement: 1890–1920* (New York: W. W. Norton, 1981), 262.

53. Frank R. Kent, "Women's Faults in Politics," *Woman Citizen*, March 1927, 23, 46–47.

54. "Women Who Won," *Woman Citizen*, November 18, 1922, 8–10, 29; "More Women Who Won," *Woman Citizen*, December 22, 1922, 10–11.

55. Chafe, *The American Woman*, 131.

56. Chafe, *The American Woman*, 131.

57. Lucinda Desha Robb, "Lessons from the Woman Suffrage Movement," in *A Voice of Our Own: Leading American Women Celebrate the Right to Vote*, ed. Nancy M. Neuman (San Francisco: Jossey-Bass, 1996), 40–41.

11

Memory, Interrupted

A Century of Remembering and Forgetting the Story of Women's Suffrage

CAROLYN KITCH

The lines formed early in the morning on Election Day, November 8, 2016, outside Mount Hope Cemetery in Rochester, New York. By evening, more than seven thousand people had come to visit the grave of Susan B. Anthony, "the simple burial site that has become a shrine to women's rights," according to the *Rochester Democrat & Chronicle*. Its reporter interviewed visitors, mostly women—some dressed in white, in tribute to the fashion choice of suffragists more than a century earlier—who had cast their votes and then had come to the cemetery to affix their "I Voted Today" stickers to Anthony's headstone. "I'm voting for the first woman president," one told the journalist. "As a woman I can vote because of the sacrifices she [Anthony] made." Another woman, pregnant and carrying a fourteen-month-old daughter, said of the toddler, "I want her to know that she was part of this. When Hillary wins, I want her to be part of it."[1]

Throughout the day, news websites worldwide republished Instagram and Facebook posts from the cemetery while providing some explanation of the past that was being recalled. *Time* magazine's site captioned its photographs of the stickered gravestone with this information: "A key figure in the American suffragist movement—she was arrested for illegally casting a ballot in the 1872 presidential election—Anthony's impact on politics is still being felt today."[2] *Newsweek* followed a television news reporter as he walked through the crowd and "shifted his camera from the gravesite to a 99-year-old woman in a white pantsuit slowly edging her way to the front of the line. 'We have a woman who's a World War II veteran!' he said."[3]

The ebullient mood in Rochester, and in news coverage, did not last. Hillary Clinton did not become the first woman president of the United States. Yet news media reports from that day in Rochester seemed to affirm that, nearly a century after the passage of the Nineteenth Amendment, the American women's suffrage movement was well remembered.

Such a conclusion would have been unlikely only two decades earlier. American news media barely mentioned women's suffrage in the many century-summary special issues and series they produced in 1999, the same year that Ken Burns released a new film meant to recount a history that he said he "had never heard of." That PBS documentary, *Not for Ourselves Alone: The Story of Elizabeth Cady Stanton and Susan B. Anthony*, told the "little-known story" of two women "who have been unjustly neglected" and "written out of history," said coproducer Paul Barnes.[4] Reviewers echoed this claim: "Virtually ignored during the latter half of the 20th century, the[ir] selfless revolution . . . finally gets its due," wrote *Variety*.[5]

That end-of-century amnesia was remarkable after decades of women's efforts to keep suffrage memory alive in public consciousness. During the 1930s the National Woman's Party successfully petitioned "to rename public parks, schools, playgrounds, bridges, and highways after Susan B. Anthony" and sent press releases and radio programs about her to thousands of news outlets, according to historian Julie Des Jardins.[6] Such publicity built on the foundation Anthony herself had laid by cowriting the earliest history of suffrage, one largely featuring herself and Stanton, in order to create "an origins story" for the movement's future, as historian Lisa Tetrault has argued.[7] During the middle decades of the twentieth century, Anthony's face appeared on postage stamps and a dollar coin, and during the 1980s the National Park Service created the Women's Rights National Historic Park in Seneca Falls, New York. Stanton and Anthony also were recalled, along with other suffragists, in news coverage of feminism's second wave, including some of the same media that failed to recall suffrage history in 1999.

The goal of this chapter is to trace how the American women's suffrage movement has been alternately remembered and forgotten in mainstream journalism, which has also alternated (and sometimes combined) celebration and dismissal of feminism. Most of the chapter's evidence comes from US newsweekly magazines, a form of journalistic storytelling that has fallen from prominence (and, with one exception, out of print form), but was an influential genre through most of the twentieth century, peaking in reach during the second wave of feminism. By the time of suffrage's fiftieth anniversary in 1970, *Life* had a paid circulation of 8.5 million readers per week; *Time* sold more than 4 million copies and *Newsweek* more than 3 million copies per week. The latter two publications maintained those circulation figures through the turn of the twenty-first century.[8] From their beginnings in the 1920s and 1930s, the mission of newsmagazines was not only reporting but also interpretation, with cover stories explaining social and political trends.

My analysis in this chapter draws on two main theoretical perspectives about the nature of news. One is that journalism is a form of familiar narrative, a structure and a lesson that seems to make sense because we have heard the story before. "The facts, names, and details change," wrote S. Elizabeth Bird and Robert Dardenne, "but the framework into which they fit—the symbolic system—is more enduring."[9] The other premise is the seemingly obvious notion that news must be new, or must seem new. Yet, as sociologists who study news production have determined, "journalists create novelty," in the words of Herbert Gans, who observed the editorial process at national news media (including *Time*) during the 1960s and 1970s. Journalists, he wrote, "increase the supply of novelty . . . by being ahistorical; in the 1960s, for example, they 'rediscovered' American poverty and hunger."[10] Gaye Tuchman, another sociologist whose newsroom research coincided with feminism's second wave, further noted how "craft traditions" of journalism, which privilege novelty, events, and conflict, shaped news coverage of the women's movement.[11] Journalism historian Patricia Bradley made a similar case that such news norms impeded public understanding of the movement, yet she added that they served as a national stage on which at least some of its goals were publicized to "millions of women who otherwise might never have been connected to the movement at all."[12]

This chapter provides an analysis of newsmagazine cover stories about the women's movement published in *Time*, *Newsweek*, and *Life* during the second half of the twentieth century. Collectively, this journalism constructed a temporal arc with three stages: first, puzzled and cautious concern over women's unhappiness; second, acknowledgment of gender inequities and the movement's promise; and, third, coverage of women running for political office during a postfeminist period continuing into the twenty-first century.[13]

Especially in its discussions of women as politicians and voters, this coverage referenced the women's suffrage movement in ways that sometimes provided historical perspective, but more often denied the movement's continuity, instead interpreting each episode of activism as an unanticipated development, a new event unconnected with events of the past. When historical connections were made, they were most often to a distant past (in particular, to Susan B. Anthony), a reference that did not interfere with assertions that current events were a surprise.

The following sections consider how these national news media constructed public understandings of the longer history of the American women's movement, during and since that movement's second wave. Although some coverage included information about women's history, most of this journalism was remarkably ahistorical in nature. Over time, that aspect of news coverage has ensured the repeated interruption of public memory of women's suffrage. While confirming the power of the news value of novelty, journalism's relentless emphasis on the unexpectedness of women's protest does not deviate from the seemingly different model of news as a form of familiar narrative; it has *become* the familiar narrative.

Mid-Century Musings on Women's Unhappiness[14]

None of the newsweeklies I study existed when the Nineteenth Amendment became law in 1920, but a popular humor magazine titled *Life* had chronicled the final decade of the suffrage movement, alternately poking fun at and prais-ing suffragists. After their success, famed illustrator Charles Dana Gibson created a cover image depicting a classically attired "America" shaking hands with a modern young woman and saying, "Congratulations."[15] When *Time* founder Henry Luce purchased the name of the old humor magazine and relaunched it as a photographic newsweekly in 1936, he inherited content that would become useful in *Life*'s midcentury musings on American woman-hood, leading up to and during the second wave of the women's rights move-ment. On its September 4, 1970, cover, marking the fiftieth anniversary of the achievement of suffrage, *Life* reprinted the 1920 Gibson drawing, with the new coverline "Women Arise: The Revolution That Will Affect Everybody."

Life had been the first of the newsweeklies to publish a cover story on what it termed "the woman problem" in 1956, with its special issue on "The American Woman: Her Achievements and Troubles." This subtitle succinctly established the narrative premise for the newsmagazines' coverage of the coming second wave of feminism: as women achieve, their problems multiply. The issue combined tributes to women's accomplishments, photo spreads of "beauties," profiles of the ideal American mother and housewife, and puz-zled essays wondering why so many American women still seemed anxious and unhappy. One article claimed that after gaining the vote, women had "earned places in politics" as "tireless workers" in civic groups and campaigns. Another essay declared in its title, "Women Are Misguided: They Are Still Waging a Shrill, Ridiculous War over the Dead Issue of Feminism."[16] Here, a reference to the suffrage movement assured readers that its politics were finally dead . . . in 1956.

Four years later, in 1960, a *Newsweek* cover featured an illustration of a diaper pin and a Phi Beta Kappa key within the silhouette of a woman's head, accompanied by the astonishing coverline "Young Wives with Brains." This

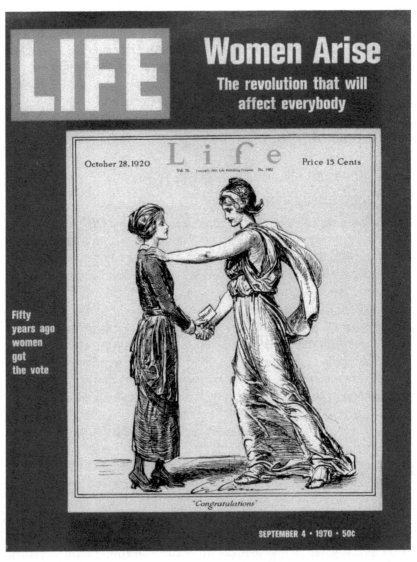

FIGURE 11.1. September 4, 1970, *Life* magazine cover, featuring 1920 *Life* magazine cover, "Women arise." LIFE logo and cover design © TI Gotham Inc. LIFE and the LIFE logo are registered trademarks of TI Gotham Inc. used under license.

cover story, billed as a "Special Science Report," addressed why a certain type of young woman—despite "her brains, her good looks, her car, her freedom"—was so unhappy. The experts responded that a good education merely gets women's hopes up, when in fact "in almost every field there is a barrier . . . beyond which few women progress."[17] The magazine persisted with this conclusion in its 1966 cover story on the same subject. Because of the civil rights movement and other activism of the 1960s, the unsigned article explained, young, college-educated women expressed "a new idealism" and wanted to do "important work," but experts warned that the working world was likely to disappoint them, making it risky to delay marriage. Even so, the report found that "the career drive is strong," even in students who planned to marry. For a companion piece, the magazine assembled a roundtable discussion by eight recent graduates of Vassar who were asked, among other things, whether they were concerned about appearing to compete with men. They were not.[18]

The most politically conservative of the newsmagazines, Time, was critical of all the era's social movements, and by 1969 it foresaw a backlash, with the coverline "Counterattack on Dissent." Though focused mainly on antiwar activism and the civil rights movement, this overview identified a third force, "the angries," a "Women's Liberation Movement" for whom "sexism is their target and battle cry—as racism is the blacks'." The magazine printed statistics documenting economic and legal prejudice discrimination against women as problems that needed to be solved; it also recalled some history, including "the redoubtable Elizabeth Cady Stanton, mother of seven and one of the few first-rate intellects in the suffrage movement." Nevertheless, Time concluded, "Women's rising expectations . . . are increasingly out of kilter with reality."[19]

This story, Time's first foray into reporting on second-wave feminism, was typical of much of what would follow, confirming various kinds of discrimination against women but dismissing women's protests as unseemly or ridiculous. By "taking feminism seriously one minute, mocking it the next," notes historian Susan Douglas, "news media exacerbated quite keenly the profound cultural schizophrenia about women's place in society that had been building since the 1940s and 1950s."[20] Such ambivalence was woven through coverage even as the movement became a regular news topic.

By the 1970s, "the press simply could not ignore the massive changes in American society, including successful suits by women against major news organizations such as the New York Times and Newsweek," writes journalism critic Caryl Rivers.[21] In the case of Newsweek, forty-six female employees announced that they were suing the magazine on the very same day that it published its cover story titled "Women in Revolt," with a cover illustration of a blurrily naked woman with her fist raised. The editors' introduction explained, "In an age of social protest, the old cause of U.S. feminism has flared into new and angry life in the women's liberation movement. It is a phenomenon difficult to cover." A freelancer, Helen Dudar, was hired to write the article "since the editors didn't believe any of the women in-house were up to the task," a later account claimed. [22] In the article itself, Dudar admitted that she had been chosen by "the men who run this magazine" because of her "ambivalence" about feminism.

Her report must have come as a surprise to the editors. Although both *Newsweek* and *Time* frequently described the "women's lib" movement as an imitation of the civil rights movement, Dudar saw the activism of her day as the continuation of the suffrage movement, which had begun as "a wide-ranging effort to change the status of women. . . . The vote for women arrived in 1920, along with a few other reforms that went part way toward converting women from property to people," although significant inequities persisted, she wrote. The five-page article was deeply researched, including findings from studies done by women academics and personal accounts from women whose consciousness had been raised by the movement. Dudar was one of them, she revealed in her self-reflective conclusion: "The ambivalence is gone; the distance is gone. What is left is a sense of pride and kinship with all those women who have been asking all the hard questions. I thank them and so, I think, will a lot of other women."[23]

Taking Feminism (and Suffrage History) Seriously at the Movement's Peak

That same issue's installment of a department titled "Where Are They Now?" profiled National Woman's Party founder Alice Paul, reporting that "the elderly suffragette" was, at age eighty-five, still pursuing passage of the Equal Rights Amendment, which she had first proposed in 1923. Asked what she thought of "the new women's lib groups," Paul replied that they were "a welcome addition to the movement."[24] Similarly, she told *Life* magazine: "The movement for women's rights has been going on for years and years. . . . I don't see any lack of continuity in the fight. It's been one long struggle. The only change has been that more people have come in. There are generations of unknown women who have brought it up to this particular point."[25]

Paul was speaking to *Life* on the occasion of the Women's Strike for Equality, held across the country on August 26, 1970, to publicize suffrage's fiftieth anniversary and to protest present problems. In addition to documenting women's lower pay, low representation in the professions, and various kinds of legal barriers, *Life* paid significant attention to history in this issue that reprinted Gibson's 1920 illustration. Its cover story explained: "When the forerunners of those suffragists who finally won the vote in 1920 held a Women's Rights Convention in Seneca Falls, N.Y., in 1848, their demands . . . were much as they are today. . . . Considering the length of the struggle . . . and the simple validity of many of their demands, it is nothing short of appalling that great inequities continue to exist in 1970."[26]

In its own coverage of the strike, *Newsweek* acknowledged "several 70- and 80-year-old veterans of the suffragette movement taking part or looking on as honored guests," adding that "in New York's Duffy Square, six women placed a 'symbolic' plaque on the site of a hoped-for statue to Susan B. Anthony."[27] Although *Time* used more belittling language, wondering at the "fury" of "the diffuse, divided, but grimly determined Women's Liberation movement," it also chronicled differences in pay and opportunities for women, and it mentioned Lucretia Mott and Elizabeth Cady Stanton in a summary of the "sentiments" declared in 1848, concluding, "Except for suffrage, those demands have yet to be met." Of the march itself, *Time* reported that "women dressed in suffragette costumes stood a 'silent vigil' for women's rights during the day at the Federal Building" in Washington, DC.[28]

Other national news coverage was more negative, according to television scholar Bonnie J. Dow, who quotes CBS anchor Walter Cronkite's description of the marchers as "a militant minority." Noting "the parallels between press reactions to early-twentieth-century suffrage parades and to the 1970 strike," she remarks, "For Alice Paul, watching the networks' coverage of the strike might have produced a profound sense of déjà vu."[29] Even so, Paul was an effective symbol in 1970 news coverage, "a living link between the uncontroversial (in retrospect) goals of the first wave" and those of the second, writes Dow. "Much as the Nineteenth Amendment had given women political rights, the ERA would give them legal ones, and the amendment's support by an elderly first-waver . . . made clear that this was no fringe issue."[30]

Life continued its role as a public historian, devoting a ten-page section in 1971 to a fuller account of the suffrage past. It began colloquially: "On July 19, 1848, in a Methodist chapel in Seneca Falls, N.Y., a handful of nervous but determined housewives rose before a crowd of farmers and their families and read aloud a manifesto." Yet it went on to recount the activism of Lucretia Mott, Sojourner Truth, Lucy Stone, the Grimké sisters, Anna Howard Shaw, and Carrie Chapman Catt. It pictured a member of the National Woman's Party picketing the White House and provided brief histories of the Women's Christian Temperance Union, women's colleges, the settlement house movement, and the Women's Trade Union League. Its joint profile of

Stanton and Anthony began with wording almost identical to the synopsis of the Ken Burns film that, two decades later, claimed to have rescued this history:

> For more than 50 years of their legendary friendship, they thought out the movement's goals, masterminded its strategy, and built up its strength until it became a national force—although neither of them lived to see the final victory. A less likely-looking pair of radicals could hardly be imagined—or two people as different from each other. . . . Yet the two women complemented each other perfectly. For Mrs. Stanton was one of the most original minds of her age, a prolific writer, a powerful orator, and the movement's philosopher and theoretician. Miss Anthony was its organizer and executive.[31]

This same year, *Newsweek* described the 1971 formation of the National Women's Political Caucus as a fulfillment of the "dream" that was "implicit in the suffragette movement a century ago" and recognized "strides taken" in the organization's goal of increasing women's representation in Congress and at major political-party conventions.[32] In 1972, in a special issue titled "The American Woman," *Time* similarly lauded these goals, claiming: "For the first time since the women's suffrage movement, American male politicians are responding earnestly to women's demands." A sidebar titled "Madam President" pointed out that Shirley Chisholm, on the ballot for the Democratic presidential nomination, was not only a woman but a black woman, and predicted that "the only surprise would be if there were not a woman running for President—or at least Vice President—on a major ticket well before the year 2000."[33] Covering the caucus's 1973 meeting, *Newsweek* predicted that the event would be "a valuable training ground and troop mobilizer for those women who move onto the front lines of party politics."[34]

In 1974, *Newsweek* celebrated "The Year of the Woman," featuring many women congressional candidates as well as its cover subject, Ella Grasso, who was running for governor of Connecticut. The opening of this cover story featured an early twentieth-century photograph of a woman with an open-backed dress revealing the words "Votes for Women" painted onto her bare skin, along with a photo of women at a Grasso rally, captioned "The New Suffragettes: After half a century, politics in their own behalf." The magazine explained that women were running for office partly because the downfall of a disgraced president [Richard Nixon] had "made old-line politicos more vulnerable . . . improv[ing] the prospects of all women."[35]

Seeming to confirm the movement's success, *Time* declared that its 1975 "Man of the Year" would be "Women of the Year," with a cover picturing prominent American achievers including Congresswoman Barbara Jordan and tennis player Billie Jean King. The wording of the cover story was more disingenuous. "They have arrived like a new immigrant wave in male America," it began, describing a societal shift that was "spiritually equivalent to the discovery of a new continent." So powerful was this transformation that the movement might no longer be necessary: "A measure of just how far the idea has come can be seen in the many women who denigrate the militant feminists' style ('too shrill, unfeminine') and then proceed to conduct their own newly independent lives." In fact, *Time* reported, feminist leaders had fallen "into factional disputes" and many ordinary women, while happy to have opportunities, were "hobbled by a fear of success," worried "that the risks of succeeding are 'loss of femininity,' loss of womanly identity. The 'fear' is also practical—in the face of expected discrimination, a woman may decide that the effort to succeed is not worth it."[36]

With that parry—and the special section's enigmatic title, "Great Changes, New Chances, Tough Choices"—*Time* set the tone for its future coverage of women's issues within a culture of backlash against the second wave of the movement.[37] In cover stories of the 1980s and 1990s, the magazine repeatedly cautioned that women were frazzled by trying to "have it all" and announced the "news" that feminism was dead, most notably on a 1998 cover featuring the disembodied heads of Susan B. Anthony, Betty Friedan, Gloria Steinem, and the fictional television character Ally McBeal, who stood for "the culture of celebrity and self-obsession" into which feminism had sunk. That article expressed nostalgia for the time when "feminists made big, unambiguous demands of the world."[38] *Time* had forgotten its own earlier coverage, which had characterized those demands as "out of kilter with reality." *Time* also ignored the women's movement at the end of the 1990s in its series naming the 100 most important people of the century—not one of them a leader of either the first or second wave of American feminism.[39]

Assessing "the Feminization of Politics" in a Postfeminist Era

It was against this backdrop that the newsmagazines continued to cover the increasing numbers of women running for office, hailing them as unexpected forces in American politics. When Geraldine Ferraro was nominated as the Democratic vice presidential candidate in 1984, *Time* editorialized: "History, so this is how it's made.... Come November, a woman from Tulsa (Hartford, Butte) will hear the curtain of the voting booth shut behind her, and she will be alone with America and her own life. Another woman's name will be on the ballot before her. However she votes, her thoughts about her place in the world will not be the same again."[40] With Ferraro's nomination, *Time* asserted: "Feminism has scored no more spectacular triumph since women won the right to vote."[41] A four-page history of women in politics located the origins of Ferraro's milestone not in 1970s feminism but in 1848 Seneca Falls.[42]

Newsweek also turned to a more distant past, writing that Ferraro's "stunning" nomination "seemed certain to change the face of American politics permanently—for it declared, more plainly than any single event since the adoption of the 19th Amendment, that women have arrived."[43] Forgetting its own proclamation of the "Year of the Woman" a decade earlier, *Newsweek* heralded "the feminization of politics" in a story that began: "More than 200 years after Abigail Adams penned that warning to her husband—and 64 years after winning the right to vote—American women have emerged as a powerful and rebellious political force."[44]

Geraldine Ferraro did not become vice president, the Reagan era continued, and *Time* returned to its preoccupation with masses of women opting out of careers lest they "find [themselves] at 35 with no family."[45] By March of 1992, the magazine reported a "war against feminism," in which women rebelled against "denigrating motherhood, pursuing selfish goals and wearing a suit."[46] Only eight months later, it reversed its position, announcing "The Year of the Woman" again, as dozens of women were elected to Congress along with Bill Clinton's first win of the White House. "From coast to coast, women candidates, thrust forward by Anita Hill–inspired outrage[47] . . . were in contention as never before," the cover story explained. In the same issue, Margaret Carlson, *Time*'s first woman columnist, wondered if the election also had ushered in "a different kind of First Lady" who was not merely democracy's version of a queen but in fact "a woman who could be king."[48]

A great deal has been written about Hillary Clinton's own political campaigns, first successfully for the US Senate and then unsuccessfully in two presidential election cycles. In the second instance she became the first woman to lead the ticket of a major party, dressing in a white pantsuit to accept that nomination at the 2016 Democratic National Convention, a political moment widely covered as historic. During the campaign, the mainstream press largely did not hold Clinton's opponent accountable for his open misogyny. Later, those news media seemed surprised to discover how many women did. On January 21, 2017, two months after Susan B. Anthony's grave was decorated with voters' stickers, millions of women around the world marched in support of women's rights; nearly a million were in Washington, DC, where suffragists had staged a spectacular parade more than a century earlier. Speaking there, Kirsten Gillibrand, who succeeded Hillary Clinton as the junior US senator from New York, recalled the 1913 suffrage parade, contending that "today . . . we are marching on Washington for similar reasons. . . . This is the moment of the beginning of the revival of the women's movement."[49]

Time magazine seemed to confirm Gillibrand's claim—featuring the words "The Resistance Rises: How a March Becomes a Movement" over a knitted, pink "pussyhat" on its cover—but the story inside was cautious. Noting that the word feminist "remains an epithet in parts of society, evoking [a] scolding tone," it suggested that the march, "even in its striking success, offered more in the way of catharsis than clarity" and that it was plagued by "intramural dissent." In one of the magazine's first references to the intersectionality of women's activism, *Time* characterized diversity as a reason the movement already was falling apart. Its preview story published the prior week had similarly warned, "The barriers to success are high. . . . No one knows what this coalition looks like moving forward."[50]

Time provided an answer a year later, in January of 2018, with a coverline introducing "The Avengers: First They Marched. Now They're Running," over the faces of nearly fifty women political candidates. "Skeptics wondered if the people who marched would go home and sink back into their ordinary lives," its cover story observed, without acknowledging that *Time* had been one of those skeptics. Instead, it now reported, the Women's March and the #MeToo campaign (which exposed widespread sexual harassment across American institutions) had fomented "a nationwide reckoning with the politics of gender." The "unprecedented surge" in women political candidates was "part of a grassroots movement that could change America. Call it payback, call it a revolution, call it the Pink Wave, inspired by marchers in their magenta hats, and the activism that followed."[51] Repeating its phrase the following November, the magazine declared that a "pink wave" had "crash[ed] on the capitol" when eighty-four Democratic women (as well as a significant number of candidates of color) gained congressional seats in midterm elections. Their success was explained as the outcome of continuing collective action:

> Like all meaningful transformations, this one required persistent struggle. . . . Millions surged into the streets for the Women's March, the biggest single-day protest in U.S. history. . . . By Election Day, 183 Democratic women were on the ballot for the House. . . . The political infrastructure that pushed those candidates over the line may last, as the grassroots groups turn their attention to pressuring their new representatives on issues like health care and paid family leave.[52]

It is tempting to read this as a new kind of news narrative, one interested in continuity. Yet, unlike the magazine's previous coverage of women's protests, or years-of-the-woman, this article's only reference to history was to the Women's March held the year before. The magazine's cover story on the Women's March itself was similarly history-free, except for a mention of Woodstock. *Time*'s 2018 coverage described a brand-new landscape, declaring with surprise that women had "crashed" into political importance—an old refrain, indeed.

Conclusion

The question of *Time*'s present and future coverage may not seem to matter much, since it is the only traditional newsweekly to survive today in print. Yet, along with its competitors, it provided prominent, national coverage of the women's movement during the century following the achievement of suffrage, and the newsmagazines interpreted subsequent women's activism in ways that both remembered and forgot the suffrage past. Therefore, this journalism offers some insights on how feminism may, or could, be remembered in the future.

Most scholarship on mainstream news coverage of women has analyzed it as a product of antiprogressive ideology and/or sexism. While such assessments may be supportable, the journalism surveyed in this chapter suggests that the news value of novelty—the need for "fresh" trends to report—is perhaps a more compelling factor in coverage, at any given time, and over time. As a core element of newsworthiness, novelty is a requirement that supersedes journalist bias (and that is one explanation for why coverage of feminism has not changed as much as one might assume as more women have risen to the top of the masthead). Writing about coverage of the 1992 "Year of the Woman," communication scholar Mary Douglas Vavrus notes that the *New York Times* explained the election of women that year "as a unique phenomenon, occurring as a result of the peculiarities of Hill-Thomas gender politics" and characterized them as political actors who "surged out of nowhere" to speak for a "no-longer-silent majority." Not only was this description ahistorical, Vavrus writes, but "creating the impression that women came out of nowhere to thrust themselves into politics casts them as a flash-in-the-pan phenomenon."[53]

The newsmagazines explained women's political candidacies and elections similarly: as discrete but explosive reactions to specific stimuli (usually abuses of power by individual, prominent men), as negative, retaliatory bursts rather than next steps in a constructive trajectory of political engagement. Journalists aided the perception that women's gains were isolated incidents by contextually grounding them in distant history, comparing the 1984 vice presidential nomination of Geraldine Ferraro and the 1974 and 1992 "Years of the Woman" to precedents from 1920, 1848, and 1776, rather than the feminist movement just a decade or two earlier, too close in the rear-view mirror for the latest developments to be understood as distinctly new. Thus, these gains were understood as exceptions to history rather than part of its core.

Writing in 1981, journalism historian Catherine Covert argued that historical (and journalistic) narratives structure time from a male perspective, organizing American life as a series of episodes involving triumphant individuals and dramatic events. Instead, she proposed, if we view the past through the lens of (most) women's experiences, or more generally the experiences of ordinary people, we might see history as a flow of "recurring motifs" and "reiterated values."[54] Historian Nancy Hewitt further contends that artificial divisions of time simplify the historical complexity of the women's movement, a history of "compelling stories filled with diverse characters and contentious struggles"; what's more, she writes, the "wave" metaphor promotes the false assumption that eras before or between the movement's most visible events were "feminist-free zones."[55] They were not, of course; women's progress during those periods was advanced by the "generations of unknown women who have brought it up to this particular point" whom Alice Paul remembered in her 1970 interview with *Life* magazine. Paul's own long life of steady activism is a case in point.

One conclusion that can be drawn from this study is that the press and the public might develop a different memory of American women's political activism if we were to understand it as an ongoing process—not as a series of separate episodes about achievers or "angries," but as a continuous story with many coexisting characters and themes. An uninterrupted narrative would enhance our ability to perceive and normalize its diversity and its complexity, offering fresh insight not only on history but also on the current moment, a time when both the press and progressive movements must seek new ways of connecting and collaborating with other cultural institutions and actors. As sociologist Robin Wagner-Pacifici observes, memory "vibrates" according to "the social acts of . . . [its] translation."[56] So, too, new formulations of feminism's present and past may enable new kinds of journalism that refocus and sustain public memory of the American women's movement.

Notes

1. Steve Orr, "Susan B. Anthony Grave Draws Huge Crowds Tuesday," *Rochester Democrat & Chronicle*, November 11, 2016, https://www.democratandchronicle.com /story/news/2016/11/08/hundreds-flock-to-susan-b-anthonys-grave/93431564/.

2. Josh Raab, "See Susan B. Anthony's Grave Covered in 'I Voted' Stickers," *Time*, November 8, 2018, http://time.com/4562785/susan-b-anthony-gravesite-election -day/; Abigail Jones, "How the Susan B. Anthony Tombstone Became a Monument of Hope for Hillary Clinton Supporters," *Newsweek*, November 8, 2016, https://www .newsweek.com/susan-b-anthony-tombstone-i-voted-hillary-clinton-518629. This story also was told in a short documentary, aired on Rochester, NY, public television: Linda Moroney, prod. and dir., *Election Day 2016* (Low to the Ground Productions and EPIC10 Films, 2017).

3. Orr, "Susan B. Anthony Grave Draws Huge Crowds Tuesday."

4. Ken Burns and Paul Barnes, prods., "The Making of *Not for Ourselves Alone*," special feature on the DVD of *Not for Ourselves Alone: The Story of Elizabeth Cady Stanton & Susan B. Anthony* (Florentine Films, 1999); promotional description on http://kenburns.com/films/alone. The producers' lack of knowledge is even more surprising given that, only four years earlier, PBS had aired another documentary, *One Woman, One Vote*, about not only Stanton and Anthony but also the rest of the suffrage movement (Ruth Pollak, prod., *One Woman, One Vote* [Educational Film Center, 1995]).

5. Ray Richmond, "*Not for Ourselves Alone: The Story of Elizabeth Cady Stanton & Susan B. Anthony*," *Variety*, November 4, 1999, https://variety.com/1999/tv/reviews /not-for-ourselves-alone-the-story-of-elizabeth-cady-stanton-susan-b-anthony -2-1200459879/.

6. Julie Des Jardins, *Women and the Historical Enterprise in America: Gender, Race, and the Politics of Memory, 1880–1945* (Chapel Hill: University of North Carolina Press, 2003), 197–98.

7. Lisa Tetrault, *The Myth of Seneca Falls: Memory and the Women's Suffrage Movement, 1848–1898* (Chapel Hill: University of North Carolina Press, 2014), 8.

8. Norberto Angeletti and Alberto Oliva, *Magazines That Make History* (Gainesville: University Press of Florida, 2004); Philip B. Kunhardt Jr., ed., *Life: The First Fifty Years* (Boston: Little, Brown, 1986); Audit Bureau of Circulations (Schaumburg, IL), June 30, 2000. *Life* ceased weekly publication in 1972, but relaunched as a monthly from 1978 to 2000; it also regularly has issued special issues and books that repackage history on various themes.

9. S. Elizabeth Bird and Robert W. Dardenne, "Myth, Chronicle, and Story: Exploring the Narrative Qualities of News," in *Media, Myths, and Narratives: Television and the Press*, ed. James W. Carey (Newbury Park, CA: Sage, 1988), 69.

10. Herbert J. Gans, *Deciding What's News: A Study of CBS Evening News, NBC Nightly News, and Time*, 25th anniv. ed. (1979; reprint, Evanston, IL: Northwestern University Press, 2004), 167–68.

11. Gaye Tuchman, *Making News: A Study in the Construction of Reality* (New York: Free Press, 1978), 135–55.

12. Patricia Bradley, *Mass Media and the Shaping of American Feminism, 1963–1975* (Jackson: University Press of Mississippi, 2003), 4.

13. *Time* and *Newsweek* coverage of the middle stage also is discussed in Laura Ashley and Beth Olson, "Constructing Reality: Print Media's Framing of the Women's Movement, 1966 to 1986," *Journalism & Mass Communication Quarterly* 75, no. 2 (Summer 1998): 263–77. These authors analyzed journalists' framing of both feminists and antifeminists, concluding that the press trivialized both groups.

14. For access to some of the reporting discussed in this section, including the full issue of *Life* magazine's suffrage-anniversary issue that is pictured here, I am grateful for the resources of the Alice Marshall Women's History Collection in the Penn State Harrisburg Library, Middletown, PA, and for the help of archivist and humanities reference library Heidi Abbey Moyer and her team, Katie Gorrell and Tesa Burns.

15. Cover, *Life* [humor magazine], October 28, 1920. I thank Rachel Podmajersky and Amy Wong at the Meredith Corporation for supplying this image.

16. "Earned Places in Politics" and Cornelia Otis Skinner, "Women Are Misguided: They Are Still Waging a Shrill, Ridiculous War over the Dead Issue of Feminism," special issue: "The American Woman: Her Achievements and Troubles," *Life*, December 24, 1956, 49–55, 73, 75.

17. Edwin Diamond, "Young Wives," *Newsweek*, March 7, 1960, 57, 58.

18. "What Educated Women Want: Marriage, Yes—But the Career Drive Is Strong" and "The Talk of Vassar, 1966," *Newsweek*, June 13, 1966, 68–74, 74–75.

19. "A Letter from the Publisher" and Ruth Brine, "The New Feminists: Revolt against 'Sexism,'" *Time*, November 21, 1969, 1, 53–56.

20. Susan J. Douglas, *Where the Girls Are: Growing Up Female with the Mass Media* (New York: Times Books, 1994), 165.

21. Caryl Rivers, *Slick Spins and Fractured Facts: How Cultural Myths Distort the News* (New York: Columbia University Press, 1996), 105.

22. "'Women in Revolt': A *Newsweek* Cover and Lawsuit Collide" [online feature], *Newsweek*, October 28, 2016, https://www.newsweek.com/women-revolt-newsweek-cover-and-lawsuit-collide-514891.

23. Helen Dudar, "Women's Lib: The War on 'Sexism,'" *Newsweek*, March 23, 1970, 71–78.

24. "Where Are They Now?" *Newsweek*, March 23, 1970, 18.

25. "The Personal Views of Eight Women Who Succeeded in It," *Life*, September 4, 1970, 21. (This title's phrasing follows the title of a feature above it, cited in the next note.)

26. "A Long and Painful Record of Little Progress in a Man's World," *Life*, September 4, 1970, 18–19.

27. "The Women Who Know Their Place," *Newsweek*, September 7, 1970, 16–18.

28. "Who's Come a Long Way, Baby?" *Time*, August 31, 1970, 18–25; "Women on the March," *Time*, September 7, 1970, 20–21.

29. Bonnie J. Dow, *Watching Women's Liberation: 1970: Feminism's Pivotal Year on the Network News* (Urbana: University of Illinois Press, 2014), 159.

30. Dow, *Watching Women's Liberation*, 69–70.

31. Edward Kern, "Votes for Women," *Life*, August 20, 1971, 40–49, Alice Marshall Women's History Collection, Penn State Harrisburg, Middletown, PA. *Life's* most comprehensive treatment of the women's history was a special issue titled "Remarkable American Women," published for the nation's Bicentennial, four years after the magazine had ceased periodical publication. Its encyclopedia-style format included women from all fields as well as a section titled "Women for Women: Pioneers in the Struggle for Equal Rights," which included a broad range of reformers including suffrage activists and leaders of the movement's second wave (*Life: Remarkable American Women, 1776–1976*, 1976, 94–102.)

32. "Never Underestimate . . . ," *Newsweek*, July 26, 1971, 29–30.

33. "Toward Female Power at the Polls" and "Madam President," special issue, "The American Woman," *Time*, March 20, 1972, 43–44.

34. Helen Dimos Schwindt, "This Beautiful Force," *Newsweek*, February 26, 1973, 31–32.

35. "The Year of the Woman," *Newsweek*, November 4, 1974, 20–27.

36. "Great Changes, New Chances, Tough Choices," *Time*, January 5, 1976, n.p.

37. Susan Faludi, *Backlash: The Undeclared War against American Women* (New York: Crown, 1991).

38. Cover and Ginia Bellafante, "Feminism: It's All about Me!" *Time*, June 29, 1998, 54, 57.

39. One of its choices was Margaret Sanger, who was a suffragist but was not remembered as such for this series. *Time: People of the Century* [six-part series], 1998–99. *Newsweek* briefly mentioned both waves in the final cover story of its own similar series, on "How Ordinary Americans Made History" (Kenneth Auchincloss, "Fanfare for the Common Man," *Newsweek: People of the Century*, December 20, 1999, 48–53). Only *Life* printed pictures of suffragists, including Alice Paul, on a two-page spread in its 400-page retrospective book (Richard B. Stolley, ed., *Life: A Century in Pictures* [Boston: Bulfinch Press, 1999], 86–87).

40. Roger Rosenblatt, "Mondale: 'This Is an Exciting Choice,'" *Time*, July 23, 1984, 12.

41. Kurt Anderson, "Ripples throughout Society," *Time*, July 23, 1984, 28.

42. Otto Friedrich, "Braving Scorn and Threats," *Time*, July 23, 1984, 30–33.

43. Tom Morganthau, "Making History," *Newsweek*, July 23, 1984, 16.

44. Melinda Beck, "The Feminization of Politics," *Newsweek*, July 23, 1984, 29.

45. "The Dreams of Youth," *Time*, November 1, 1990, 4, 10–14.

46. Nancy Gibbs, "The War against Feminism," *Time*, March 9, 1992, 50–55.

47. During the 1991 confirmation hearings for Supreme Court nominee Clarence Thomas, attorney Anita Hill alleged that he had sexually harassed her when she worked with him in federal agencies. Senate Judiciary Committee members' dismissive treatment of Hill prompted public outcry.

48. "From Anita Hill to Capitol Hill," *Time*, November 16, 1992, 21; Margaret Carlson, "A Different Kind of First Lady," *Time*, November 16, 1992, 40–41.

49. "Senator Gillibrand Speaks to the Women's March on Washington," C-SPAN, https://www.c-span.org/video/?c4650727/senator-gillibrand-speaks-womens-march -washington.

50. Cover and Karl Vick, "The Other Side," *Time*, February 6, 2017, 26, 28, 29; Charlotte Alter, "New Friends, Common Foe," *Time*, January 30, 2017, 42.

51. Cover and Charlotte Alter, "Meet the Candidates," *Time*, January 29, 2018, 29, 28.

52. Charlotte Alter, "A Pink Wave Crashes on the Capitol," *Time*, November 19, 2018, 36–37.

53. Mary Douglas Vavrus, *Postfeminist News: Political Women in Media Culture* (Albany: SUNY Press, 2002), 87, 93.

54. Catherine L. Covert, "Journalism History and Women's Experience: A Problem in Conceptual Change," *Journalism History* 8, no. 1 (Spring 1981): 2–6.

55. Nancy Hewitt, "Introduction," in *No Permanent Waves: Recasting Histories of U.S. Feminism*, ed. Nancy Hewitt (New Brunswick, NJ: Rutgers University Press, 2010), 2, 5. Susan Ware bolsters this case by documenting the history of women's political activism and progress during the decades between the first and second "waves" in *Beyond Suffrage: Women in the New Deal* (Cambridge, MA: Harvard University Press, 1981).

56. Robin Wagner-Pacifici, "Memories in the Making: The Shape of Things That Went," *Qualitative Sociology* 19, no. 3 (1996): 301, 302.

Afterword

Women's Suffrage, the Press, and the Enduring Problem of White Supremacy

KATHY ROBERTS FORDE

Journalism has been central to US public and political life, including the more than seventy-year movement for women's suffrage, from Seneca Falls in 1848 to Nashville in 1919. The authors of this volume have charted the multidimensional role journalism played in this long—and enduring—struggle, covering a broad range of periodicals and topical concerns.

To wit: suffrage periodicals provided women the forum to imagine themselves as a community of political beings and to negotiate among competing notions of women's political identity. Antisuffrage periodicals promoted the maintenance of gendered separate spheres, an argument white southerners put to use as a strategy to protect segregation and states' rights. A Mormon periodical promoted women's suffrage in Utah and helped gain the franchise for Utah women well before the Nineteenth Amendment became law. The black press—including conventional black newspapers of the late nineteenth and early twentieth centuries and radical periodicals of the New Negro era—covered and engaged the suffrage struggle, often providing a platform for well-known black women suffragists to voice their arguments. Black public discourse on women's suffrage in the early twentieth century was particularly complex, evincing both robust support and patronizing paternalism. Radical journals of this same period demonstrated the degree to which white supremacy shaped the women's suffrage struggle. Anxieties about white masculinity, race, and political power inflected white Tennessee newspaper editorial positions on the state's decision to ratify the Nineteenth

Amendment. Elites across the color line, including powerful men as well as women, provided much of the infrastructure, influence, and resource base needed in the 1910s finally to achieve the federal amendment securing voting rights for women. In the years since the ratification of the Nineteenth Amendment in 1920, the women's suffrage movement has been remembered, distorted, and even forgotten in news coverage that has fatefully shaped public memory. This volume goes a long way toward fulfilling Linda Lumsden's call in chapter 1 for studies that explore "how movement media influenced and interacted within the larger political and cultural climates."

Racial Division as the Rule

Race, like journalism, has also been central to the enduring struggle for women's suffrage. As several authors have demonstrated here, racial divisions shaped the movement for women's suffrage and inflected much of the journalism that helped suffragists collectively imagine women as political beings, persuade others that women should play a direct role in electoral politics, and finally secure the vote through ratification of the Nineteenth Amendment. These racial divisions proved tragic. If the Nineteenth Amendment ever promised a new era of racial democracy in America, that promise was lost when white suffragists abandoned the citizenship aspirations of black women (and men) in the South to the forces of white supremacy.

Although some black and white suffragists made common cause early in the suffrage movement, as the nineteenth century progressed, they increasingly divided. They worked in separate if parallel organizations. Suffrage and antisuffrage organizations alike produced newspapers and magazines that reported on campaigns, activities, and issues, and promoted causes related to the struggle, with women publishers and editors at the helm. But racial division came to be the rule. White women belonged to white suffrage and antisuffrage associations that published journals meant for white women. Excluded by their white sisters, black women banded together in their own suffrage associations with their own journals.[1]

When the women's suffrage movement began in the mid-nineteenth century, more than three million black Americans were enslaved and about four hundred thousand, the majority living in the North, were free.[2] By 1870, when the last of the Reconstruction era amendments was ratified, the black population had expanded substantially. For the first time in the history of the US Census, the 1870 Census—the first after emancipation—showed the numbers of "colored" and "free colored" persons living in the country to be the same number, almost five million.[3] Only half a million had been previously "free."

The United States was founded on a politics of racist exclusion that limited "the privileges of citizenship to white men," Eric Foner noted. The Reconstruction era amendments were "a radical repudiation of the nation's actual practice [of democracy] of the previous seven decades."[4] The Thirteenth Amendment wiped out the institution of slavery, surely a radical transformation of American life. But the next two amendments entirely revised the relationship of black Americans to the nation. The Fourteenth Amendment promised citizenship and equal protection under the law (while at the same time identifying the ideal voter as "male"). And the Fifteenth Amendment went beyond civil rights, specifically promising the right to vote regardless of "race, color, or previous condition of servitude." These amendments, which enfranchised black men but left women out of the political equation, broke what Elaine Weiss called "the feminist-abolitionist alliance" that had begun at Seneca Falls.[5]

Newly freed black Americans exercised their liberty energetically. They built schools, businesses, churches, banks, neighborhoods, and networks of kinship and sociability. Black men eagerly embraced citizenship and the political opportunities it conferred, serving in Reconstruction era legislatures across the South and showing up at the ballot box. But when Reconstruction ended in 1877, and federal troops withdrew from the South, white southerners systematically began to reestablish white supremacy and curtail so-called "Negro rule." The North acquiesced.[6] As W. E. B. Du Bois wrote, "The slave went free; stood a brief moment in the sun; then moved back again toward slavery."[7]

The Fantasy of a New South

Very shortly, a "New South" emerged. In the 1880s, Henry W. Grady, editor of the *Atlanta Constitution*, used his popular speeches and columns, reprinted in newspapers throughout the country, to spread his fantasy of a New South of racial harmony, sectional unity, and industrial enterprise.[8] The overt purpose was to attract northern capital to fuel southern industry, but Grady also meant to persuade northern whites that the South's so-called "race problem" must be left to the South to resolve. Grady, of course, meant the white South because the "problem" was black political power. Fear of black electoral influence led white southern Democrats to promote one-party rule and the "solid South" of white supremacy. So long as white southerners voted together as Democrats, they could vanquish the mostly Republican black vote, which Grady derided as "impulsive, ignorant and purchasable."[9]

Grady spoke and wrote often of suffrage—"the suffrage of the weak and shiftless" and the "ignorant or corrupt suffrage"—but he was not referring to women's suffrage.[10] In fact, Grady cared little about women's suffrage, committed as he was, Marjorie Spruill Wheeler observed, to "the preservation of the Southern Lady in her traditional role."[11] Although violence sometimes broke out, Grady claimed, black men in the South voted largely undisturbed. But violent intimidation of black voters was more common than Grady let on, and the ability to vote increasingly curtailed. Grady perhaps put the white supremacist case most plainly in a speech at the Texas State Fair two years before his death in 1889: "The supremacy of the white race of the South must be maintained forever, and the domination of the negro race resisted at all points and at all hazards—because the white race is the superior race."[12] In other words, the white South would do anything necessary to control the "negro vote."

This particular form of white supremacy—control of the ballot box—came to be enforced across the South using various tools of racial control, including poll taxes, grandfather clauses, literacy tests, and white primaries. But these were not the first tools of control. In the 1880s, the decade of Grady's most significant work and influence, voter suppression tools included byzantine ballots, gerrymandering, onerous registration requirements, and violent intimidation.[13]

Historians have examined Grady's role in Georgia politics, but few have noted his prominent role in constructing the state's white supremacist political economy and social order.[14] As a kingmaker for the Democratic Party in Georgia in the 1880s, Grady helped elect and appoint governors and US senators who amassed great wealth working mostly black convicts leased from the state in their private businesses. The convict lease system in Georgia, and throughout the South, targeted black men, women, and children to provide cheap labor for railroad construction, iron and coal mines, turpentine farms, and other industrial concerns. They were arrested for misdemeanors and sham crimes like vagrancy and then sentenced to hard labor at convict camps.[15] It was a brutal, inhumane system that David Oshinsky has called "worse than slavery" and Douglas Blackmon "slavery by another name."[16] Grady knew a great deal about the convict lease because the *Constitution* reported on it exhaustively. What's more, Grady's former partner at the *Atlanta Herald*, Robert Alston, was murdered in the statehouse after presenting a damning report on the convict lease system in the legislature. (His murderer was involved in the convict lease and intimately connected to Grady's "Atlanta Ring" of politicians who basically controlled the convict system.)[17] And then there was lynching, which the *Constitution* reported with unsettling levity, drawing readers' attention with headlines like "The Triple Trapeze: Three

Negroes Hung to a Limb of a Tree" and "Two Minutes to Pray before a Rope Dislocated Their Vertebrae."[18]

Convict lease and lynching—which Ida B. Wells-Barnett, the pioneering black suffragist and journalist, called the "twin infamies" of the South—were tools of New South racial terror meant to constrain black political participation, economic opportunity, and self-expression.[19] C. Vann Woodward described Grady's vision of the New South as "a cheerful gospel of progress, prosperity, industry, and nationalism with a sugary icing of reconciliation of all classes, sections, and races—all of course under proper white supremacy."[20] Grady's "sugary icing" and "proper" white supremacy barely concealed the threat of chilling violence at the hands of the state and the lynch mob. Wells-Barnett blamed Grady's New South fantasy for national acceptance of the terrible lynchings she described in her pamphlet *Southern Horrors*—and the role of the "malicious and untruthful white press" in the events.[21]

Suffragists' North–South Alliance

Women's suffrage did not gain a foothold in the South until the 1890s. And it only emerged then, Wheeler explained, "*because* suffragists from both South and North believed the South's 'negro problem' could be the key to victory for their cause."[22] If white women could vote, it was supposed, white control of the South's political affairs would be ensured, given widespread disenfranchisement of black southerners. The leading suffragist periodical in the South—the *New Southern Citizen*, the organ of the Southern States Woman Suffrage Conference—embraced white supremacy with vigor. Its motto: "Make the Southern States White."[23] Not all white southern suffragists were so rabidly racist, but none "was moved to come forward as champion of the political rights of Southern blacks."[24]

At Seneca Falls, Frederick Douglass stood proudly with Elizabeth Cady Stanton, but by 1895, when the National American Woman Suffrage Association (NAWSA) met for the first time in a southern city, his support was understood to be a liability. Susan B. Anthony disinvited him from the Atlanta convention, a clear signal that white southern support was more important to NAWSA than black American support.[25] The New South had arrived, and Douglass was not welcome in it. As the suffrage struggle moved into the twentieth century, racial concerns moved front and center. In 1903, NAWSA capitulated completely to southern prejudice, agreeing to make suffrage the "medium through which to retain supremacy of the white race over the African," as Belle Kearney, a white suffragist from Mississippi, argued at the

NAWSA convention. "The enfranchisement of women," she noted, "would insure immediate and durable white supremacy."[26] At the same convention, held in New Orleans, the executive board recognized the right of southern chapters to exclude black women from membership.[27]

When the NAACP was founded in 1909, its primary goal was to reclaim black voting rights.[28] But leading white suffragists had already capitulated to the New South demands of those who viewed women's suffrage as a means to maintain white political control in the South. Black Americans thus faced a daunting struggle as they pursued voting rights. The Nineteenth Amendment could theoretically empower black women, but practically, at least in the "solid South" with its Jim Crow voter restriction rules and violent intimidation of black voters, it would empower mainly white women. At least, that's the way many white suffragists, particularly southerners, understood the situation.

Black citizens had other ideas. The Nineteenth Amendment encouraged many black women and men across the South "to reassert their place at the polls," Lorraine Gates Schuyler wrote. Black women led the way, organizing voters' leagues, registration drives, and citizenship schools.[29] In the wake of modest wartime gains for black men, achieving women's suffrage spurred hope that the ballot box might be within reach.

In Florida, Mary McLeod Bethune called this moment the "newest era of Reconstruction." In 1920, as Paul Ortiz documented in his brilliant book *Emancipation Betrayed*, black Floridians across generations, social class, and gender built a mass social movement aimed at destroying white supremacy by claiming their right to the ballot. Bethune, president of the State Federation of Colored Women's Clubs, and Eartha White, secretary of the federation, led the movement, mobilizing black Floridians through a vast network of secret societies and churches. The fraternal order Knights of Pythias mobilized more than fifteen thousand members, urging them to pay their poll taxes and register to vote. Black newspapers covered the movement, providing a critical forum for discussion and organizing. Influential black editors like Matthew M. Lewey of the *Florida Sentinel* and W. I. Lewis of the *Florida Metropolis*'s special section "News of the Colored People" spoke at citizens' meetings. NAACP leaders James Weldon Johnson (who had left Florida long ago) and Walter White supported the movement from afar, lobbying Congress to reduce congressional representation in states that violated black voting rights. Black Floridians, long experienced in protest and struggle, prepared to remake American democracy.[30]

When white newspapers like the *Tampa Tribune* and *Palm Beach Post* indignantly reported that black women were outregistering white women, white Floridians began their own voter registration drives for women. As the final day of voter registration approached, Representative Frank Clark of Florida, a powerful Democrat known throughout the South for his protection of white supremacy in the US Congress, promised violence if black Floridians "tried to govern this country." The governor's Democratic machine asked white women to vote to save Florida from Negro rule. Officials arrested black women for supposedly falsifying their voting qualifications when registering. And in the days leading up to the election, the Ku Klux Klan and other white terrorists attacked black men across the state suspected of helping black women in their efforts to register to vote.[31]

When election day finally arrived on November 2, 1920, "African Americans across the state locked arms and prepared to vote," Ortiz wrote. Black Floridians turned out to vote en masse. But white Democrats had devised plans to quash black voting. They set up separate voting stations for whites and blacks, moving white voters through quickly but gumming up the works so the majority of black voters never made it to the ballot box. They turned away registered voters with false claims they had registered improperly. They placed armed men at the polls to keep black voters away. And finally, they organized violent reprisals and repression, crushing black voting efforts across the state. The worst of the violence happened in Orange County, where white intimidation of black voters in Ocoee escalated from mob violence to lynchings to a full-blown massacre. Historians cannot say how many black lives were lost in the Ocoee Massacre and across Florida that election day. Walter White, who traveled to Florida to investigate, was told fifty-six black Floridians were killed in Ocoee alone; the NAACP ultimately estimated between thirty and sixty were killed across the state. White citizens of Ocoee drove out their remaining black neighbors and seized their land, turning Ocoee into a whites-only town for the next sixty years. Black Americans in Florida and across the country asked the federal government to investigate. Nothing was done.[32]

Continuing Struggles for Voting Rights

Despite the passage and ratification of the Nineteenth Amendment, and its valuable expansion of the "circle of we" in US public life, democracy in America remained an unfulfilled project until the Voting Rights Act of 1965. This federal legislation, which finally enforced the Fifteenth and Nineteenth Amendments for African Americans, would not have been possible without the efforts of black voting rights activist Amelia Boynton Robinson. When the civil rights movement shifted to Selma, Alabama, the goal was voting rights—and Robinson had been seeding the ground for decades through her local education and organizing efforts in the Dallas County Voters League. As a child, she had passed out leaflets supporting women's suffrage. As an adult, she began working in the 1930s to register black voters in Selma and Dallas County, Alabama. By the time John Lewis of the Student Nonviolent Coordinating Committee and Dr. Martin Luther King of the Southern Christian Leadership Conference arrived in 1965 to push for a federal voting rights law, she had prepared the way. When black demonstrators marched across the Edmund Pettus Bridge, both she and John Lewis were savagely beaten by Alabama state troopers. The national press coverage, which dramatized white supremacist brutality in broadcast footage and news photos of the carnage, pressured the federal government to pass the Voting Rights Act.[33]

The struggle for voting rights continues. In 2013, in *Shelby County v. Holder*, the United States Supreme Court eliminated the key provision in the Voting Rights Act meant to combat racial discrimination in voting.[34] Since then, voter identification laws have reappeared; voters, often those who are black or Latinx, have been disenfranchised. Discrimination in voting is a growing concern.[35] In the governor's election in Georgia in 2018, African American democratic gubernatorial candidate Stacey Abrams—a long-time Georgia voting rights activist—narrowly lost to Republican Bryan Kemp. Kemp ran for governor as he performed his duties as sitting secretary of state. He understood these duties to include voter suppression, including purges of voter rolls, registration blocks, and intimidation of groups attempting to register minority voters.[36]

This volume has explored the history of women's suffrage and the media that served interests on all sides of the long struggle. It reminds us that media are central to social movements, social change, and social justice. This afterword suggests that the struggle for voting rights in the United States is not over, mired as it is in the country's seemingly endless struggle to achieve racial equality. The constitutional amendments that have expanded the franchise—including the Nineteenth—mean little if they are not vigorously protected and enforced. Our history has taught us that much, even if five Supreme Court justices are innocent of that history. In her dissent in *Shelby County v. Holder*, Justice Ruth Bader Ginsburg wrote that abandoning the protections of the Voting Rights Act was "like throwing away your umbrella in a rainstorm because you are not getting wet."[37] Ginsburg knows her history.

The project of democracy is never-ending and fragile. Henry Grady and the *Atlanta Constitution* helped construct a "New South" that excluded African Americans from this democratic project. White Democrats in Florida followed suit in the election of 1920, with the help of the white Florida press.

White leaders of the women's suffrage movement followed the same path when they decided to support a southern strategy to achieve the Nineteenth Amendment, with the help of the white suffrage press. Black Americans forcefully resisted these antidemocratic moves, and they used their own press outlets to organize, agitate, regroup in defeat, and rejoin the effort.

The press can serve democratic ends—and it can serve antidemocratic ends. The woman's suffrage press—divided as it was into separate spheres of black and white endeavor, like the woman's suffrage movement itself—achieved voting rights for white women across the country and some black women. But it miserably failed black women—and men—throughout the South. Voting rights in the United States, especially those of marginalized communities, continue to be attacked and eroded. White supremacy endures. We desperately need a press that fights for democracy for all of us.

Notes

1. Rosalyn Terborg-Penn, *African American Women in the Struggle for the Vote, 1850–1920* (Bloomington: Indiana University Press, 1998).

2. US Census Bureau, *1850 Census: The Seventh Census of the United States*, table 1, "Population of the United States Decennially from 1790 to 1850," ix, https://www2 .census.gov/library/publications/decennial/1850/1850a/1850a-02.pdf#.

3. US Census Bureau, *1870 Census: The Ninth Census of the United States*, table 1, "Population, 1870–1790, by States and Territories, in Aggregate, and as White, Colored, Free Colored, Slave, Chinese, and Indian," https://www2.census.gov/library /publications/decennial/1870/population/1870a-04.pdf#.

4. Eric Foner, *Forever Free: The Story of Emancipation and Reconstruction* (New York: Vintage, 2006), 122–23.

5. Elaine Weiss, *The Woman's Hour: The Great Fight to Win the Vote* (New York: Viking, 2018), 135. For an excellent analysis of the struggle over the Fifteenth Amendment and black male voting rights in suffragist activism after the Civil War, see Faye E. Dudden, *Fighting Chance: The Struggle Over Woman Suffrage and Black Suffrage in Reconstruction America* (New York: Oxford University Press, 2011).

6. See, for example, Foner, *Forever Free*.

7. W. E. B. Du Bois, *Black Reconstruction in America* (1935; reprint, New Brunswick, NJ: Transaction Publishers, 2013), 26.

8. Kathy Roberts Forde, "Afterword: Ida B. Wells-Barnett and the 'Racist Cover-Up,'" in *Political Pioneer of the Press: Ida B. Wells-Barnett and Her Transnational Crusade for Social Justice*, ed. Lori Amber Roessner and Jodi L. Rightler-McDaniels (Lanham, MD: Lexington Books, 2018).

9. Henry W. Grady, speech, Augusta Exposition, November 1888, in *Joel Chandler Harris' Life of Henry W. Grady Including His Writings and Speeches*, ed. Joel Chandler Harris (New York: Cassell, 1890), 126.

10. Grady, *Harris' Life of Henry W. Grady*, 190, 193.

11. Marjorie Spruill Wheeler, *New Women of the New South: The Leaders of the Woman Suffrage Movement in the Southern States* (New York: Oxford University Press, 1993), 8.

12. Henry W. Grady, speech, "The South and Her Problems," Texas State Fair, October 26, 1887, in *Harris' Life of Henry W. Grady*, 100.

13. Alexander Keyssar, *The Right to Vote: The Contested History of Democracy in the United States*, rev. ed. (New York: Basic Books, 2000), 86–88.

14. Forde, "Ida B. Wells-Barnett," 180–81.

15. Alex Lichtenstein, *Twice the Work of Free Labor: The Political Economy of Convict Labor in the New South* (New York: Verso, 1996); Matthew J. Mancini, *One Dies, Get Another: Convict Leasing in the American South, 1866–1928* (Columbia: University of South Carolina Press, 1996).

16. David M. Oshinsky, *"Worse Than Slavery": Parchman Farm and the Ordeal of Jim Crow Justice* (New York: Free Press, 1996); Douglas A. Blackmon, *Slavery by Another Name: The Re-enslavement of Black Americans from the Civil War to World War II* (New York: Anchor Books, 2009). See also Talitha L. LeFlouria, *Chained in Silence: Black Women and Convict Labor in the New South* (Chapel Hill: University of North Carolina Press, 2015).

17. Derrell Roberts, "Duel in the Georgia State Capitol," *Georgia Historical Quarterly* 47, no. 4 (December 1963): 420–24.

18. Harold E. Davis, *Henry Grady's New South: Atlanta, a Brave and Beautiful City* (Tuscaloosa: University of Alabama Press, 1990), 151.

19. Ida B. Wells, ed., *The Reason Why the Colored American Is Not in the World's Columbian Exposition* (Chicago, 1893), http://digital.library.upenn.edu/women/wells/exposition/exposition.html.

20. C. Vann Woodward, *The Future of the Past* (New York: Oxford University Press, 1989), 281.

21. Ida B. Wells-Barnett, *Southern Horrors: Lynch Law in All Its Phases* (New York: New York Age, 1892), https://www.gutenberg.org/files/14975/14975-h/14975-h.htm.

22. Wheeler, *New Women of the New South*, xv.

23. Elna C. Green, *Southern Strategies: Southern Women and the Woman Suffrage Question* (Chapel Hill: University of North Carolina Press, 1997), 133.

24. Wheeler, *New Women of the New South*, 108.

25. Weiss, *The Woman's Hour*, 136.

26. Deborah Gray White, *Too Heavy a Load: Black Women in Defense of Themselves, 1894–1994* (New York: W. W. Norton, 1999), 103. See also Belle Kearney, "The South and Woman Suffrage," *Woman's Journal*, April 4, 1903, in *Up from the Pedestal: Selected Writings in the History of American Feminism*, ed. Aileen S. Kraditor (Chicago: Quadrangle Books, 1968), 262–65.

27. Keyssar, *The Right to Vote*, 160.

28. R. Volney Riser, *Defying Disfranchisement: Black Voting Rights Activism in the Jim Crow South* (Baton Rouge: Louisiana State University Press, 2010), 4–6.

29. Lorraine Gates Schuyler, *The Weight of Their Votes: Southern Women and Political Leverage in the 1920s* (Chapel Hill: University of North Carolina Press, 2006), 7.

30. Paul Ortiz, *Emancipation Betrayed: The Hidden History of Black Organizing and White Violence in Florida from Reconstruction to the Bloody Election of 1920* (Berkeley: University of California Press, 2005), 169 (quotation), 172–208.

31. Ortiz, *Emancipation Betrayed*, 190 ("tried to govern"), 186–215; "Register More White Women Than Negroes," *Tampa Morning Tribune*, September 29, 1920; "More White Women Register This Week," *New Smyrna Daily News*, October 1, 1920; "White Women Urged to Vote Democratic Ticket in November," *Palm Beach Post*, October 2, 1920.

32. Ortiz, *Emancipation Betrayed*, 216 ("locked arms"), 216–23; "Fla. Town Where Blacks Were Massacred Renounces Racist Past," *U.S. News & World Report*, November 19, 2018, https://www.usnews.com/news/best-states/florida/articles/2018-11-19/fla-town-where-blacks-were-massacred-renounces-racist-past.

33. Margalit Fox, "Amelia Boynton Robinson, a Pivotal Figure at the Selma March, Dies at 104," *New York Times*, August 26, 2015, https://www.nytimes.com/2015/08/27/us/amelia-boynton-robinson-a-pivotal-figure-at-the-selma-march-dies-at-104.html; Gary May, *Bending toward Justice: The Voting Rights Act and the Transformation of American Democracy* (New York: Basic Books, 2013); Gene Roberts and Hank Klibanoff, *The Race Beat: The Press, the Civil Rights Struggle, and the Awakening of a Nation* (New York: Vintage Books, 2007).

34. *Shelby County v. Holder*, 557 U.S. 193 (2013).

35. Vann R. Newkirk, "How *Shelby County v. Holder* Broke America," *Atlantic*, July 10, 2018, https://www.theatlantic.com/politics/archive/2018/07/how-shelby-county-broke-america/564707/.

36. Carol Anderson, "Brian Kemp, Enemy of Democracy," *New York Times*, August 11, 2018, https://www.nytimes.com/2018/08/11/opinion/sunday/brian-kemp-enemy-of-democracy.html.

37. *Shelby County v. Holder* at 2650 (Ginsburg dissent).

About the Contributors

MAURINE BEASLEY is a professor emerita of journalism at the University of Maryland. Her books include *Women of the Washington Press, Eleanor Roosevelt: Transformative First Lady*, and *First Ladies and the Press*. She is coeditor of *The Eleanor Roosevelt Encyclopedia* and *Taking Their Place: A Documentary History of Women and Journalism*. She has won major research awards from the Association for Education in Journalism and Mass Communication and the American Journalism Historians Association and is a past president of both organizations. She has written for the *Kansas City Star* and the *Washington Post*.

SHERILYN COX BENNION, a former Fulbright scholar, spent most of her teaching career at Humboldt State University in California, where she chaired the Department of Journalism and the Women's Studies program and retired as a professor emerita. She also taught at Indiana University and the University of Utah. She is the author of *Equal to the Occasion: Women Editors of the Nineteenth-Century West*, as well as numerous book chapters and periodical articles. She has served on the boards of the Mormon History Association, the Utah Foundation for Open Government, and the Utah League of Women Voters.

JINX COLEMAN BROUSSARD is a professor and the Bart R. Swanson Endowed Memorial Professor in the Manship School of Mass Communication at Louisiana State University. Broussard is the author of the national award-winning book *African-American Foreign Correspondents: A History* as well as *Giving a Voice to the Voiceless: Four Pioneering Black Women Journalists* and *Public Relations and Journalism in Times of Crisis: A Symbiotic Rela-*

tionship. An expert on the history of the black press, Broussard researches representation of racial and ethnic minorities, public relations, and crisis communication.

TERI FINNEMAN is an assistant professor of journalism at the University of Kansas. She is the author of *Press Portrayals of Women Politicians, 1870s–2000s*, and has contributed to several other books including *A Companion to First Ladies*. She has worked in the print and broadcast news industry, including through a fellowship at *ABC News* in Washington, DC.

KATHY ROBERTS FORDE is an associate professor of journalism at the University of Massachusetts–Amherst. She is the author of *Literary Journalism on Trial: Masson v. New Yorker and the First Amendment*, which received the Frank Luther Mott-KTA and the AEJMC History Division book awards. She is the coeditor of the book series Journalism & Democracy at the University of Massachusetts Press; former associate editor of the journal *American Journalism*; and former chair of the AEJMC History Division.

LINDA M. GRASSO is a professor of English at York College and of liberal studies at the Graduate Center, the City University of New York. She is the author of *Equal under the Sky: Georgia O'Keeffe and Twentieth-Century Feminism*, *The Artistry of Anger: Black and White Women's Literature in America, 1820–1860*, and numerous essays on nineteenth- and twentieth-century US women's literature and culture.

CAROLYN KITCH is a professor of journalism at Temple University. She has authored four books, including *The Girl on the Magazine Cover: The Origins of Visual Stereotypes in American Culture* and *Pages from the Past: History and Memory in American Magazines*, the latter receiving the James W. Carey Media Research Award. She serves on the editorial boards of eleven academic journals and edited an online special issue titled "Women in the Newsroom: Status and Stasis" for *Journalism & Mass Communication Quarterly*. She previously worked as a magazine editor at *McCall's* and *Good Housekeeping*.

BROOKE KROEGER is a professor of journalism at New York University, where she served as the Arthur L. Carter Journalism Institute's inaugural director and now directs NYU Journalism's graduate Global and Joint Program Studies. Her books include *The Suffragents; Fannie: The Talent for Success of Writer Fannie Hurst; Nellie Bly: Daredevil, Reporter, Feminist;* and *Undercover Reporting: The Truth about Deception*. She worked for *Newsday* and United Press International with postings in Chicago, Brussels, Tel Aviv, where she served as bureau chief, and London, where she was chief editor for Europe, the Middle East, and Africa.

LINDA J. LUMSDEN is a professor of journalism at the University of Arizona. She is the author of *Journalism for Social Justice: A Cultural History of Social Movement Media from Abolition to #womensmarch*; *Black, White, and Red All Over: A Cultural History of the Radical Press in Its Heyday, 1900–1917*; *Inez: The Life and Times of Inez Milholland*; and *Rampant Women: Suffragists and the Right of Assembly*. She was a Fulbright scholar at the National University of Malaysia in 2012–13.

JANE MARCELLUS is a professor at Middle Tennessee State University. She is author of *Business Girls and Two-Job Wives: Emerging Media Stereotypes of Employed Women* and a coauthor of *Mad Men and Working Women: Feminist Perspectives on Historical Power, Resistance, and Otherness*. A former head of the AEJMC Cultural and Critical Studies Division and former chair of the AEJMC Publications Committee, she now chairs the AJHA Blanchard Dissertation Prize Committee. Her work has appeared in peer-reviewed journals, newspapers including the *Washington Post*, and literary journals including the *Gettysburg Review*. She received a *Best American Essays* "Notable" in 2018.

JANE RHODES is a professor and head of African American Studies at the University of Illinois–Chicago. Her books include *Mary Ann Shadd Cary: The Black Press and Protest in the Nineteenth Century*, named the AEJMC best book in mass communication history in 1999; and *Framing the Black Panthers: The Spectacular Rise of a Black Power Icon*, now in a second edition. Her current project, *Rebel Media: Adventures in the History of the Black Public Sphere*, is a collection of critical essays on radical black media from the early twentieth century to the present.

LINDA STEINER is a professor of journalism at the University of Maryland. Among her coauthored or coedited books are *News of Baltimore: Race, Rage, and the City*; *Journalism, Gender, and Power*; *Women and Journalism*; *The Routledge Companion to Media and Gender*; *Critical Readings: Gender and Media*; *The Handbook of Gender and War*; and *Key Concepts in Critical-Cultural Studies*. She is editor of Journalism & Communication Monographs, a former editor of Critical Studies in Media Communication, and a past president of the AEJMC.

ROBIN MAZYCK SUNDARAMOORTHY is a PhD student at the University of Maryland. Her research interests include new media trends and their effects on women, girls, and diverse populations. She has twenty years of TV news experience and covered the campaign and election of President Barack Obama. She earned her master's in journalism from Michigan State University; her thesis title was "Time for Action: World War II through the Eyes of an African-American Cartoonist."

Index

Selling Free Enterprise: The Business Assault on Labor and Liberalism, 1945–60
  Elizabeth A. Fones-Wolf
Last Rights: Revisiting *Four Theories of the Press*   *Edited by John C. Nerone*
"We Called Each Other Comrade": Charles H. Kerr & Company, Radical
  Publishers   *Allen Ruff*
WCFL, Chicago's Voice of Labor, 1926–78   *Nathan Godfried*
Taking the Risk Out of Democracy: Corporate Propaganda versus Freedom
  and Liberty   *Alex Carey; edited by Andrew Lohrey*
Media, Market, and Democracy in China: Between the Party Line and the
  Bottom Line   *Yuezhi Zhao*
Print Culture in a Diverse America   *Edited by James P. Danky and
  Wayne A. Wiegand*
The Newspaper Indian: Native American Identity in the Press, 1820–90
  John M. Coward
E. W. Scripps and the Business of Newspapers   *Gerald J. Baldasty*
Picturing the Past: Media, History, and Photography   *Edited by Bonnie Brennen
  and Hanno Hardt*
Rich Media, Poor Democracy: Communication Politics in Dubious Times
  Robert W. McChesney
Silencing the Opposition: Antinuclear Movements and the Media in the
  Cold War   *Andrew Rojecki*
Citizen Critics: Literary Public Spheres   *Rosa A. Eberly*
Communities of Journalism: A History of American Newspapers and
  Their Readers   *David Paul Nord*
From Yahweh to Yahoo! The Religious Roots of the Secular Press
  Doug Underwood
The Struggle for Control of Global Communication: The Formative Century
  Jill Hills
Fanatics and Fire-eaters: Newspapers and the Coming of the Civil War
  Lorman A. Ratner and Dwight L. Teeter Jr.
Media Power in Central America   *Rick Rockwell and Noreene Janus*
The Consumer Trap: Big Business Marketing in American Life   *Michael Dawson*
How Free Can the Press Be?   *Randall P. Bezanson*
Cultural Politics and the Mass Media: Alaska Native Voices   *Patrick J. Daley
  and Beverly A. James*
Journalism in the Movies   *Matthew C. Ehrlich*
Democracy, Inc.: The Press and Law in the Corporate Rationalization of the
  Public Sphere   *David S. Allen*
Investigated Reporting: Muckrakers, Regulators, and the Struggle over Television
  Documentary   *Chad Raphael*

The University of Illinois Press
is a founding member of the
Association of University Presses.

———————————————

Composed in 10.5/13 Adobe Minion Pro
with Avenir display
by Jim Proefrock
at the University of Illinois Press
Cover designed by Dustin Hubbart
Cover image: Florence Luscomb selling copies
of the Woman's Journal. Photographer Elmer
Chickering, 1912. Courtesy Schlesinger Library,
Radcliffe Institute, Harvard University.

University of Illinois Press
1325 South Oak Street
Champaign, IL 61820-6903
www.press.uillinois.edu